BIBLICAL RECEPTION 2 (2013)

BIBLICAL RECEPTION 2 (2013)

Sheffield Phoenix Press
2013

Copyright © 2013 Sheffield Phoenix Press
Published by Sheffield Phoenix Press
Department of Biblical Studies, University of Sheffield
Sheffield S3 7QB

www.sheffieldphoenix.co

A CIP catalogue record for this book
is available from the British Library

Typeset by the HK Scriptorium
Printed by Lightning Source

ISBN-13 978-1-909697-14-0
ISSN 2051-400X

CONTENTS

ABBREVIATIONS

2 Clem.	*2 Clement*
AB	Anchor Bible
ABD	David Noel Freedman (ed.), *The Anchor Bible Dictionary* (New York: Doubleday, 1992).
Augustine, *Civ.*	Augustine, *De civitate Dei*
b.	Babylonian Talmud
BAGD	Walter Bauer, William F. Arndt, F. William Gingrich and Frederick W. Danker, *A Greek–English Lexicon of the New Testament and Other Early Christian Literature* (Chicago: University of Chicago Press, 2nd edn, 1958).
BDB	Francis Brown, S.R. Driver and Charles A. Briggs, *A Hebrew and English Lexicon of the Old Testament* (Oxford: Clarendon Press, 1907).
BL	British Library
CCCM	Corpus christianorum continuatio mediaevalis
ConBNT	Coniectanea biblica, New Testament
Douay–Rheims	Douay–Rheims Bible
Exod. Rab.	*Midrash Exodus Rabbah*
Gen. Rab.	*Midrash Genesis Rabbah*
Hippolytus, *Cant.*	Hippolytus, *Canticles*
Ignatius, *Eph.*	Ignatius, *Ephesians*
Jerome, *Qu. Hebr. Gen.*	Jerome, *Quaestiones hebraicae in Genesim*
JPS	Jewish Publication Society Version
JSNT	*Journal for the Study of the New Testament*
JSNTSup	*Journal for the Study of the New Testament* Supplement Series
JSOTSup	*Journal for the Study of the Old Testament* Supplement Series
KJV	King James Version (Authorized Version]
LAB	*Liber antiquitatum biblicarum*
LSJ	H.G. Liddell, Robert Scott and H. Stuart Jones, *Greek–English Lexicon* (Oxford: Clarendon Press, 9th edn, 1968).
LXX	Septuagint translation of the Old Testament
NABRE	New American Bible Revised Edition
NASU	New American Standard Bible, 1995 update

NICNT	New International Commentary on the New Testament
NIV	New International Version
NJPS	New Jewish Publication Society Version
NKJV	New King James Version
NRSV	New Revised Standard Version
NTV	Nueva traducción viviente
Philo, *Gig.*	Philo, *De gigantibus*
Philo, *Mos.*	Philo, *De vita Mosis*
Philo, *Opif.*	Philo, *De opificio mundi*
Philo, *Quest. in Exod.*	Philo, *Quaestiones in Exodum*
Philo, *Somn.*	Philo, *De somniis*
PL	J.-P. Migne (ed.), *Patrologia cursus completus … Series prima [latina]* (221 vols.; Paris: J.-P. Migne, 1844–65).
Sanh.	Talmud tractate *Sanhedrin*
SBLDS	Society of Biblical Literature Dissertation Series
Tertullian, *Marc.*	Tertullian, *Adversus Marcionem*
VTSup	*Vetus Testamentum* Supplements
ZAW	*Zeitschrift für die alttestamentliche Wissenschaft*

David J.A. Clines is Professor Emeritus of Biblical Studies in the University of Sheffield. His publications include *The Dictionary of Classical Hebrew* (8 vols., Sheffield Academic Press and Sheffield Phoenix Press, 1993–2011), and the three-volume commentary on Job in the Word Biblical Commentary series (Word Books and Thomas Nelson, 1989–2011). He is currently working on a book to be called *Play the Man! Biblical Imperatives to Masculinity*. Email: d.clines@sheffield.ac.uk.

Colleen M. Conway is a professor in the Department of Religion and in the University Honors Program of Seton Hall University, South Orange, New Jersey. She specializes in the study of the New Testament and Early Christianity with a particular interest in gender critical approaches. Her publications include *An Introduction to the Bible: Sacred Texts and Imperial Contexts* (Wiley–Blackwell, 2010), co-authored with David M. Carr, and *Behold the Man: Jesus and Greco-Roman Masculinity* (Oxford University Press, 2008). Her current research is focused on the reception history of Judges 4–5. Email: conwayco@gmail.com.

Nathan P. Devir is Assistant Professor of Hebrew, Jewish Studies, and Comparative Literary and Cultural Studies at the University of Utah. His doctoral and post-doctoral research focused on the intersection between literary discourse, hermeneutics, and biblical exegesis in modern Judaic cultural production. His more current research, situated between Ethnography and Religious Studies, involves discourse analyses of heritage narratives from so-called 'neo-Jewish' and 'Lost Tribe' communities in India and sub-Saharan Africa. Email: nathan.devir@utah.edu.

Yaffa Englard lectures in the Department of Biblical Studies at the University of Haifa. Former Head of Biblical Studies at Gordon College of Education, Haifa, and art consultant for the Reches textbook series, her academic interests focus on mediaeval artistic representations of biblical narratives. Her recent publications include 'Mosaics as Midrash: The Zodiacs of the Ancient Synagogues and the Conflict between Judaism and Christianity', *Review of Rabbinic Judaism* 6 (2003), pp. 189-214, and 'The Creation of

Eve in Art and the Myth of Androgynous Adam', *Ars judaica* 5 (2009), pp. 23-36. Email: jaffa@research.haifa.ac.il.

J. Cheryl Exum is Professor Emerita of Biblical Studies at the University of Sheffield and a Director of Sheffield Phoenix Press. The author of numerous articles on the Hebrew Bible, her books include *Tragedy and Biblical Narrative: Arrows of the Almighty*; *Fragmented Women: Feminist (Sub)versions of Biblical Narratives*; *Plotted, Shot, and Painted: Cultural Representations of Biblical Women*; and *Song of Songs: A Commentary*. She is currently writing a book on the Bible and the arts. Email: j.c.exum@ sheffield.ac.uk.

Mark Finney is Lecturer in Religion at the University of Sheffield. His research interests include religion and violence in its ancient and modern contexts, constructs of the afterlife in the ancient world, and the Bible and the arts. He is the author of *Honour and Conflict in the Ancient World: 1 Corinthians in its Greco-Roman Social Setting* (T. & T. Clark, 2012). Email: m.t.finney@sheffield.ac.uk.

Deirdre Good is professor of New Testament at the General Theological Seminary in New York City. Her most recent publication is *Studying the New Testament: A Fortress Introduction* (with Bruce Chilton, 2010). Email:good@gts.edu.

Christine E. Joynes is Director of the Centre for Reception History of the Bible at the University of Oxford. Her research focuses on the reception history of Mark's Gospel and she is currently writing the Blackwell Bible Commentary on *Mark's Gospel through the Centuries*. She is particularly interested in the interpretation of the Bible in visual art. Email: christine.joynes@trinity.ox.ac.uk.

Helen Leneman received her PhD under Athalya Brenner in Amsterdam. Leneman, a professional musician, specializes in musical retellings of biblical narratives. Publications include *Love, Lust and Lunacy: The Stories of Saul and David in Music* (Sheffield Phoenix Press, 2010); and *The Performed Bible: The Story of Ruth in Opera and Oratorio* (Sheffield Phoenix Press, 2007). Email: cantorl@gmail.com.

Katherine Low is Assistant Professor of Religion and Chaplain at Mary Baldwin College in Staunton, Virginia. She is currently researching biblical family structures from a gender-critical perspective. She is the author of *The Bible, Gender, and Reception History: The Case of Job's Wife* (Bloomsbury T. & T. Clark, 2013). Email: klow@mbc.edu.

Andrea M. Sheaffer received a PhD in Hebrew Bible in 2013 from Graduate Theological Union in Berkeley, California, and is now Director of Admissions there. Her current research interests are women and marginalized figures in the Bible and visual arts. She is the author of *Envisioning the Minority: Art Illuminates Minor Characters in the Book of Judith* (Sheffield Phoenix Press, 2013). Email: andrea.sheaffer@gmail.com.

James W. Watts is Professor and Chair of the Department of Religion at Syracuse University. His research focuses on the interplay of ritual and rhetoric in the Pentateuch and in other texts. He is the author of *Leviticus 1–10* (Peeters, 2013) and the editor of *Iconic Books and Texts* (Equinox, 2013). Email: jjwatts@syr.edu.

Carmen Yebra Rovira is Assistant Professor of Introduction to the Bible and Hermeneutics at Salamanca Pontifical University, Spain. She researches new visual sources and methods for investigating the history of the reception and transmission of the Bible. She focuses especially on the influence of biblical engravings and illustrated Bibles in European society, culture and religion. Email: cyebraro@upsa.es.

ART

Illustrating Leviticus:
Art, Ritual and Politics[1]

James W. Watts

Abstract

The book of Leviticus has rarely attracted much attention from Christian interpreters, much less artists, either in antiquity or modernity. The same situation obtained in the Middle Ages, except in one tradition of thirteenth- to fifteenth-century illuminated manuscripts, called *Bibles moralisées*, 'moralized Bibles'. They give considerable space and attention to an unusual selection of chapters from Leviticus due to the politics of biblical interpretation and of changes in the ritual of the Eucharist during these centuries. The history of Leviticus's depiction in art illustrates the capacity of parts of scripture to lie fallow until special circumstances draw interpretive and artistic interest to them.

Background

Leviticus is little read and less often followed. This is especially the case among Christians who have, since antiquity, regarded its ritual rules and even many of its other laws as superseded by Christ's crucifixion and teachings. Apart from the love commandment in 19.18 and a few other famous verses, Leviticus has not drawn much attention from Christian readers and interpreters, unless they make the effort to work through the entire Pentateuch or Bible. This tendency to avoid the book is so deep seated and widespread as to suggest that exceptions were motivated by extraordinary circumstances. What does it mean when Christians' silence about Leviticus is broken?

Among Jews, the situation is different. Rabbinic *halakhah* (legal interpretation) gives the book much attention. Synagogue liturgy continues to reflect facets of ancient temple practices. Yet the ritual discontinuity about animal offerings places many of the book's ritual instructions in the liminal

1. I am very grateful that this paper has benefited from the comments and suggestions of participants in the symposium Passions and Transgressions: Medieval and Renaissance Studies, at Syracuse University on April 16, 2010, and in the session on Reception of Bible in Art at the International Society of Biblical Literature Meeting in Amsterdam, July 26, 2012.

legal situation of being closely studied but never practiced. Like Christians, then, Jewish interpretation and preaching from Leviticus must consciously straddle the differences between the rituals depicted by the text and those being practised by contemporary readers.

Aaron and Leviticus in Art

These interpretive tendencies apply to art as much as they do to preaching and verbal commentary. Two- and three-dimensional art illustrating biblical themes usually consists either of iconic portraits of key figures or illustrations of dramatic narrative scenes. Leviticus contains a small cast of key figures: God, who speaks the instructions and laws; Moses, who hears them and consecrates the Tabernacle and its priesthood (Leviticus 8–9); and Aaron, who officiates as high priest after his consecration (Leviticus 9–10, 16) and also hears God speak some of the instructions (Lev. 10.8-11; 11.1; 16.1). The figure most distinctive to Leviticus is Aaron, though interpretation and art still draw more attention to his depiction in Exodus and Numbers than in Leviticus.

Moses and Aaron frequently appear together in both Jewish and Christian art. Aaron can be identified by his distinctive vestments, especially his turban and jeweled breastplate (Exodus 28) (Fig. 1). He usually holds a censor (Lev. 16.12; Num. 17.11 [Eng. 16.46]) or sometimes his flowering rod (Num. 17.23-26 [Eng. 17.8-11]), but he rarely appears with animal offerings. The iconic depiction of Aaron holding a censor, in this case paired with Melchizedek holding bread (Gen. 14.18), appears already in the eleventh century on a portable silver altar from Fulda, Germany.[2] Aaron appears in European art commonly in this guise on the frontispieces of early printed Passover Haggadot (for example, the Amsterdam Haggadah of 1695 and many others), occasionally in sculptures of baroque churches (for example, in Rome's sixteenth-century Santa Maria Maggiore and Dresden's eighteenth-century Frauenkirche), but rarely in portraits (exceptions are by Pier Francesco Mola [c. 1650] and by Anton Kern [1710–1747]). Another motif in Christian icons portrays Aaron as a prophet (Exod. 7.1) by showing him holding a scroll. This theme appeared already in a twelfth-century sculpture from the Cathedral of Noyon[3] and often in Eastern Orthodox icons.[4]

Apart from portraits of its two main characters, Leviticus has been neglected by artists because it contains very little narrative. Literary genre impacts art and performance this way in various religious traditions: 'Narrative genres (for example, the Ramayana, the Gospels) tend to evoke dra-

---

2. Now in the Musée National de l'Age Médiévale, Paris.
3. Now in the Metropolitan Museum of Art, New York.
4. See the sixteenth-century example in the Bulgarian National Art Museum, Sofia.

Fig. 1. Gable stone from of the sixteenth-century 'Aaron house' in the Jewish quarter of Amsterdam, now preserved in the back wall of the Moses and Aaron Church that was built on the site. Photo by J. W. Watts, 2012.

matic performances and artistic portrayals of their contents, while hymnic and hortatory genres (the Vedas, the Adi Granth, the Qur'an, much of the Torah) are more likely to find expression in performances of their words through recitation, memorization, calligraphy and the like'.[5] When artists do illustrate Leviticus, they usually illustrate only the book's two dramatic stories, the deaths of Nadab and Abihu (10.1-2) and the stoning of the blasphemer (24.10-23). Of course, illustrations regularly depict the frame narrative of God speaking to Moses, but it is unusual for that motif to include the ritual contents of the divine instructions. One exception is Holbein's woodcut depicting Moses listening to God while Aaron officiates over a burning altar in the background (Fig. 2). Otherwise, instructions and laws rarely get illustrated. When they do, artists focus first on those that stimulate their visual imaginations, such as the lists of unclean animals in Leviticus 11.

Far more stimulating for artists than Leviticus's contents has been its setting in the Tabernacle. The later chapters of Exodus describe its construction, along with its furnishings and the priests' vestments.[6] A very early illuminated Bible, the Ashburnham Pentateuch (fifth or sixth century CE), provides one full-page illustration that shows Moses receiving the law, reading the law, and the Tabernacle.[7] It replaces Israel's offerings on the altar with the Eucharistic bread and cup on the altar, a common feature of mediaeval

5. James W. Watts, 'The Three Dimensions of Scriptures', *Postscripts* 2 (2006), p. 146 = in *Iconic Books and Texts* (London: Equinox, 2013), p. 18.

6. For traditional Christian and Jewish interpretation of the Tabernacle account, including some references to art, see Scott M. Langston, *Exodus through the Centuries* (Oxford: Blackwell, 2006), pp. 221-30.

7. Bibliothèque Nationale de France, Ms. nouv. acq. lat. 2334, fol. 76r.

Fig. 2. 'The Burnt Offerings', Leviticus 1.2. Woodcut from an early-sixteenth-century design by Hans Holbein. From *Icones Veteris Testamenti: Illustrations of the Old Testament, Engraved on Eood,* from *Designs by Hans Holbein* (London: William Pickering, 1830; first published 1538). In the public domain.

Christian illustrations of Israel's Tabernacle altar. The type-scene of Aaron standing before the Tabernacle already appears in the third-century frescos in the synagogue at Dura-Europos in Syria. There animals stand ready to serve as offerings, though the only scene showing a bull burning on an altar depicts Elijah's offering (1 Kgs 18.36-39).

Interest in the architecture and furnishings of the Tabernacle dominate late mediaeval Jewish illuminations of the Torah's instructions. Jewish codices often devote several pages to illuminations of the furnishings described in Exodus, but they provide no similar art for Leviticus (for example, the Perpignan Bible of 1299[8] and the Farhi Bible of 1366–1383[9]). Others interleave full-page illustrations of the Tabernacle furnishings with abstract carpet pages that separate the Torah from the Prophets (for example, the Kennicott Bible of 1476[10]). Perhaps their influence led the fourteenth-century Christian Hebraist Nicholas of Lyra to include many illustrations in his commentary on Exodus 25–28.[11] With the development of printing, illustrated Bibles included

8. Bibliothèque Nationale de France, Ms. hébr. 7, fol. 12v.
9. Letschworth, England, Sassoon Collection, Ms. 368, fol. 182.
10. Bodleian Library, Oxford University, Ms. Kennicott 1, fols. 120b, 121a.
11. See Bernice M. Kaczynski, 'Illustrations of Tabernacle and Temple Implements in the *Postilla in Testamentum Vetus* of Nicholas de Lyra', *Yale University Library Gazette* 48.1 (1973), pp. 1-11.

increasingly detailed renderings of the Tabernacle, its contents and priests. These scenes sometimes contain a burning altar, but they focus on objects, not ritual practices. That tendency even extends to the Temple Institute in Jerusalem, which for 25 years has been preparing for the restoration of the Jerusalem Temple primarily by creating furniture and vestments.[12] Popular interest among Jews and Christians in such scenes frequently led in modern times to the construction of scale models of the Tabernacle and Temple. In Holland, for example, Rabbi Jacob Judah Leon became known as 'Templo' for publishing detailed designs and displaying scale models of the Jerusalem Temple and Tabernacle. Many Christians came to see them, which contributed to turning Amsterdam's Jewish Quarter into a tourist attraction already in the seventeenth century.[13] In the same city two hundred years later, the Revd Leendert Schouten also attracted visitors with a model of the Tabernacle. Its furnishings can still be viewed in the Bible Museum that he founded. In late nineteenth-century America, summer campers could visit a full-size model of the Tabernacle at Chautaqua, New York. Replicas appear today at Holy Land Experience in Orlando, Florida, at the Mennonite Information Center in Lancaster, Pensylvania, at New Holy Land in Eureka Springs, Arkansas, and at Timna Park near Eilat, Israel.[14] Several manufacturers sell kits for constructing scale models of the Tabernacle, which appear on display in the educational rooms of many congregations (Fig. 3).

The modern fascination generated by the detailed description of sanctuary, furnishings and vestments in Exodus extends only to a limited extent to Leviticus's instructions for using them to make animal offerings. The Mennonite Information Center shows cut-out figures of priests frozen in various poses while conducting sanctuary rituals. New Holy Land shows a video to represent how offerings dramatize, in Long's (2003: 80) words, 'Christ the Lamb of God as the singularly important "burnt offering"'. Holy Land Experience in Orlando, Florida, actually stages a live re-enactment of the Day of Atonement ritual (Leviticus 16) every half hour. An actor plays the role of Aaron ministering at the altar and inside the Holy Space while

12. See the Temple Institute's website (http://www.templeinstitute.org).

13. The Amsterdam Jewish Museum contains a permanent display about Rabbi Jacob Judah Leon 'Templo'.

14. For Chatauqua and New Holy Land, see Burke O. Long, *Imagining the Holy Land: Maps, Models, and Fantasy Travels* (Bloomington, IN: Indiana University Press, 2003), pp. 7-41, 70-87; for Holy Land Experience, see Timothy Beal, *Roadside Religion: In Search of the Sacred, the Strange, and the Substance of Faith* (Boston: Beacon, 2006), pp. 49-70; for the Mennonite Visitor Center, see Julia O'Brien, 'Field Trip to the Tabernacle Reproduction', online at http://juliamobrien.net/index.php/blog/field-trip-to-the-tabernacle-reproduction.html (accessed December 10, 2012); see also examples listed in 'Replicas of the Jewish Temple', Wikipedia online, at http://en.wikipedia.org/wiki/Replicas_of_the_Jewish_Temple (accessed December 10, 2012).

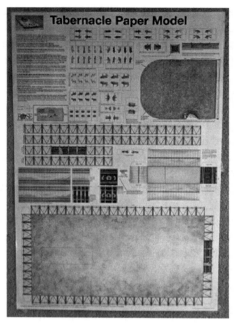

Fig. 3. Tabernacle paper model sold in gift shop at Holy Land Experience
in Orlando, Florida. Photo by J. W. Watts, 2012.

a recorded narration summarizes and quotes the biblical instructions. The
model uses a backlit screen for the Tabernacle wall so that the audience
can see the high priest's actions in the Holy of Holies without themselves
entering the tent. In this way, the Torah's restriction of the inner sanctum to
the High Priest alone is respected while simultaneously allowing full visual
access. The narrator assumes the voice of another priest. He provides little
additional interpretation and sticks closely to the biblical text, except at the
end, when he wonders if someday God will provide 'his perfect lamb for the
sins of the world', and then quotes John the Baptist's proclamation of Jesus
as that lamb. It is left to the live actor to provide a more explicit message of
Christian supersessionism. After concluding the rituals, he approaches the
audience, doffs his priestly turban and steps out of the role of Aaron. Now,
he tells the audience, these rituals are no longer needed because Christ died
to atone for everyone's sins. He suggests that this is better, because 'can you
imagine having to ask a priest to sacrifice a sheep whenever you need for-
giveness? Now you can just ask Jesus'. He concludes by inviting audience
members to accept Christ as their saviour, if they haven't already.

At Holy Land Experience, as Beal (2006: 59) observed, 'the emphasis
appears to be less on the actual physical structure and more on the ritual
practices performed in it'. He explained this unusual emphasis as due to the

apocalyptic expectation that a re-built Jerusalem Temple will play a key role in events leading up to the return of Christ. The performance I witnessed, however, did not make that hope explicit. It focused instead on traditional Christian typological interpretations of the Tabernacle and Temple rituals as foreshadowing and being superseded by Christ's atoning sacrifice (Heb. 2.17–10.18). Consistent typological interpretation also dominates the Tabernacle tours in Lancaster and Eureka Springs (Long 2003: 79; O'Brien 2009). Portrayals and reenactments of Israel's offering rituals function as concrete examples of atonement with blood.

Perhaps this explains their attraction for Christians: Israel's animal offerings are blood rituals that atone. Illustrating and reenacting them normalizes the idea of blood atonement for its application to the unique and unritualized crucifixion of Christ. Of course, the ritual of the Eucharist / Lord's Supper memorializes the crucifixion as blood atonement too, but the Tabernacle rituals are more graphic. They nevertheless stop short of using real animals and their blood: besides conflicting with health regulations and rules against animal cruelty, doing so might seem to cross the line between reenacting a superceded ritual and reviving the ritual itself. Thus modern Christian replicas, like mediaeval illuminated Bibles, use the Tabernacle and its blood rituals typologically to point to Christ.

Religious communities that still invest priests with important responsibilities can sometimes be drawn to illustrations of the ordination of Aaron and his sons in Leviticus 8. The twelfth-century Pantheon Bible[15] shows Moses receiving the law on its Leviticus incipit page and otherwise illuminates only the ordination scene from that book. It depicts Moses, Aaron and his sons in typical mediaeval fashion as king and tonsured clerics respectively. The image shows no animal offerings, but only a codex book on the altar and only a bowl for the anointing liquid. Clearly, the choice of this scene for illustration has more to do with the importance of priesthood in twelfth-century Rome than it does with any broader interest in Leviticus. The same scene as rendered by a modern artist, Harry Anderson, appears frequently in Latter Day Saints' literature.[16] Anderson's rendering makes a greater effort to reproduce the Pentateuch's descriptions of the Tabernacle and the priests' clothing, as is typical of modern realistic illustration. But its theme reflects the contemporary significance of 'Aaronic priesthood', which, in the LDS Church, should include every male church member over the age of 12.

15. Vatican Library 12 958, fol. 29v, reproduced in Joachim M. Plotzek and Ulrike Surmann (eds.), *Biblioteca Apostolica Vaticana: Liturgie und Andacht im Mittelalter, herausgegeben vom erzbischoflichen Diozesanmuseum Köln* (Stuttgart: Belser Verlag, 1992).

16. Harry Anderson, 'Aaron Is Called to the Ministry', on display in the Conference Center of the LDS Church in Salt Lake City, Utah.

Another spectacular exception to the tendency to focus on objects rather than rituals appears in the Leon Bible completed in 960.[17] At the beginning of Leviticus it presents a full-page illumination of Aaron officiating inside the sanctuary near the ark while the Israelites look on. Aaron touches an upright object on the altar, either its horn or a censor or a bottle of anointing oil.[18] The structure is clearly a stone building and the lamp and altar reflect contemporary church designs. Isidore of Seville (c. 560–636) had taught that the Tabernacle is an allegory of the church. The liturgy of Leon Cathedral in this period included Leviticus 9 as an antiphon for Lauds. Thus, though reflecting the contents of Leviticus and Exodus more closely than usual, the illuminators of the Leon Bible present Leviticus, in John Williams's words, 'as a timeless reference to the very worship they engaged in daily and to their role as priests'.[19] Like illustrations of the priests' ordination, this scene recognizes that Leviticus emphasizes priesthood and visually redirects its rhetoric to priests of its own time and tradition.

Bread Offerings in the Bibles moralisées

One family of mediaeval illuminated manuscripts gives Leviticus an extraordinary amount of space and attention. The *Bibles moralisées* (moralized Bibles) consist of seven extant manuscripts, dating from the thirteenth to the fifteenth century. They are picture books whose pages are filled with detailed illuminations accompanied by a loose paraphrase of bits of the Bible in Latin or French. Every page of a moralized Bible consists of four pairs of roundels. In each pair, the top roundel depicts a biblical text / scene while the bottom depicts its typological or allegorical 'moralization' accompanied by a sentence explaining the interpretation. These very elaborate and expensive books were probably produced for the court of France in Paris. They influenced the illuminations in other late mediaeval manuscripts, such as the famous *Rohan Book of Hours,* which copied some of their roundels for its marginal illustrations.[20]

---

17. Archivo Capitular de la Real Colegiata de San Isidoro de León, Ms. n.2, fol. 50r.

18. John Williams thinks the former, in which case the scene reflects Lev. 9.9 (*Imaging the Early Medieval Bible* [College Park, PA: Penn State University Press, 2002], p. 207). The object looks independent of the altar, however, in which case it probably reflects Lev. 16.12-14. That would not undermine Williams's observation (208) that 'It is this extraordinary interdependence of picture and text, in format and in pictorial interpretation that is the signature feature of the 960 Bible'.

19. Williams, *Imaging*, p. 207.

20. Bibliothèque Nationale, Paris, Ms. Latin 9471, fol. 211v ff.; see Millard Meiss and Marcel Thomas, *The Rohan Master: A Book of Hours* (New York: George Braziller, 1973), p. 13.

The two earliest *Bible moralisée* manuscripts, created in Paris between 1210 and 1220, devote to Leviticus seven pages containing twenty-nine pairs of roundels.[21] By contrast, reference to Leviticus is entirely missing from the other influential late mediaeval and early Renaissance typological collections, such as the *Speculum humanae salvationis*, the *Pauper's Bibles*, the thirteenth-century *Book of Old Testament Miniatures* in the Pierpont Morgan Library, and other Books of Hours.

Only select portions of Leviticus, however, make an appearance in the *Bibles moralisées*. Unlike other mediaeval illustrated Bibles, they devote considerable space to the offering instructions, especially to the bread offerings. This begins conventionally enough with a pair of roundels on Exod. 35.4-9, 20-22 that provide a typical Christian spiritualization of Israel's offerings: 'That Moses commanded them to cry out to God for mercy and to make offerings to God signifies God who commands his people to make confession and to make offerings of their bodies and their souls to God and they do so, and God receives them'. Then three pages cover the animal and bread offerings of Leviticus 1–2 while four more interpret material from just four other chapters of Leviticus. The cleansing of a person suffering from skin disease in chap. 14 represents the crucifixion and resurrection of Christ while the unclean animals and people with illnesses or physical defects in chaps. 11, 21 and 24 represent 'wicked princes, usurers, corrupt bishops, deceptive women, gluttons, . . . usurers, the lustful, and heretics'. The condemnation of the blasphemer to stoning in chap. 24 shows that 'God commands kings and counts and princes to kill all miscreants and all heretics and all those who mock God'. Entirely omitted from Leviticus are the sin and guilt offerings (Leviticus 4–5), the ordination of priests and injunctions to priests (Leviticus 8, 10) and the Day of Atonement (Leviticus 16), chapters that, on the basis of other Christian exegesis, would seem to be theologically more useful.

Gerald Guest characterized the glosses of the *Bibles moralisées* as 'political' commentary about the ills of mediaeval society but also especially about contemporary controversies over the Waldensians and their vernacular biblical texts and paraphrases.

> The present Bible, for example, features its own commentary, thereby deliberately tackling the thorny problem of scriptural interpretation by providing the reader with his or her own explanation of biblical history. It is also interesting to note that the books of the Bible most often mentioned in connection with the translation of scripture and the problem of heresy— books such as the Psalter, the Gospels, and the Pauline Epistles—are all absent from the present manuscript.

He concluded,

---

21. Österreichische Nationalbibliothek, Vienna codex 1179 and codex 2554.

> The moralized Bible as a genre performs two important and linked ideo-
> logical functions. First, it presents a tendentious view of mediaeval soci-
> ety with, among other things, a virulent critique of heretics, Jews, corrupt
> churchmen, and godless leaders. Second, it stands out as a self-conscious
> study in hermeneutics (interpretation)....[22]

However, neither Guest nor other commentators on the *Bibles moralisées* explain its interest in the bread offerings of Leviticus 2. Christian
preachers and commentators working serially through the Bible, when they
reach Leviticus 2, have often identified the bread offering as a type of Christ
(for example, the mediaeval *Glossa ordinaria*, which quotes Hesychius's
fifth-century commentary to allegorize the unleavened bread as pointing to
Christ's virgin birth; compare the collected Victorian sermons in *The Pulpit
Commentary*[23] and the notes of the *Scofield Reference Bible* that allegorize
'the oven, the unseen sufferings of Christ—His inner agonies . . . the pan,
His more evident sufferings'[24]). This association arises naturally from the
fact that bread is one of the two Eucharistic elements and that the New Testament frequently associates Christ with bread (for example, 1 Cor. 11.23-
26; Mk 14.22; Jn 6.35-59). Reading the rather obvious allegorizations of
the moralized Bibles therefore creates surprise at how little other Christian
interpretive traditions have made of the bread offerings. Beyond exegesis
dictated by the sequence of the Pentateuchal text, Leviticus's bread offerings have received little use or reflection. Pictorial illustrations of biblical
scenes portray animals rather than flour and bread, if they depict the instructions for offerings at all rather than just focusing on the narratives. The
most prominent exception to this pattern are early Christian portrayals that
substitute the bread and wine of the Eucharist for levitical offerings on the
Tabernacle altar (for example, see above on the Ashburnham Pentateuch).
But they do not depict the levitical bread offerings themselves.

The *Bible moralisée* manuscripts devote eight pairs of scenes to the
offerings of Leviticus 1–7, and six of these pairs depict the bread offerings
(Fig. 4).[25] Glosses to the 'moralizations' make the typologies explicit:

> That the bread was placed in the oven at God's command signifies that
> Jesus Christ was placed in the womb of the Virgin at the command of the
> Father in Heaven and by the Annunciation of the angel.

22. Gerrald B. Guest, *Bible moralisée: Vienna, Oesterreichische Nationalbibliothek,
Cod. Vind. 2554* (Vienna: Österreichische Nationalbibliothek, 1995), pp. 25, 29.

23. *Leviticus* (ed. Frederick Meyrick, Richard Collins and A. Cave; The Pulpit Commentary; London: Kegan Paul, Trench, & Co., 1882).

24. *The Scofield Reference Bible* (Oxford: Oxford University Press, rev. edn, 1917).

25. E.g., the Vienna codex 2554, fols. 27v, 28r.

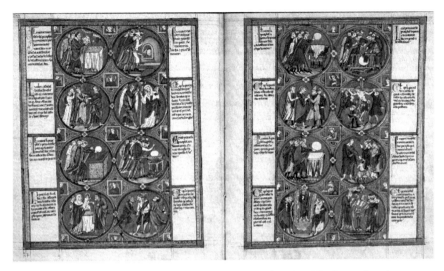

Fig. 4. *Bible moralisée,* Vienna codex 2554, fol. 27v, 28r. Reproduced by permission of the Österreichische Nationalbibliothek.

The bread that was in the oven and was offered to God signifies Jesus Christ who was in the womb of the Virgin and was offered to the Father of Heaven in the temple when Simeon received Him.

That the bread was put in a pan and fried in oil signifies that Jesus Christ was tied to the column and beaten and tormented.

That the fried bread was offered to God signifies that Jesus Christ was offered to the world.

That the bread was put on the grill and roasted signifies that Jesus Christ was put on the Cross and was roasted and tormented at His Passion

That the people offered the bread that was roasted and God received it signifies Jesus Christ who was roasted and tormented on the Cross, who offered Himself at the Ascension to the Father of Heaven, and He received Him.[26]

This interest by the *Bible moralisée* tradition in linking Jesus to the bread offerings of Leviticus 2 presents a remarkable contrast to the prevailing tendencies in Christian interpretation.

Why did this emphasis on bread that minimized blood offerings arise in the thirteenth through fifteenth centuries, rather than earlier or later? I think that the moralized Bibles focused on the bread offering to emphasize the significance of Communion bread in a time when laity were increas-

26. Translations by Guest, *Bible moralisée*, pp. 84-85.

ingly being given only bread. The wine of Communion was beginning to be reserved for priests. The rationale for restricting lay access to Communion wine was summarized by Patrick Toner in the 1910 *Catholic Encyclopedia* as 'safeguarding the reverence due to this most august sacrament and of facilitating and encouraging its frequent and fervent reception'.

> The danger of spilling the Precious Blood and of other forms of irreverence; the inconvenience and delay in administering the chalice to large numbers— the difficulty of reservation for Communion outside of Mass: the not unreasonable objection on hygienic and other grounds, to promiscuous drinking from the same chalice, which of itself alone would act as a strong deterrent to frequent Communion in the case of a great many otherwise well-disposed people; these and similar 'weighty and just reasons' against the Utraquist practice are more than sufficient to justify the Church in forbidding it.[27]

He estimated that this custom prevailed generally, though not universally, since at least the beginning of the thirteenth century. The practice of 'Communion under one kind' led to the Utraquist controversy (from *sub utraque specie* 'under both kinds'). Popular movements rejecting priestly monopolies on the cup eventually fed the Hussite rebellion and the establishment of independent churches in Bohemia in the fifteenth and sixteenth centuries, and became a central issue for sixteenth- and seventeenth-century Protestant Reformers. Against these rebellions, the Councils of Constance (1415) and Trent (1550s) ensconced the 'custom' of Communion under one kind with the status of canon law.[28] In the twentieth century, however, bishops increasingly granted permission for giving laity Communion under both kinds, a practice validated by the Second Vatican Council.[29]

The intended readers or viewers of the *Bibles moralisées* were lay people in the upper classes who could afford to buy such sumptuously illustrated books. I suspect that the books' orientation to lay readers in a time when priests began to distribute only the bread of the Eucharist to laity may account for their interest in the rules for bread offerings. They focus on Leviticus 2 to emphasize the theological importance of bread to lay readers

---

27. Patrick Toner, 'Communion under Both Kinds', *The Catholic Encyclopedia*, IV (New York: Robert Appleton Company, 1908), http://www.newadvent.org/cathen/04175a.htm; accessed October 1, 2012.

28. The 1967 revision of the *Catholic Encyclopedia* blames the Utraquist 'heresy' for changing Catholic practice, rather than vice versa: 'It was ultimately the intrusion of this unfortunate error that forced Rome to look on the practice of Communion under one species in a more sympathetic light than her reverence for tradition may otherwise have authorized' (J.J. Megivern, 'Communion under Both Species', *The New Catholic Encyclopedia* [San Francisco, CA: McGraw–Hill, 1967], pp. 44-46).

29. *Sacrosanctum Concilium*, 1963, paragraph 55; see Megivern, 'Communion under Both Species', p. 46.

while ignoring the rituals that emphasize blood (wine). As the history of later controversies and schisms shows, emphasizing the typological importance of lay bread offerings certainly had political implications. At the beginnings of these developments, the six pairs of roundels depicting Leviticus 2 in *Bibles moralisées* witness to attempts to convince rich and powerful lay people that Christ is really present in bread as much as in the wine. They do so by attaching the typologies usually reserved for blood sacrifices to the bread offerings of Leviticus. Though innovative in their application of the bread offering to Christ, the *Bibles moralisées* also recognize Leviticus's concern for the prerogatives of priests and lay people. They use the bread offerings that in ancient Israel represented priestly perquisites to reassure lay people in the late Middle Ages of the value of *their* sacrificial portions.[30]

Conclusion

The history of Leviticus's depiction in art is very thin. Most mediaeval manuscripts leave the text of Leviticus unilluminated, except perhaps for elaborate incipit letters. Similarly, when the creators of the Saint John's Bible, a twenty-first-century hand-lettered and decorated manuscript of the NRSV, decided to illuminate the pivotal teachings of Leviticus 19, they chose elaborate calligraphy of several key verses rather than any representational art.[31] Fascination with the Tabernacle, its furnishings and the priests' vestments have fueled their illustration and even re-creation in recent centuries, but the book's ritual instructions get portrayed in art and drama only rarely, and then only to illustrate Christian supersessionist theology.

It seems to require unusual circumstances for artists to pay Leviticus more attention. The desire to legitimize orders of priests sometimes draws artistic interest to Leviticus 8. The politics of ritual change in early thirteenth-century Paris also created circumstances to motivate innovation in Bible production and illumination. The *Bible moralisée* manuscripts use the bread offerings in Leviticus 2 as an innovative exegetical basis for showing that Communion bread alone carries the same salvific power as the wine, which has usually represented the blood of Christ. This argument seems intended to support the liturgical innovation of offering laity only the bread of Communion, while reserving the cup for priests. Scriptural texts that lay fallow in Christian tradition for more than a millennium were resurrected to address new issues in contemporary society and religion.

---

30. On the symbolism of bread offerings for the perquisites of Aaronide priests in ancient Israel, see James W. Watts, *Leviticus 1–10* (HCOT; Leuven: Peeters, 2013), pp. 244, 254-55, on Leviticus 2.

31. *The Saint John's Bible: Pentateuch* (Donald Jackson, artistic director and illuminator; Collegeville, MN: Liturgical Press, 2006).

ISHMAEL PLAYING? EXEGETICAL UNDERSTANDINGS AND ARTISTIC REPRESENTATIONS OF THE VERB *Mᵉṣaḥēq* IN GENESIS 21.9

Jaffa Englard

ABSTRACT

This article demonstrates that the artistic representations of Ishmael's conduct as depicted in Gen. 21.9 reflect less the 'artistic liberty' taken by artists attempting to give a visual rendering of the biblical text than interpretations of the verb *mᵉṣaḥēq* in early Jewish and Christian traditions. These become part of mediaeval Christian exegesis, and portraits of this scene by painters of this period also reflect the influence of European history, in particular Christianity's conflict with Islam.

Biblical scenes and protagonists have been a principal subject of the Western tradition of visual art since a very early period. Typically, some texts have lent themselves to representation more easily than others. The disparity in treatment, however, demands an explanation. In this article, I shall examine the way in which Ishmael has been portrayed in Western art. In contrast to Isaac, who became a popular figure in Jewish and Christian art as early as the third century, Ishmael has been relatively neglected.

As witnessed by the numerous places in which Isaac's binding (Genesis 22) is depicted in synagogue buildings, Isaac's binding was perceived as highly significant in Jewish eyes.[1] From its earliest appearance in a fresco at Dura Europos in the third century through the fourth- and sixth-century floor mosaics at Sepphoris and Beth Alpha and mediaeval prayer books and illuminated Haggadot, this scene has dominated the Jewish visual tradition.[2] Isaac's status as a 'type' of Christ similarly led, since the third and fourth century, to

---

1. The issue of Jewish visual art in light of the biblical prohibition against making 'images' is, of course, hotly debated, most recently in Lee Levine, *Visual Judaism in Late Antiquity: Historical Contexts of Jewish Art* (New Haven, CT: Yale University Press, 2012).

2. See Yaffa Englard, 'Mosaics as Midrash: The Zodiacs of the Ancient Synagogues and the Conflict between Judaism and Christianity', *Review of Rabbinic Judaism* 6.2–3 (2004), pp. 189-214. This theme is very popular in contemporary Israeli art, where it is given concrete contemporary significance.

the frequent portrayal of his sacrifice on Mount Moriah—as, for example, in wall paintings in the catacombs in Rome and sarcophagi reliefs.[3]

In contrast, Ishmael plays an ambiguous role in Genesis (16; 21).[4] His character is never fully developed; he has virtually no independent action, and while in some narratives he is the focus of the plot, he is ultimately merely a passive participant—not given voice by the narrator or heard even by his mother. Despite having been circumcised with Abraham, he is cast out of his father's house and becomes a nomad. At the same time, his birth was orchestrated by God, and his plight ultimately heeded by him (Gen. 21.17). Like Esau—with whom he has dual family ties via his daughter Mahalath/Basemath (Gen. 28.9; 36.3)—he is a marginalized figure whose role in *Heilsgeschichte* was too minor to attract artistic attention. Even when Dutch artists began displaying an increasing interest in the narrative of his expulsion in the sixteenth and seventeenth centuries, the focus of their paintings remained Hagar.

The earliest visual expressions of Ishmael occur principally in some twelfth- and thirteenth-century initials of Paul's allegoric interpretation of Genesis 21 in Gal. 4.22-28[5] and illuminated manuscripts dealing with episodes deemed to be of theological and/or hermeneutical interest—such as Sarah's giving of Hagar to Abraham and Abraham's willingness to take her to wife (hinting at polygamy) and the cause of Ishmael's banishment from his father's home. Herein, I will focus on the latter incident. Noting first the various exegeses of it, I will then examine the historical circumstances that influenced the various interpretations and the visual representations that reflect them.[6]

---

3. See, for example, the Priscilla catacomb (third century), the Via Latina catacomb (c. 320), Lateran Museum sarcophagus no. 174 (fourth century) and the sarcophagus of Julia Latronilla in Rome (c. 330–340).

4. See, for example, Carol Bakhos, *Ishmael on the Border: Rabbinic Portrayals of the First Arab* (Albany, NY: SUNY Press, 2006), pp. 13-27.

5. See Madrid, Fundacion Lazaro Gldiono, inv. 15289 fol. 295 (Galatians); Paris, Bibl. Sainte-Geneviève Ms. 1180 fol. 34 (Galatians); Philadelphia, Free Lib. Lewis Ms. 185 fol. 34 (psalter).

6. Ælfric of Eynsham's eleventh-century Anglo-Saxon paraphrase of the Hebrew Bible (Canterbury, 1025–1050; BL Ms. Cotton, Claudius B IV, fol. 36) elaborates the story at length: see Ruth Mellinkoff, 'Sarah and Hagar: Laughter and Tears', in *Illuminating the Book: Makers and Interpreters* (ed. M.P. Brown and S. McKendrick; Toronto: University of Toronto Press, 1998), pp. 37-38. Other illuminated manuscripts—such as the sixth-century Vienna Genesis (Vienna, Österreichische Nationalbibliothek, Cod. Theol. Gr. 31) and the mid-thirteenth-century *Morgan Picture Bible* (*Old Testament Miniatures, a Medieval Picture Book with 283 Paintings from the Creation to the Story of David* [ed. Sydney C. Cockerell and John Plummer; London: Phaidon, 1969])—ignore it.

Fig. 1a. *Isaac's Weaning Feast, Ishmael Playing with Isaac,* Ælfric of Eynsham. Vernacular biblical paraphrase, Canterbury, England, 1025–1050. London, BL MS Cotton, Claudius B IV, fol. 36. Photo © British Library, London.

Fig. 1b. *Ishmael Playing with Isaac,* Ælfric of Eynsham. Vernacular biblical paraphrase, Canterbury, England, 1025–1050. London, BL MS Cotton, Claudius B IV, fol. 36, detail. Photo © British Library, London.

According to Gen. 21.9, when 'Sarah saw the son of Hagar the Egyptian whom she had borne to Abraham מצחק', she demanded that Abraham banish his maidservant and her son.[7] The verb *mᵉṣaḥēq* apparently signifying the grounds for Sarah's demand that Abraham cast out Hagar and Ishmael, commentators from ancient to modern times have wondered what exactly Sarah imputed to Ishmael.[8]

The earliest interpretation of the verb is 'playing'—as in *Jubilees* ('And Sarah saw Ishmael playing and dancing', 17.4), the Septuagint ('And Sarah having seen the son of Agar the Egyptian who was born to Abraham, playing [παίζοντα] with Isaac her son'), the Vulgate ('And when Sara had seen the son of Agar the Egyptian playing [*ludentem*] with Isaac her son, she said to Abraham . . .'), and other translations up until today.[9]

---

7. All biblical quotations here follow the NASB unless otherwise stated.
8. The Septuagint and some Vulgate codices read 'with her son Isaac'. Whether or not this represents the original text, the verb *mᵉṣaḥēq* still requires elucidation.
9. Cf. NABRE, Douay–Rheims, NJPS.

Assuming that the illustrators had either the Septuagintal or Vulgate text before them, art historian Ruth Mellinkoff regards Ælfric of Eynsham's eleventh-century Old English Hexateuch representation of the boys' playing together (Figs. 1a and 1b) as a visual rendition of this biblical scene and a *Weltchronik* manuscript image portraying the boys' fighting each other (Figs. 2a and 2b) as evidence of the 'artistic liberty' taken by the illustrators.[10]

Fig. 2a. *Ishmael and Isaac Fighting* (over idol worship). *Weltchronik*, Bavaria, c. 1400–1410. Los Angeles, J. Paul Getty Museum, Ms. 33, fol. 33. Photo © J. Paul Getty Museum.

Fig. 2b. *Ishmael and Isaac Fighting* (over idol worship). *Weltchronik*, Bavaria, c. 1400–1410. Los Angeles, J. Paul Getty Museum, Ms. 33, fol. 33 detail. Photo © J. Paul Getty Museum.

I would like to propose that these works neither exemplify a precise visual rendition of the biblical text nor a form of 'artistic liberty' but that—like other representations of this episode—are based on specific textual, exegetical and polemical traditions. As widely recognized, artistic renderings of biblical scenes and stories do not simply transpose the written text into visual form but also constitute an exegesis of it. The images they employ thus frequently reflect the religious, social, cultural and political context in

10. Mellinkoff, 'Sarah and Hagar'. The *Weltchronik* (Bavaria, c. 1400–1410) is currently in the J. Paul Getty Museum, Los Angeles, Ms. 33.

which they were created.[11] Herein, I examine the way in which the understanding of the verb *meṣaḥēq* has been moulded by hermeneutical tradition, religious polemics and historical circumstances.

Sarah's demand that Abraham banish his firstborn son and God's support of her dictate have troubled many exegetes over the ages. One of the earliest interpretations of this verse attributes the event to Sarah's resentment of Abraham's bond with Ishmael: 'When Sarah saw Ishmael playing and dancing and Abraham being extremely happy, she became jealous of Ishmael' (*Jub* 17.4).[12] Jealousy not being considered a sufficient warrant for insistence on his banishment, however, other exegetes proposed that Ishmael had mocked and ridiculed Isaac. *Targum Onqelos* and the Peshitta, for example, translate the verb *meṣaḥēq* as מְחָאֵיךְ (*maḥa'ikh*) and מגחך (*mēgaḥēkh*) respectively—the same terms with which they render Sarah's sarcastic laughter in Gen. 18.13, 15—that is, as 'jesting'.[13] This tradition was continued by the Syrian church fathers and mediaeval Jewish commentators, remaining common in modern-day versions.[14]

The *Tosefta* (6.6) and *Genesis Rabbah* (53.10) further reflect an early tradition according to which, consistent with other places in the biblical text, the verb *meṣaḥēq* refers to bloodshed, idolatry and sexual misconduct—the 'cardinal sins' of Judaism, not to be committed even on pain of death (cf.

---

11. See J. Cheryl Exum and Ela Nutu (eds.), *Between the Text and the Canvas: The Bible and Art in Dialogue* (Sheffield: Sheffield Phoenix Press, 2007), p. 1.

12. James C. VanderKam, *The Book of Jubilees* (Leuven: Peeters, 1989), II, p. 103. Cf. Bakhos, *Ishmael on the Border*, pp. 18-19. This understanding is also directly affected, of course, by the account of Sarah's harsh treatment of Hagar in Gen. 16.5-6.

13. See Yeshayahu Maori, *The Peshitta Version of the Pentateuch and Early Jewish Exegesis* (Jerusalem: Magnes, 1995), pp. 114-15 (Hebrew). A visual representation of Ishmael's mockery occurs in the painting *The Banishment of Hagar and Ishmael* by (after) Francesco Solimena: http://www.wikigallery.org/wiki/painting_312074 (accessed March 4, 2013).

14. 'Sara saw Ishmael laughing on the day of the great feast which (Abraham) had made for the weaning of Isaac. Sara, who saw how much Ishmael resembled his mother, because, just as she came into contempt in the eyes of Agar, so too Ishmael was mocking her son' (Raymond Tonneau, *Sancti Ephraem Syri in Genesim et in Exodum Commentarii* [Scriptores Syri, 72; Louvain: Peeters, 1955], II, Sec. 19:1, pp. 67-68). Cf. Ms. Mignana 553; Diyarbakir (olim) 22. See Abraham Levene, *The Early Syrian Fathers on Genesis* (London: Taylor's Foreign Press, 1951), pp. 3-4, 93; Lucas van Rompay, *Le commentaire sur Génèse–Exode 9, 32 du manuscrit (olim) Diyarbakir 22* (Scriptores Syri, 206; Louvain: Peeters, 1986), pp. 109-10; KJV/NIV: 'mocking'; JPS: 'making sport'; NTV: 'burlándose'.

b. Sanh. 74a).[15] Such conduct could indeed justify Sarah's demand on Hagar and Ishmael's expulsion.[16]

Various visual representations of Ishmael's 'abuse' of Isaac occur in Byzantine and Western art from the late Middle Ages to the Renaissance.[17] An illustrated twelfth-century Byzantine Octateuch (Fig. 3) depicts Sarah as pointing out Ishmael fleeing from a bruised and bleeding Isaac to Abraham.[18] This portrayal may reflect the Jewish interpretation of m^eṣaḥēq as bloodshed, illustrations based on Jewish legends being prevalent in the Octateuchs.[19]

The text most responsible for influencing the visual portrayals of Ishmael's actions in relation to Isaac is indubitably Paul's remark at the end of his allegorical interpretation of the biblical episode in Gal. 4.29: 'But as at that time he who was born according to the flesh persecuted him who was born according the Spirit, so it is now also'. While this typology may not have originally been anti-Judaic, it has been understood so ever since

---

15. *Gen. Rab.* 53.11 (London: Soncino, 1961), p. 470; Jacob Neusner, *Genesis Rabbah: The Judaic Commentary to the Book of Genesis: A New American Translation* (Brown Judaic Studies, 105; Atlanta, GA: Scholars Press, 1985), II, pp. 252-53. For a critical Hebrew edition, see Julius Theodor and Chanoch Albeck, *Midrash Bereshit Rabbah* (Jerusalem: Wahrmann, 1965), II, pp. 567-68; Jacob Neusner, *The Talmud of Babylonia: An American Translation: Vol. 34b: Tractate Sanhedrin* (Chico, CA: Scholars Press, 1984), pp. 252-53. These sins form part of a list of seven sins that Jews and Gentiles are expected to abjure. They are usually said to be committed by a whole society, in most cases by Gentiles. Ishmael being associated with such transgressions, he is presented as a foreigner—a sinful Gentile: see Ronit Nikolsky, 'Ishmael Sacrificed Grasshoppers', in *Abraham, the Nations, and the Hagarites: Jewish, Christian, and Islamic Perspectives on Kinship with Abraham* (ed. M. Goodman, G.H. van Kooten and J.T van Ruiten (Leiden: Brill, 2010), pp. 249-50. The roots צחק (ṣāhaq, 'laugh') and שחק (śāḥāq, 'play') are very close phonetically and possess a similar meaning: see BDB, pp. 850, 965-66.

16. For the rabbinic reworking of biblical texts, see Joshua Levinson, *The Twice-Told Tale: A Poetics of the Exegetical Narrative in Rabbinic Midrash* (Jerusalem: Magnes, 2005), pp. 22-23 (Hebrew).

17. The discussion of the artistic representations of Ishmael in this paper focuses on the relationship between the hermeneutical interpretations of the verb *meṣaḥēq* and its visual expression rather than following the chronological development of the images.

18. Vatican Library, Cod. Gr. 746, fol. 80r. Kurt Weitzmann and Massimo Bernabo *The Byzantine Octateuchs* (Princeton, NJ: Princeton University Press, 1999), fig. 297. The miniatures of the Octateuchs contain details that diverge from the biblical text and are frequently independent from the textual commentary of the catena. Weitzmann and Bernabo assume that their creation antedates 460 CE (p. 7).

19. See Weitzmann and Bernabo, *The Byzantine Octateuchs*, pp. 8, 309-10.

Fig. 3. *Isaac Bleeding, Ishmael Fleeing.* Twelfth-century Octateuch.
Vatican Library, Cod. Gr. 746, fol. 80r. Photo © Biblioteca
Apostolica Vaticana, Vatican.

Marcion and the early church fathers.[20] On this reading of Paul's text, Hagar
represents the bondage of the Mosaic covenant (Judaism), Sarah symbolizing the freedom of the New Covenant in Jesus (Christianity).[21] Under this

20. For the view that Paul's allegory is not anti-Judaic, see J. Louis Martyn,
Galatians (AB; New York: Doubleday, 1997), pp. 442-45; Martyn, *Theological Issues
in the Letters of Paul* (Nashville, TN: Abingdon Press, 1997), pp. 25-36, 77-84; Martyn,
'The Covenants of Hagar and Sarah', in *Faith and History: Essays in Honor of Paul
W. Meyer* (ed. J.T. Caroll, C.H. Cosgrove and E.E. Johnson; Atlanta, GA: Scholars
Press, 1990), pp. 164-65; Mark Nanos, 'What Does "Present Jerusalem" (Gal. 4.25)
in Paul's Allegory Have to Do with the Jerusalem of Paul's Time, or the Concerns of
the Galatians?': http://www.marknanos.com/Allegory-Web-Temp-5-2-04.pdf (accessed
October 26, 2012); Hilary Le Cornu and Joseph Shulam, *A Commentary on the Jewish
Roots of Galatians* (Jerusalem: Academon, 2005), pp. xciii-xciv, 298-320.

21. For the traditional view, see Tertullian, *Marc.* 5.4; Augustine, *Civ.* 15.2, 16.31;
The Retractions (Fathers of the Church, 60; Washington, DC: Catholic University of
America Press, 1968), p. 93; Augustine, *Four Anti-Pelagian Writings* (Fathers of the
Church, 86; Washington, DC: Catholic University of America Press, 1992), pp. 123-26;
Letters of St Ambrose (Fathers of the Church, 26; Washington, DC: Catholic University
of America Press, 1954), p. 245. Augustine is responsible, of course, for the popularity

Fig. 4. *Ishmael Persecuting Isaac.* Synagogue pedestal, south
transept portal Strasbourg Cathedral, 1176–fourteenth century.
Photo © author.

influence, Paul is understood as interpreting Ishmael's conduct as the Jewish 'persecution' of Christianity.

A visual portrayal of this idea occurs in the south transept of Strasbourg
Cathedral. On either side of the double portal stands a statue, the left figure
portraying the Ecclesia and the right the Synagogue. The pedestal under
the Synagogue's feet features two little boys (Fig. 4), the one whose lips
curved in distress is kneeling with his hands behind his back—a posture
resembling his binding—being Isaac. Behind him stands Ishmael, his right
hand grasping Isaac's arm and his outstretched left fist ready to hit Isaac's
head. Although frequently unnoticed, this statue reflects Paul's intimation
that Ishmael—the offspring of Synagogue—is 'persecuting' Isaac.

A fourteenth-century English illustrated manuscript (Fig. 5) that places
the two children in the foreground of a scene portraying Isaac's weaning
feast similarly shows Sarah's hand pointing to Ishmael—the taller of the

of the Christian image of the 'City of God', his book bearing this title being concerned
to portray human history as a conflict between the 'City of God' and the 'City of Man'.

Fig. 5. *Ishmael Striking Isaac*. Egerton
Genesis, BL Egerton Ms. 1894, fol. 10.
Photo © British Library, London.

two—as he raises his right fist toward Isaac's face. In his left hand he clasps
an unidentified object, which, while it might be an innocent ball or piece of
food, might just as easily be the hilt of a dagger.[22] Herein, Isaac is portrayed
as a fragile, innocent boy, not only unwilling to defend himself against the
strength of his older brother but also ready to 'turn his cheek' to receive the
blow (cf. Mt. 5.39). Isaac—as a prototype of Jesus—herein demonstrates
his Christian virtue in not resisting the assault of 'he who was born of the
flesh'.[23]

   While the vast majority of the portrayals of the expulsion of Hagar from
the sixteenth to the nineteenth century disregard the events leading up to the

22. Egerton Genesis, BL Ms. 1894. This fourteenth-century English Bible picture
book contains 149 scenes from the biblical text of Genesis, supplemented by legendary
material and accompanied by Anglo-Norman French inscriptions for approximately
half the folios. On the basis of its stylistic heterogeneity and Flemish features, scholars
suggest that it is the work of Michiel van der Borch, a Flemish immigrant living in
Norwich; see Mary Coker Joslin and Caroline Coker Joslin Watson, *The Egerton
Genesis* (Toronto: University of Toronto Press, 2001), pp. 1-14, 203-42.

23. Rather surprisingly, Montague Rhodes James regards this scene as representing
the brothers quarrelling: James, *Illustrations of the Book of Genesis* (Oxford:
Roxburghe Club, 1921), p. 31. See also the *Weltchronik und Marienleben*, Pomersfelden
Schlossbibliothek Cod. 303 (2897), fol. 33-1; and the Isabella Psalter, Cod. gall. 16 fol.
28v, in which Ishmael is shown striking Isaac with a whip.

Fig. 6a. *The Expulsion of Hagar,* Cornelis Engebrechtsz, c. 1500.
Photo © Vienna, Kunsthistorisches Museum.

dramatic expulsion—probably due to a transformation in attitude toward Hagar that occurred among sixteenth- and seventeenth-century Dutch artists—several artists do attend to the framing narrative.[24] Some sixteenth-century book illustrations depict Ishmael attacking Isaac and his ejection, with his mother, from Abraham's house.[25] A similar portrayal occurs in a painting by the Baroque Italian painter Francesco Allegrini, now in the Louvre.[26]

24. Christine Sellin, *Fractured Families and Rebel Maidservants: The Biblical Hagar in Seventeenth-Century Dutch Art and Literature* (New York: T. & T. Clark International, 2006). The quote is taken from the endorsement given by John Thompson (Professor of Historical Theology, Fuller Theological Seminary) on the back cover. For the rise of Christian humanism in the Netherlands, the rapid strides it made in the Low Countries between 1490 and 1520, and its impact on religious art, see Jonathan Israel, *The Dutch Republic: Its Rise, Greatness and Fall* (Oxford: Clarendon Press, 1995), pp. 41-48.

25. See François Bourgoing (trans.), *Histoire de Fl. Iosephe, sacrificateur hebreu* (Lyons: Jacques Jonte, 1562), Pitts Theology Library (Candler School of Theology, Emory University), call no. 1562 JOSE.

26. Francesco Allegrini da Gubbio (1587–1663), *Birth of Isaac, Isaac and Ishmael,* Musée du Louvre, Paris.

Fig. 6b. 'Ishmael Striking Isaac during a Game'. *The Expulsion of Hagar,* Cornelis Engebrechtsz, detail. Photo © Vienna, Kunsthistorisches Museum.

The Dutch artists Cornelis Engebrechtsz and Jan Mostaert also adduce Ishmael's violent conduct as the reason for his expulsion. In the foreground of Engebrechtsz's painting *The Expulsion of Hagar* (Fig. 6a), he depicts the barefooted Hagar and Ishmael being banished. On the right-hand side, behind Abraham, Ishmael pins Isaac to the ground, his left hand grasping a strand of Isaac's hair and his right wielding a sharp implement resembling a stake. Isaac endeavours to prevent the blow with his left hand, his right extended in front of him and holding on to the end of a thread or rope tied to a notched disc—apparently some type of game (Fig. 6b).

The foreground of Jan Mostaert's painting portrays the ejected mother with her tearful son (Fig. 7a). While it thus evokes the viewer's sympathy for the outcasts, it balances this emotion by representing Sarah as standing in front of the house, behind Abraham, watching Ishmael attack Isaac in the

Fig. 7a. *Expulsion of Hagar,* Jan Mostaert, 1525.
Photo © Museo Thyssen-Bornemisza, Madrid.

course of a game whose sticks resemble modern golf clubs (Fig. 7b). The direct link between Ishmael's aggressive behaviour toward Isaac and the expulsion is exemplified by the 'club' that Ishmael still holds in his hand as he is cast out. Both these pictures portray Ishmael as assaulting Isaac during a 'game'—a conflation of the meaning of 'playing' as in the Septuagint and Vulgate and the 'persecution' intimated by the traditional interpretation of the Pauline text.[27]

The eleventh-century Old English Hextateuch illustration discussed above (Fig. 1a)—in whose top scene Abraham presides over Isaac's weaning feast—also contains a lower one on the left (Fig. 1b) in which the two boys' play also appears to be a mixture of sport and potential violence. Here, Isaac—the smaller of the two figures—uses both hands to play while

27. See also the Greek Catena and Petrus Comestor: Agneta Sylvan (ed.), *Petris Comestoris scholastica historia: Liber Genesis* (Turnhout: Brepols, 2004), pp. 106-107.

Fig. 7b. 'Ishmael Striking Isaac during a Game'.
Expulsion of Hagar, Jan Mostaert, 1525, detail.
Photo © Museo Thyssen-Bornemisza, Madrid.

Ishmael holds a ball in his left hand and a stick in his right. This depiction seems to reflect Josephus's exegesis of the biblical text: 'As for Sarah . . . she was not willing that Ishmael should be brought up with him, as being too old for him, and able to do him injuries when their father should be dead' (*Ant.* 1.12.3).

The sole monumental-art representation of Ishmael as attacking Isaac appears to occur in the twelfth-century Romanesque church of San Isidoro de León (Fig. 8a). The binding of Isaac in the tympanum of the Puerta del Cordero—the Lamb Gate—serves as an allegorical prefiguration of the crucifixion, and the figure of Isaac appears twice on the viewer's right, once with his head ringed with a halo and riding on a donkey on his way to Mount Moriah and once removing his shoes at the holy site.[28] On the right-hand

28. The illustration in Ælfric's biblical paraphrase also depicts Isaac riding on a donkey.

Fig. 8a. Tympanum of the Portal of the Lamb in the Collegiate Church of
San Isidoro de León, Spain, twelfth century. Photo © Erich Lessing.

Fig. 8b. Tympanum of the Portal of the Lamb in
the Collegiate Church of San Isidoro de León,
Spain, twelfth century, detail 1.
Photo © Erich Lessing.

Fig. 8c. Tympanum of the Portal of
the Lamb in the Collegiate Church
of San Isidoro, León, Spain,
twelfth century, detail 2.
Photo © Erich Lessing.

edge, Sarah sits beside a house, her left hand on the door handle, an angel
standing next to Abraham holding the ram on the left. A woman—evidently
Hagar—takes up a provocative pose on his right, her head bare and her
mouth open as though singing or flinging insults In contrast to Sarah, whose
head is covered as befitting a noble woman, Hagar is obviously a woman of
inferior rank (Fig. 8b). On the far left-hand side of the tympanum, the figure

riding on a donkey and arching backward in order to shoot an arrow at the
Lamb is identified by art historians as Ishmael.[29] (Fig. 8c).

While many of these visual representations embody the classical understanding of Paul's allegory of the Jewish 'persecution' of Christianity, other
sources were also available to many mediaeval Christian artists. Thus, for
example, while the arrow may be 'drawn' from the biblical statement that
Ishmael became an archer (Gen. 21.20), it probably also reflects a Jewish
midrashic tradition: 'then Ishmael would take a bow and arrows and shoot
them in Isaac's direction, whilst pretending to be playing' (*Gen. R.* 53.10);
'He saw Isaac sitting by himself, and shot an arrow at him to slay him' (*PRE*
30).[30] This tradition fits the iconography of the tympanum, Isaac being a
prototype of Jesus—the slain lamb—according to Christian tradition.

As noted above, rabbinic midrashim also accuse Ishmael of engaging
in idolatry. This Jewish tradition was well known among mediaeval Christian scholars, largely on the basis of the reference made to it by the church
fathers. Thus, for example, Jerome's allusion to Ishmael's idolatry as an
interpretation of 'the Hebrews' was inherited by later Christian exegetes,
who continued to cite it for centuries.[31] While Jewish tradition represents
Ishmael's idolatry by the vague statement that he was doing evil deeds that
ought not to be done or engaged in a game of foreign worship, Christian
exegetes—including Braulio, bishop of Saragossa, in the first half of the
seventh century, Alcuin of York in the eighth century and Bonaventure of
Bagnoregio in the thirteenth century—magnified Ishmael's sin, asserting
that he made an image.[32] Both Braulio and Rupert of Deutz (c. 1075–1129)

29. John Williams, 'Generationes Abrahae: Reconquest Iconography in León', *Gesta*
16.2 (1977), pp. 3-14. Cf. Therese Martin, *Queen as King: Politics and Architectural
Propaganda in Twelfth-Century Spain* (Leiden: Brill, 2006), pp. 101-103.

30. The association of the angel with a ram in the scene of Isaac's binding likewise
appears to be based on a Jewish legend: see Meyer Shapiro, *Late Antique, Early Christian
and Medieval Art* (New York: G. Braziller, 1980), p. 295

31. Jerome, *Qu. hebr. Gen.* on 21.9; cf. Dennis Brown, *Vir trilinguis: A Study in
the Biblical Exegesis of Saint Jerome* (Kampen: Kok Pharos, 1992), pp. 70-82, 167-74;
Adam Kamesar, *Jerome, Greek Scholarship, and the Hebrew Bible* (Oxford: Oxford
University Press, 1993), pp. 176-91; John Thompson, *Writing the Wrongs: Women of
the Old Testament among Biblical Commentators* (Oxford: Oxford University Press),
pp. 37-38.

32. Alejandro Díez Macho, *Neophyti 1, Targum Palestinense MS la Biblioteca
Vaticana: Genesis* (Madrid: Consejo Superior de Investigaciones Científicas, 1968),
p. 119; *Sifre* 31 (*Sifre: A Tannaitic Commentary on the Book of Deuteronomy* [trans. R.
Hammer; New Haven, CT: Yale University Press, 1986], pp. 55-56); Michael Klein, *The
Fragment-Targums of the Pentateuch* (Analecta biblica, 76; Rome: Pontifical Biblical
Institute, 1980), I, p. 53; Braulio of Saragossa, Letter 44 (*Iberian Fathers* [Fathers of the
Church, 63; Washington, DC: Catholic University of America Press, 1969], II, pp. 106-
107); Alcuin, *Interrogationes et responsiones in Genesin, Inter.* 196 (PL, C, col. 543);

note that 'according to the Hebrews' the image was made of mud or clay; and Petrus Comestor (c. 1160) and Roderigo Jiménez de Rada, bishop of Toledo (1170–1247), combined Ishmael's idolatry with his physical abuse of Isaac.[33] Pedro Pascual, bishop of Jaén, likewise claimed in his anti-Islamic tract that Ishmael—Abraham's illegitimate son—acted malevolently toward his brother, compelling him to worship clay idols, which constituted the reason for his banishment.[34]

With the rise of Islam and the Muslim victories over Byzantine forces—culminating in the wresting of the Holy Land from Christian hands—the church was faced with the task of providing an explanation for these historical events. As John Tolan notes, 'when mediaeval Christians looked at Islam, they did so through the filter of the Bible and of writers such as Eusebius, Jerome, Augustine, and Isidore . . . when they first meet Muslims they will try and understand their military successes and their religion in terms familiar to them, to fit Islam into already existing Christian categories by portraying them, variously, as a divinely sent punishment, as pagan idolaters, as Christian heretics, as followers of Satan, or as devotees of Antichrist'.[35]

Following the Muslim conquest of the Holy Land and a large portion of the Christian world, Paul's alleged identification of the Jews as the descendants of Ishmael and Christianity's enemy became irrelevant. In order to adjust the biblical interpretation to the new historical circumstances, the Venerable Bede—one of the first to address the Muslim threat exegetically and theologically—explains that, while typologically Ishmael's seed may

P.P. Collegii S. Bonaventurae (eds.), *S. Bonaventurae S.R.E. episcopi cardinalis opera omnia* (Commentarii in Sacram Scripturam, 10 vols.; Rome: Ad Claras Aquas), VI, p. 190 n. 9; cf. *Exod. Rab.* 1.1, which states that Ishmael brought idols from the street, toyed with them, and worshiped them. This tradition is much later than the Christian tradition that claims that Ishmael made an idol.

33. See Rupert, *Opera omnia* (PL, CLXVII), I, p. 419; Roderigo Jiménez de Rada, *Breviarium historie catholice* 2:15-20 (ed. J. Fernández Valverde; CCCM, 72A–B; Turnhout: Brepols, 1992), p. 68; Thompson, *Writing the Wrongs*, pp. 60-66.

34. Pedro Pascual was captured by Muslim troops in 1298 and imprisoned until his death two years later. He composed an anti-Islamic tract in Castilian in an attempt to discourage other Christian prisoners from converting to Islam; see John V. Tolan, *Sons of Ishmael: Muslims through European Eyes in the Middle Ages* (Gainesville, FL: University Press of Florida, 2008), pp. 35, 135, 142.

35. John V. Tolan, *Saracens: Islam in the Medieval European Imagination* (New York: Columbia University Press, 2002), p. 4. See also his *Sons of Ishmael*, pp. 35-37; Tolan (ed.), *Medieval Christian Perceptions of Islam* (New York: Taylor & Francis, 1996), p. 10. Despite the fact that Christian scholars had been familiar with Muslim literature since the middle of the twelfth century—either in translations or because of their knowledge of Arabic—they preferred to propagate debasing stories about Muhammad and Islam as part of their attempt to prevent members of the church from apostasizing and restore those who had already converted to Islam to the bosom of the church.

Fig. 9. *Ishmael Forcing Isaac to Worship an Idol,* Bible of Jean de Sy,
c. 1353. Paris BnF MS. fr. 15397, fol. 33r.
Photo © Bibliothèque Nationale de France, Paris.

be the Jews, literally and practically they are the Saracens.[36] Ishmael coming
to represent the early ancestor of Muhammad and the Muslims, his 'playing' with Isaac and 'persecution' of Christianity are thereby transferred to
the Muslims.[37] The tympanum at San Isidoro de León reflects this polemical
interaction with Islam (Fig. 8b). By placing a turban on Ishmael's head, the
artist transformed Ishmael into a mounted Muslim warrior shooting at the
Lamb of God—that is, Islam fighting against Christianity.

This image spread throughout Europe in the twelfth century via the *Chan-
sons de geste* and the liturgical works of the twelfth and thirteenth centuries,
continuing to be prevalent for centuries to come.[38] Dozens of mediaeval
texts depict Islamic worship in a manner reminiscent of the Roman pantheon, and the Saracens were thought to sacrifice to and worship gods made

36. Venerable Bede, *Opera omnia* (PL, XCI), pp. 241-42; *On Genesis* (trans. Calvin
B. Kendall; Liverpool: Liverpool University Press, 2008), pp. 26-27; Tolan, *Saracens*,
pp. 72-77; Thompson, *Writing the Wrongs*, pp. 48-51; Richard Southern, *Western Views
of Islam in the Middle Ages* (Cambridge, MA: Harvard University Press, 1962), pp.
16-17.

37. Geert Claassens, 'Jacob van Maerlant on Muhammad and Islam', in *Medieval
Christian Perceptions of Islam* (ed. J.V. Tolan; New York: Taylor & Francis, 1996),
pp. 211-24. Jacob van Maerlant—a prominent thirteenth-century Flemish poet and
Middle Dutch writer—wrote a rhymed chronicle of the world known as the *Spiegel
historiael,* in which he devotes an extensive section to Islam in general and Muhammad
in particular.

38. Tolan, *Saracens*, pp. 125, 129, 318.

Fig. 10a. *The Expulsion of Hagar,*
Pieter Aertsen (active 1543–1571).
Private collection. Photo © Christie's
Images / Bridgeman Art Library.

of stone or precious metals that were inhabited by demons who granted them special powers.[39]

In a fourteenth-century illustrated French Bible (Fig. 9), Ishmael's right hand presses down on Isaac's head, his right knee pinning him down as he kneels with clasped hands, gazing toward his parents in hope of deliverance. Isaac's kneeling before a statue resembling Jupiter indicates how Ishmael is compelling him to worship an idol—a symbol of the way in which Christians were forced to convert to Islam. Two centuries later, in the background of the left side of Pieter Aertsen's (1508–1575) *The Expulsion of Hagar* (Fig. 10a), an adolescent Ishmael behind Abraham likewise forcefully grasps the infant Isaac's arm with his left hand, leading him toward a structure on which stands a statuette (Fig. 10b). Pointing it out to Isaac, the latter appears appalled by the sight of such an outrage.[40]

In this context, we must return to Rudolf von Ems's *Weltchronik* manuscript (Fig. 2a), in which Sarah draws attention to the brothers struggling with each other.[41] While the cause of their quarrel and its initiator are obscure

39. Tolan, *Saracens*, pp. 105-34; *Sons of Ishmael*, pp. 35-60; Southern, *Western Views of Islam*, pp. 29-32.

40. http://www.christies.com/lotfinder/lot/pieter-aertsen-the-expulsion-of-hagar-and-4794279-details.aspx?intObjectID=4794279 (accessed October 26, 2012).

41. Rudolf von Ems's *Weltchronik* (mid-thirteenth century) is one of the central Middle High German texts, comprising a rhymed poem in which biblical accounts

Fig. 10b. *The Expulsion of Hagar,*
Pieter Aertsen, detail. Private collection.
Photo © Christie's Images /
Bridgeman Art Library.

at first glance, a closer examination discloses that behind Isaac stand two small clay statuettes on a terraced rock, and Isaac treads on a third with his right foot. Ishmael's left hand touching Isaac's cheek, his right pressing down on Isaac's head, the painting reflects the fusion of the two traditions of Ishmael injuring Isaac and forcing him to bow down to and worship clay images. Isaac's resistance corresponds with the accompanying poem, which states that Isaac's refusal to participate with Ishmael in idol worship prompted a fight between them (Fig. 2b).[42] In contrast to the Egerton (Fig. 4) and French Bible illustrations (Fig. 9), this *Weltchronik* illumination portrays Isaac as forcefully resisting participation in Ishmael's idolatry; Isaac thus symbolizes Christianity's opposition to Ishmael's idolatrous Muslim descendants and lauds Christian efforts to drive the Muslims out of Christian Europe.

and other historical events are combined to form a lengthy chronicle of world history. The text is based on the Bible, Petrus Comestor's *Historia scholastica* and Godfrey of Virtebo's *Pantheon.*

    42. www.mhdwb-online.de/Etexte/PDF/RWCHR.pdf (lines 5024-46) (accessed October 26, 2012).

From the twelfth to the fourteenth century, European writers and artists therefore appear to have revived the ancient Jewish interpretation of the verb *mᵉṣaḥēq* to indicate that Ishmael was involved in idolatry, enlisting it in their polemics and political and theological propaganda against the Muslims.

In summary, this brief survey demonstrates that visual representations of biblical scenes constitute not merely 'artistic license' but can be traced to earlier Jewish and Christian exegetical traditions, as well as historical developments and circumstances. This study of an enigmatic word in Gen. 21.9 demonstrates the way in which visual depictions of biblical texts necessarily represent a form of hermeneutical activity—making explicit motives and conduct that remain undisclosed in Scripture itself—as well as reflecting religious disputes and historical circumstances. It thus helps us to understand that artistic renderings of biblical scenes—such as Ishmael's 'playing'—are frequently not merely illustrative but also manipulative, serving as tools in Christianity's polemical interaction with Judaism and Islam alike.

THE MALLEABILITY OF JAEL
IN THE DUTCH RENAISSANCE

Colleen M. Conway

ABSTRACT

The article traces depictions of the figures of Jael and Sisera from the mediaeval period into the Dutch Renaissance. As the representation of Jael moves beyond the theological rendering of the church to the secular print market, the potential for interpretation of Jael widens considerably. Jael is portrayed as a model of female virtue, a celebrated heroine, or a deceptive man-killer. Somewhat surprisingly, these varying interpretations are found in the same period and sometimes by the same artist. These sometimes conflicting renderings were possible because Jael played a different function for differently gendered audiences. Depictions of Jael as a model of virtue were intended for elite female audiences, while warnings about Jael as a treacherous woman were meant for male audiences. Still, the line between the heroic and the devious Jael are not so clearly drawn. Several illustrations meant to celebrate a virtuous Jael also introduce suggestive hints of her dangerous aspects. Likewise, representations of Jael meant to warn men about women's power may have unintended consequences. For example, one powerful example of Jael from this period suggests a gender-blurring that radically undermines the binary sex–gender system. In this way, it anticipates Jael's role in empowering alternative visions of gender to future interpreters.

Introduction

But Jael wife of Heber took a tent peg, and took a hammer in her hand, and went softly to him and drove the peg into his temple, until it went down in the ground—he was lying fast asleep from weariness—and he died (Judg. 4.21 NRSV).

The picture painted by these chilling lines—a woman stealthily approaching and brutally murdering a sleeping man—has long intrigued scholar and artist alike. In casting Jael in the role of man-slayer, the biblical depictions of Jael unmans both the Israelite warrior Barak and the Canaanite general Sisera. After Barak refuses to go to battle without the company of Deborah, she predicts that Barak will not achieve glory, but, instead, the enemy Sisera will be delivered into the hand of a woman (Judg. 4.8). For his part,

Sisera ironically denies his own manhood, instructs Jael to tell anyone asking whether there is a man in the tent to say 'No' (Judg. 4.20)—not to mention the fact that he is then violently penetrated with a tent peg. As many have observed, these and other aspects of the two accounts of Jael in Judges 4–5 suggest multiple sexual and gendered allusions depending on how one translates and interprets the stories.[1] In short, for a gender theorist, there is no shortage of material to explore in these accounts, and much productive work has already been done on the biblical traditions in Judges 4–5. Here, rather than debate the gender implications of the story in its biblical context, I focus on how gender plays a role in later representations of Jael. In fact, it is precisely the ambiguity of Jael's action and the confusion of traditional gender markers in the story that make her figure a site of contest and opportunity for later interpreters. For this study, my interest is in the shifting interpretations and presentations of Jael and Sisera from the late mediaeval period to the Dutch Renaissance. I explore how the images of Jael and Sisera are affected when the illustration of their story moves beyond the theological readings of the church to include the secular interpretations of the print market.

Of particular interest will be the prints of Jael and Sisera produced in Germany and the Low Countries during the sixteenth century. These works show how the ambiguity of Jael's character in the biblical accounts results in a malleability of her image that proved useful to later artists. One can find depictions of Jael as a celebrated heroine produced alongside images that use the figure of Jael to warn of women's evil ways. Print makers rightly perceived a market for both types, mostly likely, I suggest, with differently gendered audiences in mind. In spite of this representational split between what I will call the virtuous and the villainous Jael, we will see that the lines between these contrasting images can be blurred. It is as if Jael's complex and ambiguous character in the biblical story creates a resistance to overdetermination in her later representations. In addition, because gender identity is always relational, we will see how differing depictions of Jael also influence the interpretation and representation of Sisera in significant ways.

---

1. For discussion of the erotic and maternal imagery in these traditions, see, for example, Mieke Bal, *Death and Dissymmetry: The Politics of Coherence in the Book of Judges* (Chicago: University of Chicago Press, 1988); Danna Nolan Fewell and David M. Gunn, 'Controlling Perspectives: Women, Men and Violence in Judges 4–5', *Journal of the American Academy of Religion* 58 (1989), pp. 43-57; Susan Niditch, 'Eroticism and Death in the Tale of Jael', in *Gender and Difference in Ancient Israel* (ed. Peggy L. Day; Minneapolis, MN: Fortress Press, 1989); Pamela Tamarkin Reis, 'Uncovering Jael and Sisera: A New Reading', *Scandanavian Journal of the Old Testament* 19 (2005), pp. 24-47.

Mediaeval Representations of Jael

To see the development of two distinct representations of Jael in the Dutch Renaissance, we begin with a brief discussion of mediaeval typological illustrations of Jael and Sisera. These illustrations served the theological purposes of the church and, in so doing, were only loosely connected to the events depicted in Judges 4–5. For instance, images of Jael were widely circulated in the context of the mediaeval text *Speculum humanae salvationis* (*SHS*, that is, 'Mirror of Human Salvation'). This mediaeval bestseller presented, through text and illustrations, a typological reading of the Old Testament as a prefigurement for the New Testament.[2] In this context, Jael appears with Judith and Tomyris as a prefiguration of Mary's victory over the devil.[3] The following translation from a French version of *SHS* explains the link between Jael and Mary, found in the nail that pierced the head of Sisera.

> This womanly victory was long ago prefigured by Jael, the wife of Heber. When she perceived and saw the wrongs which Sisera, a prince of the army of King Jabin, visited day after day upon the people and lineage of Israel in his desire to destroy, exile and do away with them, Jael began to reflect. She decided to make him suffer and take the severest possible revenge on him. Finding him in bed, asleep, she took a great nail, and suddenly without more ado, put it into position and placed it against his temples, then raised a heavy hammer, and, without further delay, hammered the nail into the head of Sisera, whom she murdered and killed, just as Mary, the mother of our Redeemer did with the nails with which her Son had been attached and crucified on the tree of the Cross on the hill of Calvary.[4]

Although the focus is on Jael as a type of Mary, note how the interpretation provides a motive for Jael that is missing in the Bible. She is shown to be a reflective woman, concerned about the welfare of the Israelites (though it is not clear that she is one of them). What is crucial in the interpretation of Jael and Sisera is the nail and the killing. Indeed, Sisera is 'murdered and

---

2. Over 350 manuscripts of the *Speculum* still exist. By the early fourteenth century, the Latin text had been translated into German, Dutch, French, English and Czech. See Adrian Wilson and Joyce Lancaster Wilson, *A Medieval Mirror: Speculum humanae salvationis, 1324–1500* (Berkeley, CA: University of California Press, 1984), pp. 10, 24.

3. Jael, Judith and Tomyris are all legendary manslayers, with Judith famously beheading Holofernes, and Tomyris, queen of the Scythians, commanding the beheading of the defeated King Cyrus of Persia (although the legend of Tomyris comes to us not through the Bible, but through Greek historians such as Herodotus).

4. *Le miroir de humaine salvation*, c. 1455 (trans. David Wright with the assistance of John French, Jr, pp. 90-93), Newberry Call No. folio BS478.S64. http://dcc. newberry.org/collections/wives-and-wenches-sinners-and-saints-women-in-medieval-europe#women-from-the-bible.

Fig. 1. From *Speculum humanae salvationis.*
The Illustrated Bartsch, vol. 81, cat. 496.

killed', driving home the point, so to speak. These, too, are the elements
that are emphasized in the accompanying illustrations of Jael and Sisera
in the *SHS*. Given the many translations and copies of the text, there are
many different artistic renditions of Jael and Sisera. But, those reviewed for
this study all feature a sleeping or already-slain Sisera with a surprisingly
serene-looking Jael standing above him as she takes on her task 'without
more ado'. In one hand, she holds the nail, while her other arm is raised with
mallet in hand (see, for example, the woodcut shown in Fig. 1). In the illustrations that show Sisera already dead, there is typically blood flowing from
his wound. Attention is drawn to Jael's violence in these images because
that is what connects her to Mary. They share violent 'womanly victories'
over evil by way of the nail.

This point is made even more graphically in another typological interpretation of Jael and Sisera found in the *Bible moralisée*, a mediaeval picture
Bible illustrating the moral significance of particular biblical stories. The
story and its interpretation are presented in four medallions. From the top,
we first see Jael giving milk to Sisera and then slaying him with the tent peg
(Fig. 2). Underneath, the allegorical illustration shows the church giving the
milk of the gospel to many who are asleep in mortal sin.[5] In the third medal-
lion, Jael shows Sisera's murdered body to Barak and the Israelites. Underneath this literal illustration, the allegorical interpretation depicts Christians
rejoicing that the devil has been slain by the nails from Christ's crucifixion.
The slain body that was Sisera has morphed into a dark demonic figure
lying before the spectators. Thus, in these mediaeval theological readings,
Jael is a champion of the oppressed and a slayer of evil. She is a type of

5. As per the image description accompanying this print in the Bodleian collection.
http://bodley30.bodley.ox.ac.uk:8180/luna/servlet/detail/ODLodl~1~1~34369~119487.

Fig. 2. Jael shown literally and allegorically in
the *Bible moraliseé*. French manuscript from
the mid-thirteenth century. Bodleian Library,
Oxford University. MS Bodl. 270b.

Mary, the mother of Jesus, while Sisera becomes evil incarnate as the devil
himself.

Apart from these theological purposes to which Jael was put, she also
makes sporadic appearances in the mediaeval courtly tradition of the female
'worthies'. These women 'worthies', modeled after the nine male worthies,
were intended as ideal examples of chivalric virtues. Traditionally, the worthies included three pagan, three Jewish and three Christian exemplars.[6]

6. The nine male worthies were made popular by a 1310 poem by Jacques de Longuyon,
Les voeux de paon (*The Vows of the Peacock*), which celebrates three exemplary pagan,
three Jewish and three Christian men. By the late 1300s, the balladeer Eustace Dechamps
introduced nine female worthies, but his women were all pagan and mostly Amazon
warriors. John Ferne's prose work *The Blazon of Gentrie* (1586) lists three Jewish

Fig. 3. Hans Burghmair, Esther, Judith, and
Jael from a cycle of Nine Worthies, engraving,
c. 1519. *The Illustrated Bartsch*, vol. 11. B.
VII.219.67.

Although the choice of nine women worthies varied, Jael was sometimes
featured as one of the 'three good Jews', as in the print by German artist
Hans Burghmair (Fig. 3). In his rendering of the women, Judith holds center
place, flanked by Esther and Jael. All three bear identifying attributes—
Queen Esther wears her crown, Judith carries her sword and the head of
Holofernes, and Jael clasps her mallet and peg. But apart from these attrib-

women worthies including Jael, Deborah and Judith. Notably, their mention raises an
objection from one of the interlocutors, the Ploughman, who suggests that more genteel
and meek women should be used for examples rather than 'sturdy, manly' women. See
Ann McMillan, 'Men's Weapons, Women's War: The Nine Female Worthies, 1400–
1640', *Mediaevalia* 5 (1979), pp. 113-39 (129-30).

utes, the women are isolated from the biblical narrative context. Together, their figures alone are meant to call to mind virtuous conduct.

These, in brief, are the main images of Jael seen in mediaeval iconography. In the theological illustrations, the violence of Jael was acceptable, indeed meritorious, because it symbolized the defeat of the devil and the salvation offered through the crucifixion. Indeed, these images of Jael *focus* on the blood spilled, since one is to recall the nails of the crucifixion and the blood spilled in the defeat of the devil. Although not at all villainous (indeed, quite the contrary), she is obviously violent. The presentation of this typological Jael contrasts with the 'virtuous Jael' of the worthies, insofar as this latter type of representation distances the woman from her act of violence. As we move into the Renaissance period, we find that both the image of the active, violent Jael and that of the stately, virtuous Jael persist, although both will be put to different uses.

Didactic Uses of Jael in Fifteenth–Sixteenth-Century Literature and Art

To understand the uses to which the malleable Jael was put in the fifteenth and sixteenth centuries, we should consider that in this period a major function of European artwork was didactic. That is, in addition to the aesthetic pleasures that art certainly must have brought, as Renée Pigeaud notes, 'the moralizing function of art was accepted as a matter of course . . .'.[7] This is not surprising, given the widespread popularity of instructional literature during this time.[8] In what follows, I argue that the 'virtuous' and the 'villainous' representations of Jael in fifteenth- and sixteenth-century prints are linked to two different types of instructional texts. Further, I suggest that the image of the virtuous Jael, like the texts on which it was based, was intended primarily for women while the images of the villainous Jael were meant primarily for men.

In the sixteenth century, the popular mediaeval idea of a mirror continued to prove useful as a metaphor for the function of illustrations of biblical scenes. However, whereas illustrations in the mediaeval period focused on biblical figures as mirrors reflecting back God's plan for human salvation (resulting in an emphasis on Jael's violent act), the secular instructional

7. Renée Pigeaud, 'Woman as Temptress: Urban Morality in the 15th Century', in *Saints and She-Devils: Images of Women in the 15th and 16th Centuries* (ed. Lène Dresen-Coenders and Petty Bange; London: Rubicon Press, 1987).

8. Ilja Veldman notes that visual admonitions for female conduct became increasingly popular in the sixteenth century, corresponding to an increase of instruction books intended for women (Ilja M. Veldman, 'Lessons for Ladies: A Selection of Sixteenth- and Seventeenth-Century Dutch Prints', *Simiolus: Netherlands Quarterly for the History of Art* 16 [1986], pp. 113-27 [114]).

texts that became popular during the Renaissance used biblical characters to mirror back ideal conduct for women. The biblical women became models of female virtues, with chastity taking precedence; but others virtues, such as modesty, humility and moderation were also important.[9] That the intended audience for such models was women has been convincingly demonstrated by art historian Yvonne Bleyveld.[10] She cites multiple instances of literature from this period that implicitly and often explicitly provide instruction to elite girls and women for their moral edification. For example, the Dutch translator of Christine de Pisan's famous catalogue of women (*Le livre de la cité des dames*, 1404–1405) includes an epilogue stating, 'It is a book full of honor, full of virtues and full of dignities, a mirror and example to all women' that the translator hopes, will 'edify or convert many women'.[11]

Another popular text, the *Book of the Knight of the Tower*, was written by the French nobleman Geoffrey IV de la Tour Landry for the instruction of his daughters in proper conduct. De la Tour Landry's book was translated twice into English, as well as into German (1495) and Dutch (1515). As in de Pisan's catalogue, the author presents biblical women as exemplars of good conduct, though he is not adverse to using some as negatives examples as well. In 1523, Juan Luis Vives dedicated his manual for the education of women, *De institutione feminae christianae,* to Catherine of Aragon for the instruction of her daughter. Once again, Vives draws on examples of women from the Bible, as well as from classical traditions, to support his arguments for proper conduct. This manual became one of the most frequently translated and printed treatises of the time.[12]

Finally, we should mention yet another quite popular text in the Netherlands, known as *Zielentroost*, which in this case used the typology of the

---

9. See, for example, Juan Luis Vives, *The Education of a Christian Woman: A Sixteenth-Century Manual* (trans. Charles Fantazzi; Chicago: University of Chicago Press, 2000). In his section titled 'On the Virtues of a Woman and the Examples She Should Imitate', he notes that a woman 'should be aware that the principal female virtue is chastity, and it is in itself the equal of all the others in moral worth.... [T]he inseparable companions of chastity are a sense of propriety and modest behavior' (p. 116).

10. Yvonne Bleyerveld, 'Chaste, Obedient and Devout: Biblical Women as Patterns of Female Virtue in Netherlandish and German Graphic Art, ca. 1500–1750', *Simiolus: Netherlands Quarterly for the History of Art* 28 (2000–2001), pp. 219-50. I am indebted to Bleyerveld's fine article for much of the discussion that follows on the role of didactic literature and art in Dutch and German graphic art during this period. See also her monograph *Hoe bedriechlijck dat die vrouwen zijn: Vrouwenlisten in de beeldende kunst in de Nederlanden circa 1350–1650* (Leiden: Primaver Pers, 2000).

11. Quoted in 'Chaste, Obedient and Devout', p. 221.

12. Veldman, 'Lessons for Ladies'. p. 114. Notably, Jael is not used as a model in the volume.

Decalogue to focus on negative biblical exemplars for instruction.[13] When it came to violators of the fifth commandment, the author had plenty of biblical examples to choose from, but it is notable that both Jael and Judith make the list.[14] Thus, these same biblical women who in some popular secular texts served as examples of virtue could also illustrate disobedience and moral failure. For Jael and Judith, this is a pattern that will be true also in the visual arts.

The literary use of biblical women as mirrors of virtue made it quite natural for the lessons from these didactic texts to move into the visual arts, thereby providing an actual image for women to gaze on and imitate. This was also a natural progression, given the humanist understanding of the effects of visual stimuli on the human condition, especially on the female human condition.[15] Indeed, from this humanist perspective, visual examples were particularly important for women because their physical nature made women especially primed for imitation. Because a woman was thought to be lower in temperature than man, she simply absorbed what she observed 'without being able to "combust it"'.[16] For this reason, she was more likely to be affected by what she observed and was more inclined to imitation than were men.[17] Along these lines, Vives's manual instructs pregnant women to avoid occasions 'in which some ugly sight may come before their eyes' lest it have a negative effect on the child in their womb.[18] It was critically important, then, to hold before women positive models for them to see and imitate. As we have seen, to use negative models was possible in written texts, but to use them visually carried an even greater danger that exposure to such vice might result in unforeseen consequences.

The connection between didactic literature and images can be seen quite explicitly in a poem by German poet Hans Sachs and accompanying illustration by Erhard Schoën. The poem, *Mirror of Honor Illumined through*

13. Ilja M. Veldman, 'The Old Testament as a Moral Code: Old Testament Stories as Exempla of the Ten Commandments', *Simiolus: Netherlands Quarterly for the History of Art* 23 (1995), pp. 215-39 (218).

14. Veldman, 'The Old Testament as a Moral Code', p. 220.

15. Ellen Muller and Jeanne Marie Noël, 'Humanist Views on Art and Morality: Theory and Image', in *Saints and She-Devils: Images of Women in the 15th and 16th Centuries* (ed. Lène Dresen-Coenders; London: Rubicon Press, 1987), pp. 129-59.

16. Muller and Noël, 'Humanist Views on Art and Morality', p. 136.

17. Bleyerveld notes that in Cornelius Anthonisz.'s woodcut of a wise man and a wise woman, in which he provides an allegorical presentation of ideal male and female virtues, only the women's virtues are linked to celebrated women of the past. She offers this as further evidence for 'a tradition specifically for women of instructing them with the aid of exemplars' (Bleyerveld, 'Chaste, Obedient and Devout', p. 224). For another detailed discussion of this woodcut, see Veldman, 'Lessons for Ladies', pp. 113-14.

18. Vives, *The Education of a Christian Woman*, p. 268. See Muller and Noël, 'Humanist Views on Art and Morality', p. 137.

Fig. 4. Erhard Schoën's woodcut series of twelve
Old Testament women. *The Illustrated Bartsch,* vol. 13.

Twelve Old Testament Women (Der ehren-spiegel der zwölff durchleuchti-genn frawen dess Alten Testaments) (1530), offers an example of how biblical women could be used outside of church settings to model ideal virtues for women.[19] If the *Speculum humanae salvationis* provided a mirror of salvation, Sachs's poem provided a mirror of female virtue by way of biblical models. Sachs associates each of twelve biblical women with a particular virtue: Rebekah the obedient, Rachel the gracious, Leah the patient, and so on. In the case of Jael, Sachs identifies her as *die redlich*, a term that conveyed a range of meanings in sixteenth-century German, including valiant conduct in battle.[20] The verses on Jael conclude with the observation that *redliche* women should be honored because their *redligkeyt erhelt leut und land* (bravery saves people and country).[21] In this way, Sachs celebrates Jael much like Judges 5 does, as a woman who was a saviour to the people of Israel.

Schoën's illustration of Sachs's poem was done across two large wood panels, clearly designed for a wall hanging (Fig. 4).[22] Much like the women worthies, the biblical women in Schoën's woodcut are celebrated almost as the personified virtue itself, rather than actual women engaged in virtuous conduct. In other words, one effect of moving from the poetic text to its illustration is that the viewer becomes farther removed from the biblical narrative. In the case of Jael, the poem gives a brief review of Jael's actions, while Schoën's illustration narrows the focus to the figure of Jael with her

19. A. von Keller, *Hans Sachs. Werke* (26 vols.; Tübingen, 1870–1908), I, pp. 203-10; cited in Bleyerveld, 'Chaste, Obedient and Devout', p. 225 n. 28.

20. See J. and W. Grimm, *Deutsches Wörterbuch* (16 vols.; Leipzig, 1854–1960), VIII, p. 475-82, esp. 478. Among the many meanings listed are 'upright', 'good', 'honest', 'loyal' and 'innocent'.

21. Bleyerveld, 'Chaste, Obedient and Devout', p. 39.

22. In the first set of six, Erhard Schoën illustrates the first six women of Sachs's poem: from left to right are Eve, Sarah, Rebekah, Rachel, Leah and Jael. The second wood cut features Ruth, Michal, Abigail, Judith, Esther and Susanna.

attributes, the mallet and the tent peg. But the representation of Jael does more than this. Schoën's Jael stands apart from the rest of the women. She is spatially distanced, but she is also distinguished by her exotic, seductive costume. Her midriff, arms and ankles are all exposed. The clothing evokes an association with the East, perhaps suggesting that Jael's excessive act of violence, courageous though it was, should also be explained by way of her foreignness.[23] So although she stands with the other biblical women, and although the poem praises her valor as a virtue to be imitated, the visual image highlights her difference.[24] This tendency to clothe Jael in seductive dress will continue in other later images of Jael, showing that not only biblical scholars read sex into the story of Jael and Sisera. What will also continue in later images of Jael is the hint of ambivalence in what is seemingly intended as a positive representation of her character.

The tradition of presenting Old Testament women as exemplars of virtue for women continues into the late sixteenth century, with the images growing into an increasingly monumental style. Jael, like other celebrated biblical women, begins to tower over landscapes. In contrast, Sisera appears only as a diminished fallen figure in the background. Sometimes Jael is poised over him, reminding viewers of her act, and sometimes he lies alone, already dead.[25] Many of these images are accompanied by Latin inscriptions that link the image to the biblical narrative through a brief summary of events, or simply highlight her courageous act and resulting renown.

There are a number of such monumental figures of Jael from this period, enough to expect that she would indeed be remembered for her great courage. But this memory was tempered by another representation of Jael that portrayed her murder of Sisera not as a courageous act but as a deceptive, treacherous one instead. This alternative portrayal of Jael will be examined in the next section, but, as with Burgmair's woodcut, one can see hints of a negative view of Jael, even in these heroic depictions. Consider, for exam-

---

23. See the discussion of the relationship between the inversion of gender and violence and the use of Orientalism in the story of Tomyris and Cyrus to help render a legitimately violent woman (Marilynn Desmond and Pamela Sheingorn, *Myth, Montage, and Visuality in Late Medieval Manuscript Culture: Christine de Pizan's* Epistre Othea (Ann Arbor, MI: University of Michigan Press, 2003), pp. 180-84.

24. Eve is also dressed differently, but her skin-clad figure suggests primitiveness rather than seductiveness.

25. For a discussion of these monumental heroines in the context of the *femme forte* of the seventeenth century, see Mary D. Garrard, *Artemisia Gentileschi: The Image of the Female Hero in Italian Baroque Art* (Princeton, NJ: Princeton University Press, 1989). Garrard argues that while it may be remarkable that images of strong virile women, often juxtaposed with 'tiny and subordinated images of devalued and denigrated men', were so popular at this time, they were likely viewed only as 'curiosities at best, heroic only insofar as they are virile, and virile only insofar as they are imaginary' (pp. 168-69).

Fig. 5. Nicolaas Braeu after a drawing by
Hendrick Goltzius, 1589, 404 *New Hollstein,*
vol. 23, part 3.

ple, the inscription that surrounds a print by Nicolaus Braeu after a drawing by Hendrick Goltzius (1597) (Fig. 5). A rather literal translation of the
Latin reads, 'When the sad fight was joined under an inauspicious omen, the
treacherous Jael received Sisera, who was fleeing from the slaughter of his
own men, with a nail having been driven though his temples'.[26] Thus, while
the artist has drawn a figure of the celebrated Jael, the inscription seems far
more sympathetic to Sisera's perspective. It also hints at Jael's violation of
the code of hospitality, which some later readers will see as inexcusable.
Finally, a close look at Jael's expression in Goltzius's drawing suggests sly-

26. Thanks to my Seton Hall colleague Frederick Booth for his assistance with the
Latin translation.

Fig. 6. Maarten de Vos, *Women of the Old Testament,*
Philip Galle. © Trustees of the British Museum.

ness rather than noble heroism. Her eyes look teasingly into the eyes of the viewer with lips slightly upturned, as though she knows something that we do not. Here is an example of the ambivalence of Jael's story exerting itself against a clear-cut rendering of her character.

The same is true in another print of the celebrated Jael. Philip Galle's print after a drawing by Maarten de Vos is part of a series depicting heroes and heroines of the Old Testament. The print overtly displays the seductive nature of Jael, showing her provocatively dressed, looking demurely down at her ever-present tent peg (Fig. 6). Although she is seated with her legs gracefully bent under her, her head, the direction of her gaze and her left hand all parallel the murderous scene in the background depicting the moment that she slays Sisera. And is that Sisera's hat lying perched next to her, at the tip of the tent peg? In these ways, the celebrated Jael is visually linked in a more explicit way with her act of violence. The inscription under her figure refers to her daring action, for which her name will flourish, but given this image, perhaps a more fitting translation is, 'for which her name will be notorious'.[27]

In sum, if these images were intended as mirrors of female virtue, and as models for women to imitate, the message seems mixed. In a culture that stressed the chastity of women above all, depicting Jael in coy or provocative poses introduced an ambivalent aspect of her character. Even in prints that were intended to celebrate Jael, we find a more or less subtle undercutting of this celebration in the way her figure is drawn.

Jael in the Power of Women Topos

From this subtle blurring of lines between a virtuous and a villainous Jael, we move to an overtly negative use of her figure. At the same time that Jael was drawn as part of a series of celebrated women, or put on a pedestal for her courage, she was also featured in a number of print series depicting the popular mediaeval *topos* known as the *Weibermacht*, or 'Power of Women'. This theme warned against the power of deceptive women over even the most famous of men, and, on the flip side, the foolishness of men who succumbed to love/desire for a woman. The originating and most popular example of this theme was the legend of Aristotle and Phyllis, followed closely by the story of Virgil in a basket. Both are stories of famously wise men being tricked and humiliated by women. According to legend, Aristotle was seduced by Alexander's wife (or mistress, depending on the version), who convinced him to put on a bridle so she could ride him like an animal. From this legend, images of the 'mounted Aristotle' proliferated. A similar story circulated about the humiliation of Virgil, who was promised by the Roman emperor's daughter that she would lift him in a basket to her bedroom. Instead, she left him dangling outside her wall, helpless and humiliated for all of Rome to see.

The Power of Women *topos* first came to the visual arts in mostly decorative pieces around the beginning of the fourteenth century.[28] About two hundred years later, Lucas van Leyden was among the first to bring it to

---

27. As David Gunn suggests; see David M. Gunn, *Judges* (Blackwell Bible Commentaries; Malden, MA: Blackwell Publishing, 2005), p. 75.

28. Susan L. Smith, *The Power of Women: A Topos in Medieval Art and Literature* (Philadelphia: University of Pennsylvania Press, 1995), pp. 193-94. See also Julia Nurse, 'She-Devils, Harlots and Harridans in Northern Renaissance Prints', *History Today* 48.7 (1998), pp. 41-48.

Fig. 7. From Lucas van Leyden's
'Small Power of Women', *New Hollstein,*
vol. 3, 182/II 1517.

the graphic arts in several different print series.[29] His first Power of Women series featured the two secular legends of Aristotle and Virgil along with four examples of biblical women deemed wily in their ways—Eve, Delilah, the pagan wives of Solomon, and Salome.[30] More relevant here is van Leyden's second series, known as his Small Power of Women. In this series, van Leyden replaced his secular examples with representations of Jael and Jezebel. In his depiction of the story of Jael and Sisera, he unfolds the story before his viewer (Fig. 7). In the background, Jael invites Sisera into her

29. The first appearance of the *topos* in the graphic arts was the Housebook Master's paired prints of the mounted Aristotle and Solomon's idolatry, c. 1485 (Smith, *The Power of Women*, p. 199).

30. On the example of Solomon, Vives notes that he 'lost his mind because of women and from a wise man became the most foolish of men' (*The Education of a Christian Woman*, p. 328).

home, offering him milk. In the foreground, the viewer witnesses front and center the violence about to take place. Sisera appears deep in sleep, and, though he still holds his spear, his sword remains sheathed at his side and his crossed feet add an air of vulnerability to his pose. In the middle ground, Jael shows the fallen Sisera to Barak and other onlookers. Jael's finger and the spear in Barak's hand point to the deadly scene before the viewer. Especially the male viewer is meant to learn, along with the men in the doorway, what women are capable of doing to men.

Van Leyden's Smaller Power of Women series was popular enough to demand another run of the series, as shown in Fig. 7. In the second run of the series, the prints were enclosed by an ornately drawn frame, topped with two fanged vipers looking down on the scene. If these venomous creatures were not suggestive enough, the framed print is also accompanied with Dutch and Latin inscriptions that made clear the intended lesson. The inscription gives a brief account of the story and closes with a quote from Sir. 25.19: 'All evil is small compared to the evil of a woman'. That such uses of Jael were intended for a male audience is confirmed by the circulation of literature at the time such as *Dat dedroch der vrouwen* (*The Deceit of Women*), published in Antwerp around 1530. The subtitle of the work read, 'for the erudition and an example to all men, young and old, that they might know how deceitful and surly and how full of guile all woman are'. The title page displayed a woodcut of Jael murdering Sisera.[31]

Unlike the images of the celebrated, virtuous Jael, where Sisera is either absent or only a small figure in the background, when Jael is used for the Power of Women *topos* Sisera becomes a major feature. For the lesson to be successfully conveyed, the presence of the defeated man is as important as that of the evil woman. Thus, every depiction of Jael and Sisera intended as a warning against the evils of women shows Jael in the act of murder, with the body of Sisera prominently on display. One particularly striking example of Sisera's body is seen in a print by Jan Saenredam, after a drawing attributed to van Leyden. In this print, Sisera is shown in the background, drinking from a bowl that Jael has filled with her pitcher. His hunched figure appears small and obsequious before Jael, who stands in the doorway. But it is his dead body in the foreground that is particularly compelling. With his spiked club and helmet strewn uselessly in front of him, Sisera lies exposed to the waist before Jael and the viewer. With bare chest, head dropped back,

---

31. Quoted in Sijbolt Noorda, 'Jaël, Judith and Salome: Femmes Fatales in the Biblical Tradition', in *Femmes fatales, 1860–1910* (ed. H.W. van Os; Antwerp: Koninklijk Museum voor Schone Kunsten Antwerpen, 2002), p. 32. To be sure, an accompanying volume was published a few years later on 'The Deceit of Men', but Bleyerveld notes that in this case examples of 'deceptive' men focused on the sin of adultery rather than their own inherent deceitfulness, as in the case of women. See Bleyerveld, *Hoe bedriechlijck dat die vrouwen zijn*, p. 86.

Fig. 8. Jan Saenredam after Lucas van Leyden.
New Hollstein, vol. 3.

and knees bent together, his image evocatively recalls the crucified Christ of the Pietà (Fig. 8). Needless to say, here Jael is not intended to prefigure Mary.[32]

While it is probably going too far to see Sisera as a true Christ figure in this illustration, his role as victim in the Power of Women *topos* does suggest another interpretation of his character. If Jael becomes a treacherous and evil woman in this context, Sisera is redeemed. Whereas in early typological illustrations, Sisera was a ruthless enemy commander, and allegorically, the devil himself, in this new context he ranks alongside men such as Solomon, Samson, Virgil and Aristotle. In other words, he was a great man,

---

32. The print is paired with a drawing of Judith putting the head of Holofernes into a bag. As such, it is not part of a Power of Women series; together the prints may have been intended as a heroic representation of both women. But I would argue that Sisera's vulnerable body evokes a sympathetic response, complicating the interpretation of Jael as heroic.

Fig. 9. *The Illustrated Bartsch,* vol. 56, Netherlandish
Artists: Philip Galle after a drawing by
Maarten van Heermskerk.

who in spite of his strength and status, was tricked, in his case fatally so, by a powerful woman. While the images of the mounted Aristotle and Virgil in a basket might evoke laughter in view of the foolishness of these great men, the dead body of Sisera could well evoke a more sober response.

What is most fascinating about these images of the villainous Jael, warning men against the power of women, is that they were produced at the same time that the celebrated Jael was providing a mirror of virtue for women. The one reading of Jael did not supplant the other. Instead, these varying uses of her figure could be produced by the same artist. Figures 9 and 10 show two prints made after drawings by Maarten van Heermskerk. One (Fig. 9) is a premier example of the monumental Jael standing victorious before a radiant sun. With thumb and two fingers, she lightly holds aloft a mallet that is bigger than her head. In the other hand, she clasps an especially imposing tent peg, and the tent lines draw the eye toward more of these pegs seemingly at her disposal should she need them. This Jael is fully dressed, but only thinly so. We see through her gown to her midriff, while she lifts her gown to expose her muscular legs. Sisera, as expected, appears only in the background. With his head down and face hidden, he is a diminished and defeated foe. The one element of this drawing that seems out of place is Jael's expression. While other monumental Jaels often show a subtle smile, or serious expression, Jael's furrowed brow gives her a troubled, unhappy appearance. Perhaps again, we are seeing the influence of a more negative assessment of her act, this time written into her facial expression.

Fig. 10. *New Hollstein,* vol. 1, part 1,
(261). Maarten van Heermskerk.

The other drawing by Heermskerk (Fig. 10) is a depiction of Jael and
Sisera that is part of a Power of Women series.[33] Among the many differences between the two images is that Heermskerk here shows Sisera front
and center, taking up more than half of the frame. Likewise, rather than pos-
ing in a stately way for the artist, this Jael is in active full swing, right arm
extended just before the deadly blow. She stands, using the full force of her
body in the effort. And what a body! Heermskerk's fascination with human
musculature can be seen in both of his drawings of Jael.[34] But the effect of
this fascination on the gender construction of Jael in this print is remarkable. Is Jael a man or a woman or something else altogether? Her long
hair and breasts indicate femaleness, but what about the uplifted hand and
arm? In Heermskerk's drawing her Roman-style armor parallels Sisera's,
with both wearing Medusas, the very symbol of ambiguous and frightening

33. The series was printed by Dirk Coornhert in 1551 and includes drawings of Eve,
Lot's daughters, Jael, Delilah, Judith and Solomon's foreign wives.

34. Heermskerk spent time in Rome, where he developed a strong appreciation for
the work of Michelangelo and an interest in the meticulous representation of the human
anatomy. See Ilja M. Veldman, *Maarten van Heemskerck and Dutch Humanism in the
Sixteenth Century* (Amsterdam: Meulenhoff, 1977), pp. 120-21.

female power. While Sisera slumbers, the Medusa on his breastplate is wide awake and looking up in fright. Meanwhile, the Medusa on Jael's headpiece joins Jael in looking grimly down at her victim.

Clearly, in this drawing Heermskerk imagined the dangerous Jael as a warrior rather than seductress, and in doing so he draws a figure that blurs the traditional gender binary. Indeed, this particular image of Jael recalls Judith Haberstam's work *Female Masculinity*, especially a comment she makes about a contemporary artist's play with gender. Haberstam observes how the artist's artwork 'violates the cardinal rule of gender: one must be readable at a glance'.[35] The same could be said of this image of Jael. Heermskerk's Jael is not readable at a glance, and the more we study her, the more unclear things become. On the one hand, this image of Jael suggests that what is especially frightening about her is not her seductive powers as a woman but rather the nonconformity to a clearly defined gender identity that her figure represents. On the other hand, it points to what has been especially empowering for contemporary readers of Jael, namely, the blurring of gender in the depiction of her character that opens up the possibility of gender identities beyond the male/female binary. In this way, Heermskerk's drawing of the warrior Jael anticipates twenty-first-century readings such as the one by Robyn Fleming, who observes that as a woman warrior with a fluid gender identity, 'Jael is almost the personification of gender blur, that force most threatening to the hierarchical structure of patriarchy. If you can't tell for sure which people are men, and which are women, how can power structures based on gender inequality be maintained?'[36]

Gender Lessons from the Dutch Renaissance

So what does it mean to have these contrasting images of the villainous and the virtuous Jael produced at the same time, and sometimes by the same artist, as these two drawings by Heermskerk? At a purely economic level, it suggests that there was a market for both types of images, especially because the function and intended audience for these images differed. Images of virtuous Old Testament women were produced with elite women in mind, in some cases even clearly dedicated to particular women. Meanwhile, the long established mediaeval tradition that warned men about the dangers of powerful women flourished throughout the fifteenth and sixteenth centu-

35. Judith Halberstam, *Female Masculinity* (Durham, NC: Duke University Press, 1998), p. 23.

36. http://revena.dreamwidth.org/128023.html. Thanks to Deryn Guest, whose article pointed me to Fleming's insightful essay. See Deryn Guest, 'From Gender Reversal to Genderfuck: Reading Jael through a Lesbian Lens', in *Bible Trouble: Queer Reading at the Boundaries of Biblical Scholarship* (ed. Theresa J. Hornsby and Ken Stone; Leiden: Brill, 2011), pp. 9-43.

ries. In this context, Jael proved a malleable subject who could be read as both virtuous and deadly.

Because Judges 4 and 5 depict Jael as both praiseworthy and deadly, it is not surprising to find her shown in both these ways in her afterlives. But given the gender dynamics at work during the Dutch Renaissance, we find these two traits split into two different depictions geared toward two different audiences. When Jael is virtuous, her deadly violence recedes into the background, recalled only in the distant form of the fallen Sisera, or, when he is absent, only by her mallet and peg. Rather than the killing itself, the focus of these works is on the stately Jael, standing tall after the success of her effort. On the other hand, when Jael serves as a warning to men, the man, Sisera, becomes a central focus in the image. Men are to gaze on his fallen body as they consider what might befall them should they fall prey to a woman such as Jael. That certain artists could show her in both modes suggests that they were not overly concerned with the single 'right' reading of Judges as much as different useful and profitable readings of the story vis-à-vis their own moral universe and different markets for graphic art.

Nevertheless, as we have seen, these differing ways of depicting Jael are not always as distinct as we might expect. Aspects of the seductive and dangerous Jael sometimes spill into the heroic Jael intended as an exemplar, whether through ambiguous facial expressions, suggestive clothing, or, in some cases, inscriptions that hint at notions of treachery rather than heroism. In the other direction, images intended to warn men against women necessarily put on display the vulnerability and weakness of men, while showing the potential for women's power. In some cases, depictions of Jael undercut the very gender binary on which the patriarchal culture was built. To be sure, the possibility for the 'villainous' and gender-blurring Jael to function as positive model of resistance against oppressive patriarchal structures will take several more centuries to emerge, and must be the subject of another study. Nevertheless, the seeds of this potential may well be seen in these Power of Women images from the Dutch Renaissance.[37]

---

37. This study is part of my forthcoming book tentatively titled *Playing Jael: Sex, Gender and Power in Cultural Performances of Judges 4–5.*

Sharing a Mirror with Venus: Bathsheba and Susanna with Mirrors in Early Modern Venetian Art

Katherine Low

Abstract

Engaging a cultural and iconographical analysis of two paintings of biblical women by Tintoretto and Hans von Aachen, the author follows artistic traditions of bathing women in a number of Venetian sources. A reception history of these paintings reveals cultural traditions about women and mirrors in art, thus illuminating several reasons why Tintoretto and von Aachen place mirrors in representations of Bathsheba and Susanna. The mirror, in essence, acts as a gendered symbol. The first tradition of the mirror as gendered object stems from the Italian word *vanitas* as a feminine gendered noun for 'vanity'. Personifications of vanity as a vice include the female body and a mirror. The second tradition of the mirror comes from a woman with a mirror in her private chambers; male artists speculate and represent what happens with everyday objects such as the mirror in the secluded world of feminine primping. Cultural factors stemming from women and mirrors in ancient Graeco-Roman art and society, alongside economic factors such as the special value placed on Venetian mirrors, also inform the paintings. Finally, artists engage traditions of the goddess Aphrodite/Venus as ideal of love and beauty, and relate them to the biblical stories of Bathsheba and Susanna. Bathsheba and Susanna share a mirror with Venus, in essence, as they take on Venus-like characteristics; thus, artists interpret their stories with erotic overtones.

Introduction

During the sixteenth century in Venice, at the same time that Tintoretto begins to paint Susanna nude, he also gives her a mirror (Fig. 1). In Tintoretto's painting from c. 1557, Susanna's illuminated nude body twists toward a mirror, into which Susanna gazes.[1] In a similar manner, the German man-

This essay is a revised version of a paper I presented at the International Society of Biblical Literature meeting in Vienna, Austria, in July 2007. I am very grateful to two art historians, Dr Babette Bohn at Texas Christian University and Dr Sara James at Mary Baldwin College, for their valuable input during the revision of this paper.

    1. See Babette Bohn, 'Rape and the Gendered Gaze: Susanna and the Elders in Early Modern Bologna', *Biblical Interpretation* 9 (2001), pp. 259-86. Early Christians

Fig. 1. Tintoretto, *Susanna and the Elders.*
Kunsthistorisches Museum, Vienna, c. 1557.

nerist artist Hans von Aachen, who studied in Venice, incorporates a mirror
in his painting of Bathsheba from the late sixteenth/early seventeenth century (Fig. 2).[2] Bathsheba gazes into a mirror, held for her by her attendant;
her face reflects in the mirror.

Both Bathsheba and Susanna bathe in their biblical stories, but none do
so with a mirror, and both women fall victim to the lustful desires of men.
In early Christian interpretations, Susanna provides an upstanding example
of marital chastity.[3] Susanna's story in the Apocryphal/Deuterocanonical
group of texts of the Christian church informs the reader that her parents
instructed her according to the Law of Moses.[4] Two elders of the commu-

uplifted Susanna's virtue and marital chastity in artistic representations. In sixteenth-
century Italian paintings, however, depictions of Susanna undergo a shift from uplifting
her virtue to implying eroticism.

2. A discussion of this painting can be found in J. Cheryl Exum, *Plotted, Shot, and
Painted: Cultural Representations of Biblical Women* (Sheffield: Sheffield Academic
Press, 1996), pp. 36-43. In this article, I refer to Figs. 1 and 2 as 'Tintoretto's Susanna'
and 'von Aachen's Bathsheba'.

3. Early Christian art upholds Susanna's chastity. See K.A. Smith, 'Inventing
Marital Chastity', *Oxford Art Journal* 16 (1993), pp. 3-24.

4. Susanna, chap. 13 of the book of Daniel, is part of the Old Testament Apocrypha
for Protestants and part of the Deuterocanonical books for the Catholic Church. Jerome's

Fig. 2. Hans von Aachen, *Bathsheba.*
Kunsthistorisches Museum, Vienna, c. 1612.

nity spy on her during her walks in her garden. One day, she decides to bath
in the garden. When the elders petition that she have sex with them after
she should have sent her maids out, she refused in order not to 'sin in the
sight of the Lord'.[5] Susanna then 'cried out with a loud voice', with what
Jerome calls an 'intense vibration' out of 'the greatness of the chastity with

Latin Vulgate places Susanna as chap. 13 of the book of Daniel. Italian artists in the
sixteenth and seventeenth centuries would have consulted an Italian translation of the
Vulgate, an English translation of which is called *The Douay Old Testament.* I refer to
the *Douay Old Testament* for biblical quotes in this article.
    5. Dan. 13.23. According to Lev. 18.20 and Deut. 22.22-24, adultery is punishable
by death.

which she called out to the Lord'.[6] Jerome recognizes how Susanna upholds her chastity. Even after the elders accuse her of adultery because she would not acquiesce to their demands, 'she looked up to heaven, for her heart had confidence in the Lord' (Dan. 13.35). After Daniel intervenes by exposing the elders' plot, Susanna's parents give thanks to God 'on the ground that no immorality was found in her'.[7]

For Bathsheba, bathing comes out of necessity due to her 'purifying herself after her period', or, as the Douay Old Testament states, 'presently she was purified from her uncleanness' (2 Sam. 11.4). Biblical authors interject this information to establish Bathsheba's fertility after having been through a menstrual cycle and David's fatherhood of the child that results from him summoning her to his palace, but it also implies that she was partaking in a ritualistic purification bath when David saw her from his roof (see Lev. 15.19-28). Augustine, in a letter to Jerome, grants David the blame for the situation, not Bathsheba, for David 'committed adultery by desiring and seducing another man's wife and was guilty of a gruesome murder in killing her husband'.[8] Once David found out she was pregnant, David arranged for Bathsheba's husband, Uriah, to engage in battle on the frontline and subsequently get struck down. After Bathsheba's mourning period for the death of Uriah, David married Bathsheba.

The mirror in the two paintings of Bathsheba and Susanna under discussion in this article implicates their guilt, capturing a singular moment from their stories that reflect not their innocence but their implied vain primping and culpability. Though Daniel finds Susanna innocent in the biblical story, Tintoretto's artistic rendition of her nude body (Fig. 1) far from promotes her innocence. Her illuminated nude body centralizes the frame; she clearly enjoys viewing her body just as much as the elders do. Hans von Aachen portrays Bathsheba using the mirror for what would otherwise be a purification ritual with religious intent.

A mirror does not appear in Bathsheba's or Susanna's biblical narratives, but their stories converge in Venetian art through the iconographical link of the mirror. A reception history, centered on their use of the mirror in Tintoretto's *Susanna* and von Aachen's *Bathsheba,* reveals that artists project their own cultural and gendered expectations of behaviour onto the biblical women. This article examines several factors for why artists center on the nude bodies of Susanna and Bathsheba with mirrors in their representations of otherwise chaste biblical women.

6. Jerome, *Jerome's Commentary on Daniel* (trans. Gleason L. Archer; Grand Rapids, MI: Baker Book House, 1958), p. 154.

7. *Jerome's Commentary on Daniel*, p. 156.

8. Jerome, *The Correspondence (394–419) between Jerome and Augustine of Hippo* (trans. Carolinne White; Lewiston, NY: E. Mellen Press, 1990), pp. 82, 147.

The first factor comes from the cultural milieu of the Renaissance to revive Greek and Roman 'classical sources'; Renaissance artists draw on Graeco-Roman conventions of women with mirrors. Sexualized notions of a woman with a mirror in Graeco-Roman literature and art lend themselves to early modern Italian adaptations. Both Tintoretto and von Aachen incorporate the woman-with-a-mirror motif from classical sources in their paintings, but they do so incorporating female nudity, a signal in Christian Western art for feminine sexual availability and culpability.[9] Susanna's nudity became popular in Italian art during the sixteenth century; her nudity shifts meanings from a moralistic message to the focus on her sexuality. Bathsheba also continues to appear nude in Italian paintings during this time.[10]

Second, historical and social factors concerning Venetian mirror manufacturing provide reasons why Venetian artists put mirrors in their art. Until about 1685, Venice led the European mirror industry, holding a reputation for producing world-renowned mirrors with beveled glass borders. In the sixteenth century, polished metal mirrors were everyday objects, but Venetian glass-blown mirrors cost enough that only nobility, or those connected with the court, could afford them.[11] Hand-held mirrors, the mirror of the toilet, became common for nobility; a larger mirror cost more. Susanna's mirror in Tintoretto's painting is an extravagant display of Venetian ingenuity.

A final factor in increasingly erotic potential for artistic renditions of Bathsheba and Susanna comes from using Venus as a model. In allowing Bathsheba and Susanna to share a mirror with Venus, artists choose, in the words of Mary Garrard, 'to focus instead upon the secondary plot devices of temptation, seduction, and the erotic escapades' of the biblical stories.[12] Even when dealing with biblical subjects, artists call on social constructions of gender that clearly do not succumb to the sacred/secular dichotomy and are much dependent on their cultural contexts. The mirror links Bathsheba and Susanna into an established early modern current of women, vanity, primping and sexual culpability.

---

9. For more on this topic, see Margaret R. Miles, *Carnal Knowing: Female Nakedness and Religious Meaning in the Christian West* (New York: Vintage Books, 1989).

10. David M. Gunn, 'Bathsheba Goes Bathing in Hollywood: Words, Images, and Social Locations', in *Biblical Glamour and Hollywood Glitz* (ed. Alice Bach; Semeia, 74; Atlanta, GA: Scholars Press, 1996), pp. 75-101 (87). Nevertheless, Gunn points out that an increasingly clothed Bathsheba in illustrated Bibles in northern European areas demonstrates changing conventions of bathing at that time.

11. Sabine Melchior-Bonnet, *The Mirror: A History* (trans. Katharine H. Jewett; New York: Routledge, 2011), pp. 21-28.

12. Mary Garrard, 'Artemesia and Susanna', in *Feminism and Art History* (ed. Norma Broude and Mary D. Garrard; New York: Harper & Row, 1982), pp. 146-47 (152).

Fig. 3. Georg Pencz, *Portrait of Jakob Hofmann.*
Darmstadt, Hessisches Landesmuseum, 1544.

Vanity and the Mirror

When a man holds a mirror in Renaissance painting, he does so with clothes
on and with command of the situation. In the portrait of Jakob Hofmann by
Georg Pencz (1544), Hofmann demonstrates his status with the mirror (Fig.
3). Pencz shows influence from Northern Italy, especially since he possibly
visited Venice at least once.[13] Hofmann, a Master Goldsmith from Nurem-
berg, holds a mirror in his right hand in the portrait, but his gaze directly

13. Bernard Aikema and Andrew John Martin, 'Crosscurrents with Germany:
The Spread of the Venetian Renaissance', in *Renaissance Venice and the North:*

addresses the viewer. His body takes up the entire frame of the picture. The man does not look into the mirror, but the mirror reflects his profile. He remains fully clothed in a black robe and fur accents, sporting domination, assertiveness and self-confidence. The mirror with the elaborate frame in his hands symbolizes his wealth and status, as well as the artist's demonstration of mastering the reflection on the canvas. The mirror does not send a message of sexual availability in this case because it rests in the hands of a fully clothed and directly engaged male body.

The presence of a nude female with a mirror presents another set of assumptions. The painting *Allegory of Vanitas*, by Giovanni Bellini, c. 1490, is one of a four-part series.[14] A nude woman stands on a marble pedestal and holds a large circular mirror on her right side, which reflects a distorted male face. Her left hand points to the face in the mirror; unlike the portrait of Hofmann mentioned above, she diverts her gaze from the viewer as her eyes are shut and her head is slightly turned. The painting assumes a male gaze, as evident in the viewer reflected in the mirror, and demonstrates a moralistic message to know oneself and avoid deception from the vanity of worldly things.

The same moralistic message appears in Hans Baldung Grien's *The Three Ages and Death* (Fig. 4) from the year 1510. Art historians have based their assessment that Bellini's painting depicts *Vanitas* through comparison with Baldung Grien's personification of vice, the nude woman gazing into the mirror.[15] The old woman in Baldung Grien's painting acts as the young woman's double, the one who sees Death coming from behind. The old woman understands the futility of vanity.[16] The old woman in Baldung Grien's painting reminds the viewer that beauty fades but vanity leads one to deny such reality.[17]

Bonifazio de'Pitati, who had a workshop in Venice, includes a mirror in his pastoral landscape depiction of Lot and his daughters (Fig. 5). After the destruction of Sodom, Lot and his daughters flee to a cave. Messengers from God assist the family of Lot in the escape, but his wife looks back, turning into a pillar of salt. The eldest daughter, in thinking the destruction left a global absence of men, conceives of a plan to get pregnant by her

Crosscurrents in the Time of Bellini, Dürer, and Titian (ed. Bernard Aikema and Beverly Louise Brown; New York: Rizzoli, 1999), pp. 332-423 (386).

14. The painting can be found in Venice at the Galleria dell'Accademia.

15. Bernard Aikema and Beverly Louise Brown, 'Painting in Fifteenth-Century Venice and the "Ars Nova" of the Low Countries', in *Renaissance Venice and the North: Crosscurrents in the Time of Bellini, Dürer, and Titian* (ed. Bernard Aikema and Beverly Louise Brown; New York: Rizzoli, 1999), p. 232.

16. It is possible that von Aachen, a hundred years later, meant to use such a character type for the maid with his Bathsheba.

17. Melchior-Bonnet, *The Mirror*, pp. 210-12.

Fig. 4. Hans Baldung Grien, *Three Ages of the Woman and the Death.*
Kunsthistorisches Museum, Vienna, 1510.

father, thus carrying on humankind. She convinces the youngest daughter
to do the same; they have sex with their father consecutively in two nights
(Gen. 19.1-38). The mirror symbolizes the vanity of Lust—the daughter's
dress lowered on her shoulders accompanies this symbolization—and the
playful putti with the mask indicate the deceptiveness of Folly. As with
other women in depictions of vanity, she shows more interest in her reflection than with engaging the viewer of the painting. The mask of an old

Fig. 5. Bonifazio de'Pitati, *Lot and his Daughters*.
Chrysler Museum of Art, Norfolk, Virginia, c. 1545.

man's face satirically points to Lot, an old man who engages lustful desires, but his daughter holds the mirror and shares in the sexual culpability.[18]

Female Primping, Social Class and the Mirror

The toiletry item of the mirror signals a paradox: beauty might fade but a woman's beauty reflects her virtue, her nature and even her social class. As Clement of Alexandria writes about women and mirrors, 'The greatest extravagance is to have invented mirrors for that artificial beauty that is theirs, when really a veil should be thrown over this imposture'.[19] Baldassare Castiglione, writing his *The Book of the Courtier* in the early sixteenth century while in the Court of Urbino, reflects social conventions among the

18. Ruth Mellinkoff, 'Titian's Pastoral Scene: A Unique Rendition of Lot and his Daughters', *Renaissance Quarterly* 51 (1998), pp. 829-63 (841-42). See also J. Cheryl Exum, 'Desire Distorted and Exhibited: Lot and his Daughters in Psychoanalysis, Painting, and Film', in *'A Wise and Discerning Mind': Essays in Honor of Burke O. Long* (ed. Saul M. Olyan and Robert C. Culley; Providence, RI: Brown University Press, 2000), pp. 83-109.

19. Author's translation. Clement, *Le Pédagogue*, III (Sources chrétiennes; Paris: Editions du Cerf, 1970), p. 31.

elite concerning women, beauty and their expected primping. According to Castiglione, a courtly woman

> must clothe herself in such a way as not to appear vain and frivolous. But since women are not only permitted but bound to care more about beauty than men—and there are several sorts of beauty—this Lady must have a good judgment to see which are the garments that enhance her grace . . . and all the while she keeps herself dainty and clean, let her appear to have no care or concern for this.[20]

Castiglione warns that a woman should do her fussing over her appearance in private; she bathes in her private chambers with the expectation to adorn herself with perfume and jewels to accent her beauty. Bathing in this period usually consisted of 'wiping' with water and 'perfuming' rather than washing.[21]

Women, mirrors and expectations of beauty come to Renaissance authors and artists from Graeco-Roman traditions. From the fifth to the third century BCE in ancient Italy, families buried their female kin with mirrors and jewelry.[22] Such artifacts act as symbolic markers of gendered characteristics granted to one's sex. In Greek pottery art, mirrors accompany women in depictions of their private chambers (*gynaikonitis*), even in scenes of conjugal arrangements with courtesans.[23]

The famous Roman writer of Greek comedy Titus Maccius Plautus (254–184 BCE) utilizes the mirror to symbolize the sexual escapades of a primping courtesan in his play *Mostellaria*, or *The Haunted House*. Philolaches, the lover of a courtesan named Philematium, procures enough money for exclusive rights to her. Before he informs her of the purchase, he sneaks into her chambers to watch her bathe. Philematium asks for many toiletry items, such

---

20. Baldassare Castiglione, *The Book of the Courtier* (trans. Charles S. Singleton; New York: Anchor Books, 1959), p. 21. For more on Castiglione, see Stephen Kolsky, *Courts and Courtiers in Renaissance Northern Italy* (Burlington, VT: Ashgate, 2003).

21. Jacques Revel *et al.*, 'Forms of Privatization', in *A History of Private Life* (ed. Roger Chartier; Cambridge, MA: Belknap Press, 1989), pp. 161-225.

22. John Robb, 'Female Beauty and Male Violence in Early Italian Society', in *Naked Truths: Women, Sexuality, and Gender in Classical Art and Archaeology* (ed. Ann Olga Koloski-Ostrow and Claire L. Lyons; New York: Routledge, 1997), pp. 43-65.

23. Eva C. Keuls, *The Reign of the Phallus: Sexual Politics in Ancient Athens* (Berkeley, CA: University of California Press, 1985), p. 245. Examples of pottery art include a lekythos from Gela, Museum of Fine Arts, Boston, c. 480–470 BCE; several from a private collection shown in H.A. Shapiro, *Art, Myth, and Culture: Greek Vases from Southern Collections* (New Orleans Museum of Art; New Orleans, LA: Tulane University Press, 1981), pp. 160-61; and, especially, a third-century jug found in Centuripe, now housed at Catania University, Institute of Classical Archeology in Sicily, as pictured in P.E. Arias, *A History of 1000 Years of Greek Vase Painting* (New York: Harry N. Abrams, 1962), entry LII.

as rouge and eye make-up, fulfilling the beauty preparation and regimen expected of a highly paid prostitute: 'Give me the mirror and the casket with my trinkets, directly, Scapha, that I may be quite dressed when Philolaches, my delight, comes here'. After she uses the mirror, her maid, Scapha, orders Philematium to wipe her hands because, as she states, 'You've been holding the mirror, I'm afraid that your hands may smell of silver; lest Philolaches should suspect you've been receiving silver somewhere'.[24] The mirror connects Philematium's beauty with her sexual availability.

Given the established connection between women and mirrors in Italy, historians estimate that, by the 1650s, one in three households of various social classes owned a mirror. Small steel or tin mirrors were everyday objects in the sixteenth century; they could be bought from street venders. But the Venetian mirror was of a rare quality and requests from nobility for Venetian mirrors during the sixteenth century created a cultural mirror craze. The cost depended on the size and border, sometimes wood, ivory, silver, or crystal, but Venice definitely led the market for several centuries.[25] Tintoretto's mirror for Susanna signifies the art and ingenuity of Venice, but it also marks Tintoretto's understanding of Susanna's social class.

Adornments of women's bodies in the early modern period also related to their social standing. They wore jewelry as a public sign of their beauty and their husband's status and honor, as the husband continued to own the jewelry.[26] Especially in Venice, which hosted numerous groups of immigrants—Germans, Slavs, Albanians, Turks, Persians—elite classes encouraged established order. Three legal groups made up the social order of Venice, the top being the ruling oligarchy, or the patricians. Patrician culture set the boundaries of cultural visual representation as it had more opportunities for the patronage of art, especially in Venice.[27] Hence, in both Tintoretto's *Susanna* and von Aachen's *Bathsheba,* both women surround themselves with jewelry and perfume. Both Susanna and Bathsheba represent such beautiful married women of a specific upper class.[28] But, the symbols also lend themselves to the eroticism of the scenes, for from the fifteenth century

24. Plautus, *The Comedies of Plautus,* II (trans. Henry Thomas Riley; London: George Ball and Sons, 1906), Act I, Scene 3, pp. 13-14. For a discussion of this play, see Maria Wyke, 'Women in the Mirror: The Rhetoric of Adornment in the Roman World', in *Women in Ancient Societies: An Illusion of the Night* (ed. Leonie J. Archer, Susan Fischler and Maria Wykes; New York: Routledge, 1997), pp. 134-51.
25. Melchior-Bonnet, *The Mirror,* pp. 15-24.
26. Margaret L. King, *Women of the Renaissance* (Chicago: University of Chicago Press, 1991), p. 53.
27. Patricia Fortini Brown, *Art and Life in Renaissance Venice* (Upper Saddle River, NJ: Prentice–Hall, 1997), pp. 34-37.
28. As they are described in the biblical texts, Susanna is a 'very beautiful woman' (Dan. 13.2), and David sees that 'the woman was very beautiful' (2 Sam. 11.2).

onward in Italian painting female bathing scenes became a common way to allow voyeurs a peek into a woman's private chambers.[29]

Venus and the Mirror

In Venetian art, artistic traditions that begin with an elite woman with a mirror at her toilet morph into scenes of the goddess of love and beauty with a mirror at her toilet. As an ideal of feminine beauty, Venus regained popularity during the Renaissance. She came to represent early modern culture's re-establishment of delight in the senses, in the physical world and in indulgence of pleasures.[30] Renaissance Venus represents a whole gamut of Christian ambivalent responses to female nudity, lust, beauty and love. Venus has a dual appeal—her beauty inspires love but her appetite for frivolous and lust-filled encounters represents the delights and dangers of human urges.[31] In giving Bathsheba and Susanna visual characteristics that connect them to the theme of Venus with a mirror at her toilet, artists interpret the biblical women in terms of these delights and dangers of human sexuality.

The move to mythologize the woman at her toilet through Venus begins with those who studied under Giovanni Bellini, especially Titian. In his later work, Bellini, an influential Venetian painter in the late fifteenth and early sixteenth century, paints a *Lady at her Toilet* (Fig. 6), signed and dated in 1515, the year before he died. Bellini's choice of a female nude in this manner is unusual for his time but sets a standard for those Venetian artists who follow him, including Titian. While she holds a mirror to adjust her jeweled hair-piece, a larger circular mirror on the wall behind her reflects the back of her head. The woman sits in front of an open rectangular window, a sash barely covering her genitals. Her nude body connects to the open landscape; interior and exterior fuse together.[32] Like Susanna in the garden (Fig. 1), the woman's body becomes closely associated with the beauty and erotic qualities of nature.[33] Furthermore, like von Aachen's Bathsheba (Fig. 2), the

29. Revel *et al.*, 'Forms of Privatization', pp. 161-225 (222).

30. John Canaday, *Venus Revisited: Classical Myths in the Renaissance* (New York: Metropolitan Museum of Art, 1959), p. 6.

31. Patricia Rubin, 'The Seductions of Antiquity', in *Manifestations of Venus: Art and Sexuality* (ed. Caroline Arscott and Katie Scott; Manchester: Manchester University Press, 2000), pp. 24-38.

32. Mary Pardo, 'Artifice as Seduction for Titian', in *Sexuality and Gender in Early Modern Europe* (ed. James Grantham Turner; New York: Cambridge University Press, 1993), pp. 55-90. Pardo argues that the making of this figurative style, in and of itself, was meant to be erotic.

33. Mary D. Garrard suggests that in Tintoretto's painting (Fig. 1) Susanna rests in an 'erotically suggestive garden setting' (p. 150). See Garrard, 'Artemisia and Susanna', pp. 151-53.

Fig. 6. Giovanni Bellini, *Lady at her Toilet.*
Kunsthistorisches Museum, Vienna, 1515.

nude woman sits in front of an open window while primping with a mirror. The painting voyeuristically draws the viewer into the private quarters of a sixteenth-century Venetian woman of a significant social class. The cues from the painting, such as the mirrors, her netted hair, finely patterned material in the room, and glass vessel with sponge, remain socially dictated, idealizing the submissiveness, expected primping and subsequent beauty of a high-class Venetian wife.[34]

Unlike Bellini's early allegorical painting of *Vanitas*, the nude woman standing on the pedestal, the woman's mirror in *Lady at her Toilet* (Fig. 6) no longer reflects a male visage. The painting, therefore, requires no inner reflection on behalf of the viewer in terms of the fleeting fancies of a carnal world. In watching the woman gazing at herself, a message of vain primping rather than moral introspection emerges for the viewer. Writing in

---

34. David Alan Brown and Sylvia Ferino-Pagden, *Bellini, Giorgione, Titian and the Renaissance of Venetian Painting* (New Haven, CT: Yale University Press, 2006), pp. 219-22. See also Rona Goffen, 'Sex, Space, and Social History in Titian's Venus of Urbino', in *Titian's 'Venus of Urbino'* (ed. Rona Goffen; Cambridge: Cambridge University Press, 1997), pp. 74-75.

sixteenth-century Venice, for instance, Moderata Fonte cautions about this development, against female narcissistic behavior as a woman's vanity and self-love will 'allow herself to be tricked into releasing her grip on her own will, so that they [men] can get their hands on it, along with her honor, her soul, and her life'.[35] Just as Castiglione warns that a woman must be dainty and fresh without appearing vain, Fonte insinuates that a woman's vanity leads to her vulnerability.

The mirror in this case represents the woman's expectation for beauty and heralds an emerging motif in the late fifteenth and early sixteenth century—Venus at her toilet.[36] As one of Bellini's later works, the nude woman also signals an artistic subject emerging for the next generation of artists, especially for Titian, one of his students. Bellini worked on the cusp of an emerging style shared with Titian and Tintoretto called *de figura*, or 'figure painting'.[37] As Venetian artists, all three follow similar patterns in their depictions of nude women and mirrors. For instance, Titian's painting *Venus with a Mirror* hung in his studio until his death in 1576; the painting depicts Venus looking into a mirror held by Cupid.[38] A velvet garment drapes across her back and barely covers her genitals.[39] Venus holds her left hand on her chest while her right arm rests on her lap. Her pose is similar to that of the classical rendition of Venus as *Venus pudica* or 'modest Venus' as represented in the so-called Medici Venus in the Uffizi Gallery in Florence.

Praxiteles (in the middle of the fourth century BCE, according to Pliny) sculpted Aphrodite as the first female fully nude cult statue. The original statue, *Aphrodite knidia*, no longer exists, but Roman and Renaissance copies still resonate with the subjective classification of *pudica*.[40] The so-called modesty of the pose recalls an instance of Venus's bathing in which she, after having been startled by a voyeur, attempts to cover her breasts and pubic area. By attempting to cover herself, she draws attention to her nudity.

35. Moderata Fonte, *The Worth of Women* (trans. Virginia Cox; Chicago: University of Chicago Press, 1997), p. 79.

36. Kenneth Clark, 'Venus', in *Dictionary of Subjects and Symbols in Art* (New York: Harper & Row, 1974), pp. 318-20.

37. Tom Nichols, *Tintoretto: Tradition and Identity* (London: Reaktion Books, 1999), p. 15.

38. Painted around 1555, it currently hangs in the National Gallery of Art in Washington, DC.

39. See the webpage 'From the Tour: Titian and the Late Renaissance in Venice', Washington, DC, National Gallery of Art, 'Titian, Venus with a Mirror', in the collection http://www.nga.gov/collection/gallery/gg23/gg23-44.0.html [accessed April 2013].

40. Nanette Salomon, 'Making a World of Difference: Gender, Asymmetry, and the Greek Nude', in *Naked Truths: Women, Sexuality and Gender in Classical Art and Archaeology* (ed. Ann Olga Koloski-Ostrow and Claire L. Lyons; New York: Routledge, 1997), pp. 197-219.

Praxiteles creates a vulnerable exhibitionist in Venus; he conveys a passive construction of female sexuality.[41] Early modern artists incorporate this construction of female sexuality in other renditions of Venus, including her association with the mirror.

With a thin veneer of attention to classical mythology, Tintoretto includes Venus in his *Venus, Vulcan and Mars*, c. 1550, which is in the Alte Pinakothek, Munich. Homer's *Odyssey* indicates that Vulcan set a trap consisting of chains in the forms of cobwebs in which to snare Venus and Mars during their sexual escapades.[42] Tintoretto depicts no trap in the painting and instead incorporates a mirror. Mars hides under the bed while Vulcan examines Venus's genitals in suspicion of adultery; the mirror reflects Vulcan's back bent over Venus.[43]

Early modern Italian authors and artists, as in Tintoretto's painting, assume Venus's susceptibility to sexual advances. In his work *Concerning Famous Women*, 1355–1359, Giovanni Boccaccio, friend and correspondent of Petrarch, writes of Venus's two husbands and assumes that she first married Vulcan and then Adonis. Without a husband, her sexual drive became unfettered: 'After Adonis's death she succumbed to such enormous sexual desire that she seemed to tarnish all the splendor of her beauty with her continuous fornication'.[44] Another Italian author in the late fifteenth century in Florence, Marsilio Ficino, writes to Lorenzo de' Medici, whom he tutored, emphasizing Venus's main characteristic on the sacred feast of Saint Cosmas—'wanton Venus teased seductively'.[45] The Venus in Tintoretto's *Venus, Vulcan and Mars* exemplifies this attitude concerning Venus as a seductress who enjoys her sexual appetites.

---

41. Annette Dixon, 'Women Who Ruled: Queens, Goddess, Amazons 1500–1650: A Thematic Overview', in *Women Who Ruled: Queens, Goddesses, Amazons in Renaissance and Baroque Art* (ed. Annette Dixon; Ann Arbor, MI: University of Michigan Press, 2002), p. 169. See also Nanette Salomon, 'The Venus Pudica: Uncovering Art History's "Hidden Agendas" and Pernicious Pedigrees', in *Generations and Geographies in the Visual Arts: Feminist Readings* (ed. Griselda Pollock; New York: Routledge, 1996), pp. 69-87. Salomon traces ideological significances for the label *pudica* and its implication for the male gaze.

42. Homer, *The Odyssey*, Book 8.

43. Bette Talvacchia, *Taking Positions: On the Erotic in Renaissance Culture* (Princeton, NJ: Princeton University Press, 1999), p. 126. Writing on the erotic in Renaissance culture, Bette Talvacchia argues that mythological themes offered enough distance for artists to present erotic scenes while avoiding condemnation from the Catholic Church.

44. Giovanni Boccaccio, *Concerning Famous Women* (trans. Guido Guarino; New Jersey: Rutgers University Press, 1963), p. 17.

45. Marsilio Ficino, *The Letters of Marsilio Ficino* (trans. London Language Department of the School of Economic Science; New York: Shepheard–Walwyn, 1978), p. 21.

Susanna and Bathsheba as Venus

The culmination of the displacement of any innocence in the biblical stories of Bathsheba and Susanna in the renditions of Tintoretto and von Aachen come with Venus. For his Susanna (Fig. 1), Tintoretto employs a Venus-drying-her-foot motif for the model in what one observer calls 'Tintoretto's Venus-style transformation of Susanna'.[46] The pervasive model of Venus slightly raising her right leg to dry her foot can also be found from a German engraver, Albrecht Altdorfer, who adopts an Italian style of depicting the body in his engraving from around 1525. His engraving of *Venus after the Bath*, at the University of Cincinnati Galleries, in Ohio, incorporates the style in which Venus slightly lifts her right leg to dry her foot. Tintoretto's Susanna does just that in the painting. Associating Susanna with Venus through a visual motif, Tintoretto's Venus-like Susanna captures not her virtue and chastity but rather the erotic potential of her story.

Hans von Aachen studied in Venice early in his career and visited often. Venice and Germany had close economic ties beginning in the early sixteenth century. Employed under Emperor Rudolph II, who favored Venetian art, von Aachen traveled extensively to Italy, especially Venice, for artistic and diplomatic purposes. He became an influential painter in Prague in Rudolph's court.[47]

Rudolph II liked erotic themes, and his court artists ingeniously satisfied his desires in a variety of forms.[48] Hans von Aachen's *Couple with Mirror,* in the Kunsthistorisches Museum in Vienna (Fig.7), which hung in Rudolph's own art room,[49] offers a glimpse into the erotic potentiality von Aachen assumed when painting a woman with a mirror. In this case, however, a man holds a mirror for her and takes much delight in her watching herself in the mirror.[50] The incompatibility of her face with her reflection in the mirror could practically come from von Aachen's stylistic choices, but it also emphasizes levels of vision: Her eyes look at her own reflection,

---

46. Tom Nichols, *Tintoretto: Tradition and Identity* (London: Reaktion Books, 1999), p. 92.

47. Andrew John Martin, 'Augsburg, Prague, and Venice at the End of the Century', in *Renaissance Venice and the North: Crosscurrents in the Time of Bellini, Dürer, and Titian* (New York: Rizzoli, 1999), pp. 614-21 (614-15).

48. Wolfgang Prohaska, *Kunsthistorisches Museum, Vienna: The Paintings* (London: Scala Books, 1997), p. 9.

49. Vinzenz Oberhammer, *Great Paintings from the Kunsthistorisches Museum, Vienna* (New York: Harry N. Abrams, Inc., 1963). See also the discussion of this painting in Exum, *Plotted, Shot and Painted*, pp. 41-43.

50. Titian also painted a version of a woman with a mirror, dated 1513–1515, in the Louvre, Paris, that resonates with von Aachen's depiction here. A man stands behind her holding a small mirror, into which she gazes; he looks at her and the back of her head is reflected in a larger circular mirror on the wall.

Figure 7. Hans von Aachen, *Paar mit Spiegel* (Couple with Mirror).
Kunsthistorisches Museum, Vienna, c. 1596.

as her reflection looks back at her, all the while the man also watches her gaze at her own reflection. At any rate, the woman looks strikingly similar to van Aachen's Venus in *Pallas, Venus and Juno* at the Museum of Fine Arts in Boston, painted around the same time as *Joking Couple* but before his *Bathsheba*.

A similar reflective disjunction exists for von Aachen's *Bathsheba*, since her reflection is reversed in the mirror. Since von Aachen died in 1615, and his *Bathsheba* painting is dated 1612–1615 (his widow presented it on a list of works for Emperor Matthias in 1615), one art historian notes that possible workshop intervention could account for the faulty reverse image in the mirror and the faulty building perspective in von Aachen's *Bathsheba*

(Fig. 2). Von Aachen engaged the same facial type for his Bathsheba as for his Venus in *Pallas, Venus, and Juno*.[51] Bathsheba's pose also relates to the Venus-drying-her-foot motif that Tintoretto used for his Susanna. In Bathsheba's case, she lifts and crosses her left leg over the right to dry her foot.[52]

Tintoretto and von Aachen convey Venus motifs in their paintings of Susanna and Bathsheba. Both artists engage an interpretive thread stemming back to classical art and literature—sexualized images of women with mirrors in classical literature and art conflate with notions of Venus's beauty and eroticism in the early modern period. The mirror functions as an evident gendered sign of Tintoretto's and von Aachen's erotic interpretations of biblical women.

Conclusion

A reception history of two early modern paintings of Bathsheba and Susanna with mirrors reveals that interpreters engage their contemporary cultural symbols when making interpretive moves concerning biblical subjects. Artists insert mirrors into visual representations of Bathsheba and Susanna to interpolate interpretatively a well-established cultural signal of female sexuality into the biblical stories. With a booming market for mirror production in Venice in the seventeenth century, mirrors signal expectations of Bathsheba's and Susanna's social class, wealthy women primping in private. The mirror acts as a gendered symbol, coinciding with Bathsheba's and Susanna's nudity, to encode a sense of their sexual culpability. By allowing Bathsheba and Susanna to share a mirror with Venus, artists remove David's guilt, and they take away Susanna's guiltless marital chastity. The mirror sends no moral message nor heralds death itself, but it marks a performance of feminine gender. The mirrors belong to the spaces of feminine intimacy, particularly positioned for Venus's gaze with her lovers present or not; any guilt involved with the men in their stories dissipates through the aesthetical presence of the mirror.

51. Thomas DaCosta Kaufmann, *The School of Prague: Painting at the Court of Rudolf II* (Chicago: University of Chicago Press, 1988), p. 160.

52. Joachim Jacoby relates Bathsheba to Raphael's Venus: 'Der bildfüllende, lebensgroße weibliche Akt, der den Bildvordergrund einnimmt, variiert inhaltlich passend Raphaels *Venus nach dem Bad. . .* ' (*Hans von Aachen, 1552–1615* [Berlin: Deutscher Kunstverlags, 2000], p. 82). In 1597 von Aachen was sent to purchase works from Titian and Raphael from Cardinal Granvella's collection. He could have easily come across similar forms in Titian's and Raphael's paintings. Jacoby places this painting in the year of 1615, under Matthias's reign. In 1612, Rudolf II died and his brother, Matthias, was crowned emperor but his reign was short-lived as he died in 1619.

Images of the Indentured: Reading the Narrative of Judith's Slave Woman through Art

Andrea M. Sheaffer

Abstract

The maidservant in the book of Judith is a remarkable, yet undervalued, character in Judith studies. The apocryphal scene of the trusted maidservant actively aiding Judith in her grisly assassination of Holofernes is a common theme in Renaissance and Baroque art. The maidservant is frequently depicted collecting the severed head into her food bag while Judith looks on; this reflects her main task of provisioning ritually clean food and drink for Judith while on her mission and marks her status as servant. Modern scholarship has paid scant attention to the maidservant's important role in the narrative as accomplice, and has glossed over her identity as a slave bound to the will of her mistress. In contrast, artistic representation regularly exhibits the maidservant as an important figure in the narrative and often accurately depicts her character as subservient to Judith. Utilizing paintings from the sixteenth and seventeenth centuries as a means of highlighting the role and servile status of the maidservant in the text, this essay endeavors to illuminate the vital function of the maidservant in Judith's mission to save Israel, as well as discuss her social status as slave.

Introduction

Artemisia Gentileschi's 1625 *Judith and Maidservant with the Head of Holofernes* (Fig. 1) is a scene of dramatic suspense.[1] Judith and her maidservant have paused abruptly; the women gaze apprehensively out of the frame toward a perceived, unknown threat, reminding us that their mission is far from complete. The beheading is over, but now their lives are in peril. The two women—mistress and slave—must escape from the Assyrian camp with a concealed human head in hand.

The flame of a single, small candle illuminates the dark and intimate setting of Holofernes' tent. The candlelight functions as a spotlight, emphasizing the presence and active role of the woman who silently and obediently aided

---

1. Artemisia Gentileschi, *Judith and Maidservant with the Head of Holofernes*, c. 1625–27, oil on canvas, Detroit Institute of Arts.

Fig. 1. Artemesia Gentileschi, *Judith and Maidservant
with the Head of Holofernes.* c. 1625–27.
Oil on canvas. Detroit Institute of Arts.

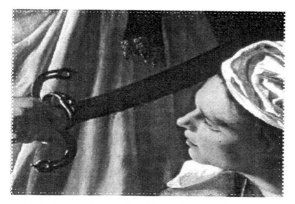

Fig. 2. Artemesia Gentileschi, *Judith and Maidservant*
with the Head of Holofernes, detail. c. 1625–27.
Oil on canvas. Detroit Institute of Arts.

Fig. 3. Artemesia Gentileschi, *Judith and Maidservant*
with the Head of Holofernes, detail. c. 1625–27.
Oil on canvas. Detroit Institute of Arts.

Judith's mission. Unlike Judith, whose shadow conceals a sizable portion of her face, the maidservant is fully revealed by the flame. The strong and capable hands of the maid adroitly place the sallow head in the food sack.

There is no doubt in the text that Judith delivered the deadly blows to Holofernes (Jdt. 13.8); this is underscored in the painting by her substantial grip on the sword, still dripping tiny droplets of blood (Fig. 2). Judith's hands are not marred with Holofernes' blood, but the maidservant's *are* (Fig. 3).[2] Indifferent to the blood smeared over her fingertips and oozing between her thick fingers, the maid dutifully places the severed head in the sack using her bare hands (Jdt. 13.10).

The soiled hands of the maidservant recall the familiar phrase echoed throughout the book of Judith that Israel's salvation would be achieved 'by the hand of a woman' (Jdt. 9.10; 13.15; 16.5). Judith's quote is likely self-referential, but Gentileschi's resolute and efficacious maid is evocative of the active hand the maidservant plays in Judith's mission.

Largely ignored in Judith studies, the maidservant's story has remained almost as silent as the character herself. But this nameless slave woman deserves recognition as the trustworthy accomplice who helps deliver Israel from destruction and enslavement under a seemingly omnipotent enemy. Artistic representation regularly exhibits the maidservant as an important figure in the narrative and often accurately depicts her as subservient to Judith. First, utilizing images from the sixteenth and seventeenth centuries to highlight the role and servile status of the maidservant in the text, I hope to illuminate the vital function of the maidservant in Judith's mission to save Israel from Assyrian forces. Second, I will discuss the maidservant's identity as a slave, a fact most translations have glossed over. This understanding of her social status will help characterize her relationship with Judith as one of master and slave rather than one of mutual respect, as some scholars have erroneously suggested. Third, I will provide a brief overview of the maidservant in art and will conclude with a survey of popular representations of the maidservant, discussing what these depictions reveal about her role in the text and about the life of a slave woman in antiquity.

A Silent Partner: The Maidservant's Active Role in Judith's Mission

The maidservant plays a crucial role in Judith's domestic and civic affairs and is all the while an integral assistant to her mistress in defeating the

---

2. Bloody hands are unique in Gentileschi's Judith *oeuvre*, and only appear in this painting on the maidservant. See Elena Ciletti, 'Gran macchina è bellezza', in *The Artemisia Files: Artemisia Gentileschi for Feminists and Other Thinking People* (ed. M. Bal; Chicago: The University of Chicago Press, 2005), pp. 63-106 (100).

Assyrians. Lawrence Wills's assertion that the maid is a 'non-character' is one example of how she has been ignored in scholarship.[3] Her silence and anonymity in the text can hide her role as heroic companion to Judith in the narrative, but in managing various aspects of Judith's mission, the maid assists in Judith's success. Judith's people's freedom is dependent on the work of a woman enslaved. Although called 'maid' or 'maidservant' in translations—as well as in this article to avoid confusion—she is not simply a servant but a chattel slave; she is Judith's property.[4] By infiltrating the enemy camp, Judith risks her own life but also the life of her maidservant. Because this maid is an unnamed slave, she is taken for granted in the narrative. I will demonstrate that the maid is Judith's accomplice, and therefore she, too, should be praised as a hero.

Servitude was a regular feature of wealthy Jewish households in the Graeco-Roman period, and slavery among Jews at this time was no different from the slavery structures of neighboring peoples.[5] In fact, 'slavery in the domestic realm in ancient Mediterranean societies was so prevalent that it continued to be the mainstay of domestic households even when the practice of slavery began to decline in late antiquity'.[6] Situating this LXX text in the larger context of the early Graeco-Roman period will prove valuable for understanding the socio-historical setting of the book of Judith.[7]

When the maidservant is introduced in the text, two important details are mentioned regarding her role as servant. First, she is in charge of all Judith's property (Jdt. 8.10). Upon the death of Judith's husband, Judith inherits precious metals, livestock, land, and male and female *slaves* (Jdt. 8.7). Indicative of her status as property, the maidservant is described as an object alongside the land and cattle. Though the maid is a component of Judith's assets, she holds a unique managerial position as the figure in charge of all Judith's property. It was unusual for a woman, let alone a slave

3. Lawrence M. Wills, *The Jewish Novel in the Ancient World* (Ithaca: Cornell University Press, 1995), p. 151.

4. On Israel's threat of being enslaved by the Assyrians, see Jdt. 7.27; 8.21-23. Concerning the maid's long tenure as Judith's chattel, this is evidenced especially in the phrase, 'She became more and more famous, and grew old in her husband's house, reaching the age of 105' (Jdt. 16.23).

5. Dale B. Martin, 'Slavery and the Ancient Jewish Family', *The Jewish Family in Antiquity* (ed. S.J.D. Cohen; Brown Judaic Studies, 289; Atlanta: Scholars Press, 1993), pp. 113-129 (113). See the book of Tobit and narrative of Susanna for examples from biblical texts.

6. Moses I. Finley, *Ancient Slavery and Modern Ideology* (London: Chatto & Windus, 1980), p. 149. For slavery as an important part of specifically Jewish household structures see Martin, 'Slavery and the Ancient Jewish Family', pp. 118-120.

7. This paper assumes the composition of the book of Judith to be some time around the Hasmonean period, in the second century BCE.

woman, to be the steward of a household, a task usually designated to male slaves or men of nonslave status.[8]

Second, the maid functions as an intermediary between Judith and Bethulia's town elders (Jdt. 8.10). While it was not uncommon for slave women to run errands for their mistresses, communicative tasks outside of the home were usually the undertaking of male slaves.[9] This unconventional responsibility over Judith's property and communications is indicative of Judith's trust in her servant's abilities to execute vital tasks, especially those related to Judith's mission.

In Gentileschi's painting, viewers are given a glimpse of the simple brown food sack that the maid is responsible for during the expedition. The sack relates the maidservant's arguably most important function toward aiding the mission: The handling of the supply of provisions while they are in the Assyrian camp, and, most notably, turning the supply sack into the vessel in which she smuggles Holofernes' head back to Bethulia (Jdt. 10.5; 12.19; 13.10). During their three-day sojourn with the enemy, the maid performs domestic tasks: She lays out lambskins for Judith so she can recline at Holofernes' banquet (Jdt. 12.15), and she prepares all of Judith's meals from the provisions in the sack that she carries from Bethulia into the camp (Jdt. 12.19). Judith's food restrictions require her to eat exclusively from the food in the sack that the maid has prepared. This demonstrates to Holofernes that Judith is committed to her dietary laws, helping to confirm the sincerity of Judith's lie that, during the siege on her town, her people plan to eat prohibited foods, which is why Judith has defected (Jdt. 11.11-16).

Gentileschi's *Judith and Maidservant with the Head of Holofernes* (Fig. 1) is a rare depiction: I have found only one other painting that shows the maid (rather than Judith) placing the head into the sack, exactly as the text describes (Jdt. 13.9-10).[10]

During their escape back to Bethulia, the maid is in charge of the food sack containing the severed head that will soon inspire the Israelites to stage an attack and terrify the Assyrians into a panic. When the women return safely to Bethulia, only Judith speaks and only Judith receives praise.

---

8. On the rarity of female slaves as household managers, see Martin, 'Slavery and the Ancient Jewish Family', pp. 122-123; Robin Gallaher Branch and Pierre J. Jordaan, 'The Significance of Secondary Characters in Susanna, Judith, and the Additions to Esther in the Septuagint', *Acta patristica et byzantina* 20 (2009), pp. 389-416 (405). Also see Gen. 24.2.

9. Brigitte Maria Egger, 'Women in the Greek Novel: Constructing the Feminine' (PhD Diss., University of California, Irvine, 1991), pp. 163-64.

10. See Jacopo Tintoretto. *Judith and her Maid Placing Holofernes' Head in a Sack*, mid to late sixteenth century, oil on canvas, National Museum of San Carlos, Mexico City.

After the Israelites defeat the Assyrians, Judith is honored for the rest of her life (Jdt. 16.20-21). But the maidservant, who was with Judith each step of the way on her dangerous expedition, is denied a place of esteem in the narrative. We hear nothing of the maid until the end of the story when she is released from bondage, well after her heroic journey with Judith that saves Israel.

The Identity of the Maidservant

In *Judith and her Maidservant with the Head of Holofernes*, the women work side by side, but there is little doubt of the maid's status. She is the slave and Judith is the master. Unlike Judith's lavish gold frock with green, velvet sash, the maid wears simple, blue garb with no ornamentation. Judith's hair is in an elaborate plait, but the maid's unruly locks jut out of her headscarf, an accessory frequently used to designate the maidservant in Gentileschi's works.[11] Perhaps the most telling aspect of the women's disparate social strata is conveyed in their physical positions: Judith stands over her maid, with hand outstretched to give a command of silence. The maid, pausing from the grisly task, is on the floor crouching low beneath Judith, with one leg bent as though in a reverential bow to her mistress.

A few scholars have questioned whether Judith's maid is an Israelite servant or non-Israelite slave.[12] Jennifer Glancy proposes that the possibility of the maidservant's status as a non-Israelite introduces a 'destabilizing element' to the narrative because Israel's survival would then be reliant on a foreign slave.[13] Does Judith trust a foreign slave to be loyal in the enemy camp? Or is the maidservant an Israelite servant who aided her people's freedom but whose own emancipation was too long deferred? I argue that the maidservant is a slave, which is not a destabilizing element in the narrative as Glancy suggests, but, rather, another fitting touch of irony that's an essential literary element in the book:[14] a widow who rescues Israel from

11. For examples, see Artemisia Gentileschi, *Judith Slaying Holofernes*, 1620, oil on canvas, Uffizi, Florence; *Judith and her Maidservant*, c. 1618, oil on canvas, Palazzo Pitti, Florence.

12. For various opinions on the maidervant's social status, see Jennifer Glancy, 'The Mistress–Slave Dialectic: Paradoxes of Slavery in Three LXX Narratives', *JSOT* 72 (1996), pp. 74-87 (84-86); Toni Craven, 'Maid of Judith', in *Women in Scripture: A Dictionary of Named and Unnamed Women in the Hebrew Bible, the Apocryphal/ Deuterocanonical Books, and the New Testament* (ed. C. Meyers, T. Craven, and R.S. Kraemer; Boston: Houghton Mifflin Company, 2000), pp. 362-63; Branch and Jordaan, 'The Significance of Secondary Characters', pp. 405-407.

13. Glancy, 'The Mistress–Slave Dialectic', p. 84.

14. In his extensive commentary on the book of Judith, Carey Moore asserts that irony is the key to the entire book. See Moore, *Judith: A New Translation with Introduction and Commentary* (Garden City, NY: Doubleday, 1985), pp. 78-86.

the mighty tyrant; a foreign persecutor-turned-ally and convert; and, finally, a slave who saves Israel from enslavement.

Scholars such as Dale B. Martin seriously doubt there was a distinction in the Graeco-Roman period between Israelite and non-Israelite slaves, as laws such as Lev. 25.35-46 and Deut. 15.12 prescribe.[15] There is substantial evidence, however, indicating that the maidservant is a slave and not simply a servant with free will.

First, Judith has long been recognized as an exemplar of religious observance, and in the narrative she is not one to disregard Torah.[16] Laws such as Lev. 25.35-46 forbid that any Israelite be treated or regarded as a slave, and command that the servant be released from debt after seven years' service.[17] Scripture, however, does not require slave owners to manumit slaves. Therefore, the maidservant's liberation at the end of Judith's long life is a likely indication that the maidservant was a slave.

Second, the language in the text concerning the maidservant's release from Judith's custody is also indicative of her slave status. A literal reading of Jdt. 16.23 is something like, 'And she set free her slave to freedom'. By using both ἀφῆκε, 'let go', and ἐλευθέραν, 'free', the text is doubly emphatic concerning a release of property from one's possession.

Furthermore, in the book of Judith the maidservant is referred to using three different terms, each denoting slave status: ἄβρα, meaning 'favorite slave'[18] (Jdt. 8.10, 33; 10.2, 5, 17; 13.9; 16.23); δούλη, 'female slave' (Jdt. 12.15,19; 13.3);[19] and παιδίσκη, 'slave girl' (Jdt. 10.10).[20] There has been

---

15. Martin, 'Slavery and the Ancient Jewish Family', pp. 116-17. See also Paul Virgil McCracken Flesher, *Oxen, Women, or Citizens? Slaves in the System of the Mishna* (Atlanta: Scholars Press, 1988), p. 36.

16. On Judith's strict adherence to Law and religious practice, see Morton S. Enslin, *The Book of Judith: Greek Text with and English Translation, Commentary and Critical Notes* (ed. S. Zeitlin; Leiden: E.J. Brill, 1972), pp. 33-34; Moore, *Judith*, pp. 60-62; Ross Shepard Kraemer, *Her Share of the Blessings: Women's Religions among Pagans, Jews, and Christians in the Greco-Roman World* (New York: Oxford University Press, 1992); Benedikt Otzen, *Tobit and Judith* (London: Sheffield Academic Press, 2002), pp. 101-106. According to Otzen, Judith's strict religious observance is a motif throughout the book that stresses the fidelity to Mosaic Law.

17. Catherine Hezser, *Jewish Slavery in Antiquity* (Oxford: Oxford University Press, 2005), pp. 9-10. Hezser argues that in ancient Israel, slaves were most often non-Israelites who became enslaved as prisoners of war, were born into slavery, or were on society's margins and became so poor the only way to survive was enslaving themselves or their children.

18. Craven, 'Maid of Judith', p. 362.

19. Jennifer A. Glancy, *Slavery in Early Christianity* (Oxford: Oxford University Press, 2002), p. 16.

20. See Lev. 25.44 in the LXX, regarding slave-owning. It contains both παιδίσκη and δούλη and both terms are translated as 'female slaves', including in the NRSV: 'As for

little recognition of this discrepancy in translating the maid's title in prominent Bible versions: the NRSV, NAB, NJB, KJV, to name a few, lack the desig-
nation of the maidservant as a slave. Perhaps translators have been—and
still are—uncomfortable regarding Judith, a biblical heroine praised for her
virtue, to be categorized as a slave owner?

It is highly likely that the maidservant is a slave; her manumission upon
Judith's death, the irony her slave status provides, and various titles, all support this conclusion.

Slave Life

The term ἄβρα, 'favorite slave', is suggestive of Judith's attitude toward
her maidservant. However, nothing in the text describes the maid's sentiments toward Judith, the mission, or anything else for that matter. It would
be fruitless to speculate on the maidservant's emotions toward her mistress,
or her motives in aiding Judith. Yet some scholars have ascribed emotional
feelings to the maid, going beyond the boundaries of the text. For example,
in *Artistry and Faith in the Book of Judith,* Toni Craven briefly mentions
the maidservant and writes that like Ruth and Naomi, Judith and her maid
'bind together for mutual support'.[21] But the story of Ruth and her mother-
in-law is quite different. Naomi has no legal obligation to her recently wid-
owed daughter-in-law, Ruth, yet expresses concern for her welfare (Ruth
1.8-14; 3.1-5). Ruth's cleaving to Naomi (1.14-17) and seeking marriage
within the family (3.6-18) demonstrate Ruth's concern for herself, as well
as Naomi's livelihood and further underscore the women's bond. There is
no such cleaving for support between Judith and the maidservant, and the
only binding to speak of is the maid's forced bondage to her mistress.[22]

While Greek novels of antiquity[23] and popular television programs such
as *Downton Abbey* (Fig. 4) frequently portray slave and servant women as
confidants of their mistresses with whom they share an emotional bond, the
book of Judith presents no evidence of such a bond between the maid and
Judith.

---

the male and female slaves whom you may have, it is from the nations around you that
you may acquire male and female slaves'.

21. Toni Craven, *Artistry and Faith in the Book of Judith* (SBLDS, 70; Chico, CA:
Scholars Press, 1983), p. 121.

22. Catherine Hezser describes the master–slave relationship as mutually dependent
but not necessarily supportive: 'The master was dependent on the slave's loyalty and
the slave dependent on the master's maintenance and humane treatment of him' (*Jewish
Slavery in Antiquity*, p. 150).

23. For examples of emotional bonds between mistresses and slaves in Greek
novels, see Egger, 'Women in the Greek Novel', pp. 98-100.

Fig. 4. *Downton Abbey.*
Carnival Films and Televsion Limited. 2011.

In their study on secondary characters in Susanna, Judith, and additions to Esther, Robin Branch and Pierre Jordaan approach the text from the viewpoint of Judith's maidservant and assert that the maid 'willingly risks her life for Judith'.[24] They extend assumptions further contending that the maid arguably 'loves Judith and accompanies her voluntarily'![25] The text, however, is as silent about the maidservant's sentiments and motives as the character herself. Perhaps in a modern, postslavery society readers would prefer to assume some type of shared affinity between the two women, prompting the maid to voluntarily risk her life to save the very people who enslave her. But we are not given the privilege of knowing the maid's feelings. We know that as a slave the maid was legally bound to follow any order Judith gave to her. Total compliance was prescribed, which meant that the maidservant had virtually no freewill in choosing whether or not to aid her mistress's mission.

In Graeco-Roman and ancient Jewish society there was general distrust of slaves, and laws that sanctioned corporal punishment (Exod. 20.21-22) undoubtedly kept slaves in line.[26] For example, the second-century BCE books of Tobit and Sirach demonstrate and appear to sanction the normali-

---

24. Branch and Jordaan, 'The Significance of Secondary Characters', p. 407.

25. Branch and Jordaan, 'The Significance of Secondary Characters', p. 407.

26. In Greco-Roman and ancient Jewish society, sayings about and prejudices against slaves circulated, presenting slaves as 'dangerous, greedy, dishonest, lazy, that is, as negatively disposed toward their masters'. See Hezser, *Jewish Slavery in Antiquity*, p. 150.

zation of slave beatings.[27] In Tob. 3.8-9, Sarah beats her slaves, and Sirach condones 'drawing blood from the back of a wicked slave' (Sir. 42.5).[28] First-century Jewish historian Josephus took the view that death was preferable to the shame, torments and cruelties that came with slavery.[29]

A perilous atmosphere permeated slave life, and examples show that female slaveholders could be just as brutal as their male counterparts.[30] Judith's maidservant would have had little choice in her duties. A slaveholding mistress and a female slave would not have had a relationship alliance simply because of a shared gender. Readers must be cautious, then, not to make more of Judith and the maidservant's relationship than what is reflected in the text: a legally bound relationship between master and slave.

Trends in Art and What They Reveal: The Old Maidservant and the Black African Maidservant

For almost as long as Judith has been depicted, her maidservant has been represented alongside her, as in the tenth-century Byzantine Bible manuscript, the Leo Bible.[31] She is usually presented in a narrative description either from part of or from the entire story, much as here. By the fifteenth century the two are depicted as individuals rather than in narrative scenes, and represented most often in what Nira Stone has classified as the 'epitomized description': during or just moments after decapitation (Fig. 5).[32] Occasionally the maid is seen as a young woman (Fig. 6),[33] but the most

27. Glancy, 'The Mistress–Slave Dialectic', p. 81.

28. In Tob. 3.8-9 Sarah's slave says: 'You are the one who kills your husbands! See, you have already been married to seven husbands and have not borne the name of a single one of them. Why do you beat us? Because your husbands are dead? Go with them! May we never see a son or daughter of yours!' Proper treatment of Hebrew servants is stressed in Lev. 25.43, but is decidedly silent concerning treatment of foreign slaves, simply stating: 'These you may treat as slaves, but as for your fellow Israelites, no one shall rule over the other with harshness' (Lev. 25.46).

29. Josephus, *Bellum judaicum* 7.379-386.

30. For further examples of abusive female slave owners, see Keith Bradley, *Slavery and Society at Rome* (Cambridge: Cambridge University Press, 1994), pp. 28-29.

31. *Leo Bible*, Folio 383r, *Judith and Holofernes*, c. 910–930, illuminated manuscript, Biblioteca Apostolica Vaticana, Vatican City, Rome.

32. Nira Stone, 'Judith and Holofernes: Some Observations on the Development of the Scene in Art', in *No One Spoke Ill of Her: Essays on Judith* (ed. J.C. VanderKam; Atlanta: Scholars Press: 1992), pp. 73-94 (75); Elisabetta Sirani, *Judith with the Head of Holofernes*, c. 1638–65, oil on canvas, Walters Art Museum, Baltimore, Maryland.

33. One of the earliest paintings of an individualized Judith with a young maidservant is Sandro Botticelli's *Return of Judith from Bethulia*, half diptych, 1476–78, tempera on wood, Uffizi, Florence.

Fig. 5. Elisabetta Sirani, *Judith with the Head of Holofernes,* c. 1638–65.
Oil on canvas. Walters Art Museum, Baltimore, Maryland.

Fig. 6. Sandro Botticelli, *Return of Judith from Bethulia,* half diptych, 1476–78.
Tempera on wood. Uffizi, Florence.

Fig. 7. Fede Galizia, *Judith with the Head of Holofernes,* 1596.
Oil on canvas, The John and Mable Ringling
Museum of Art, Sarasota, Florida.

prevalent trend throughout the late Renaissance to the Baroque period was to depict the maid as either an old (Fig. 7) or a black African (Fig. 8) slave.[34]

In this final section I will explore the implications of the maidservant as an old slave or as a black African slave, including how the maid's presence in the paintings ensures Judith's maintained chastity, central to Judith's virtuous character in the text. I will also briefly touch on the phenomenon of transference that occurs between Judith and the maid in art, in which I propose that the figure of the maid visually assumes both the negative characteristics Judith displays in the text and the evils inherent in the institution of slavery.

Caravaggio's *Judith Beheading Holofernes* (Fig. 9) is one of the first paintings to depict the maid as not only old, but hag-like, a trend that devel-

34. For an example of the maidservant as an old woman slave see Fede Galizia, *Judith with the Head of Holofernes,* 1596, oil on canvas, The John and Mable Ringling Museum of Art, Florida; as a black African slave see Paolo Veronese, *Judith with the Head of Holofernes,* c. 1583–85, oil on canvas, Kunsthistorisches Museum, Vienna.

Fig. 8. Paolo Veronese, *Judith with the Head of Holofernes*, c. 1583–85.
Oil on canvas. Kunsthistorisches Museum, Vienna.

oped around the turn of the seventeenth century.[35] The maid's aged and witch-like face is contrasted with Judith's youthful and innocent appearance. Apprehensively slicing the neck of the nude and brutish Holofernes, Judith's smooth, ivory skin and stark-white blouse radiate purity. Judith is portrayed as a virtuous young woman whose assassination of a lust-filled tyrant is justified. But the maid is Judith's antithesis.

35. Michelangelo Merisi da Caravaggio, *Judith Beheading Holofernes*, c. 1597–98, oil on canvas, Galleria nazionale d'arte antica, Rome. Also see Elisabetta Sirani, *Judith with the Head of Holofernes*, c. 1638–65, oil on canvas, Walters Art Museum, Baltimore, Maryland.

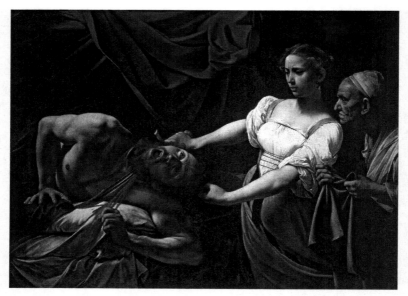

Fig. 9. Michelangelo Merisi da Caravaggio, *Judith Beheading Holofernes,*
c. 1597–98. Oil on canvas. Galleria nazionale d'arte antica, Rome.

Mary Garrard suggests that the maid's depiction as an old servant could
be understood subliminally as that of a procuress, an agent of her mistress's
sexuality.[36] This theory may be true of Judith depictions primarily from
Northern Europe, like Rubens's *Judith* (Fig. 10), which frequently represent Judith as a seductive and fatal assassin.[37] But it is more probable that
Italian representations of the maidservant saw her as protector rather than
procuress, due to the almost saintly veneration of Judith by Catholics at this

36. Mary D. Garrard, 'Judith', in *Artemisia Gentileschi: The Image of the Female
Hero in Italian Baroque Art* (Princeton, NJ: Princeton University Press, 1989), pp. 278-
336 (298).
37. Peter Paul Rubens, *Judith with the Head of Holofernes*, c. 1616, oil on canvas,
Herzog Anton Ulrich-Museum, Brunswick. Art historians Larry Silver and Susan Smith
note that, as from the early sixteenth century, female nudes became more prevalent in
the north, beginning with depictions of Eve and the Fall, as the paradigm of destructive
femininity. This theme of destructive femininity associated with the flesh undoubtedly
influenced northern artists such as Rubens, who depict Judith with counter-textual
nudity, cautioning against the pernicious power of women. See Silver and Smith, 'Carnal
Knowledge: The Late Engravings of Lucas van Leyden', *Nederlands kunsthistorisch
jaarboek* 29 (1978), pp. 239-98 (265).

Fig. 10. Peter Paul Rubens, *Judith with the Head of Holofernes,* c. 1616.
Oil on canvas. Herzog Anton Ulrich-Museum, Brunswick, Germany.

time.[38] Many paintings depict the aged maid alongside Judith in Holofernes'
bedchamber; the maidservant is a safeguard of chastity for the immacu-
late Judith. The worldly old maidservant's presence ensures that Judith's
virtue remains. Although positioning the maid in Holofernes' bedchamber
is counter-textual (Jdt. 13.2-4), the numerous works depicting the maid in
this scene underscore the importance of Judith's maintained chastity in the

38. Elena Ciletti, 'Patriarchal Ideology in the Renaissance Iconography of Judith', in
Refiguring Woman: Perspectives on Gender and the Italian Renaissance (ed. M. Migiel
and J. Schiesari; Ithaca, NY: Cornell University Press, 1991), pp. 34-70 (42).

narrative, a highly regarded virtue in both early modern Italy and in the Mediterranean social system of honor during Judith's time (Jdt. 13.16).[39]

It has been suggested that Caravaggio's characters could be an extension of *contrapposto*, in which works feature contrasting points of position, or in this case, a contrast of age and appearance between Judith and the maid-servant.[40] But it is also a situation of transference. Judith's negative and sinister characteristics associated with vengeance, lies and deception—each found in the text (see Jdt. 9.12-13; 10.13, 19)—are taken on and visually manifested in her slave woman.[41] With watchful eyes bulging and hands raised eagerly to capture her trophy, the maid's look is nefarious and blood-thirsty compared to Judith's anxious gaze. The maidservant's weathered, browned skin, wrinkles and thinning gray hair reflect a life of hardship. She represents the shrewd, deceptive and vengeful characteristics Judith exhibits toward her enemy in the text (Jdt. 9.8-11; 10.5-19). The maid is an embodiment of the evil of Judith's deed, a reminder of the darker side of tyrannicide.

Andrea Mantegna's *Judith and her Maidservant with the Head of Holofernes* (Fig. 11) is thought to be the first depiction of Judith's maid as a black African slave.[42] In the fourteenth and fifteenth centuries, the number of African slaves grew tremendously in Europe, particularly in Portugal, Spain and Italy.[43] In Italy, slaves were commonly purchased for domestic

39. The pervasive and restrictive Mediterranean social system's concern for the preservation of honor permeated the social milieu of Italian artists, and their inclusion of the maidservant as a protector of Judith's honor while in Holofernes' bedchamber reflects this concern. For a summary of Mediterranean honor in early modern Italy, see Elizabeth S. Cohen, 'Honor in the Streets of Early Modern Rome', *Journal of Interdisciplinary History* 22 (1992), pp. 597-625. Concerning maidservants' maintaining their mistresses' honor associated with chastity, see Elizabeth S. Cohen and Thomas V. Cohen, 'Moralities: Honor and Religion', in *Daily Life in Renaissance Italy* (ed. E.S. Cohen and T.V. Cohen; Westport, CT: Greenwood Press, 2001), pp. 89-107 (94).

40. For the theory that Caravaggio used *contrapposto* in relation to character appearance, see Garrard, 'Judith', p. 291; and Howard Hibbard, *Caravaggio* (New York: Harper & Row, 1983), p. 67.

41. Garrard has suggested that transference of Judith's negative traits to the maid allows 'the inclusion of both the good and evil Judiths within the same painting'. See Garrard, 'Judith', p. 298.

42. Andrea Mantegna, *Judith and her Maidservant with the Head of Holofernes*, 1491–1492, ink on paper, Uffizi, Florence. On Mantegna being the first artist to depict Judith's maid as a black African, see Paul H.D. Kaplan, 'Isabella d'Este and Black African Women', in *Black Africans in Renaissance Europe* (ed. T.F. Earle and K.J.P. Lowe; Cambridge: Cambridge University Press, 2005), pp. 125-54 (127).

43. Black African slave attendants gained popularity among European elite households around the era of the Hohenstaufen emperors of the twelfth and thirteenth centuries, quickly transforming to visual images. On the evolution of black African slaves in Italian history and art, see Kaplan, 'Isabella d'Este and Black African Women',

Fig. 11. Andrea Mantegna, *Judith and her Maidservant with the
Head of Holofernes,* 1491–92. Ink on paper.
Uffizi, Florence.

duties, and slave women between the ages of 15 and 25 drew the highest purchase price.[44] This penchant for obtaining black slave women for one's household is described by Paul Kaplan as a trend of the elite, a 'fashion for human accessories'.[45] The growing slave population and the popularity of black female slaves by the late fifteenth century are two factors that likely prompted Mantegna to depict Judith's maidservant as black.[46]

Drawing in ink, Mantegna emphasizes facial features and attributes over skin color to designate the maid as a black African. The maidservant's head-scarf and earring, as well as the treatment of her hair, nose and lips, are all indicative of her African slave identity.[47] Scale and positioning also iden-tify the maid as a slave. She is smaller in scale and relegated to the margins of the page as she dutifully offers the food sack for the severed head. The maidservant's stooped posture compared to that of Judith's standing erect in the central foreground marks the women's social disparity.

By the late sixteenth century, iconography of the black maidservant was prevalent. Prominent artists such as Titian and Veronese utilized this trend, and it is estimated that in the Renaissance there are more paintings of black African women in the role of Judith's maidservant than at any other time.[48] Although there is no textual basis describing the maidservant as black, her representations as such reinforce her status in the narrative as a slave.

Of all renderings of the maidservant as a black African, Correggio's small (about 10.5 x 7.5 inches) but powerful image of the maid titled *Judith* (Fig. 12) is at once the most disturbing and yet, I propose, the most tell-ing polemic against the institution of slavery.[49] Like Caravaggio's *Judith Beheading Holofernes*, Correggio presents a scene that can also be 'read' as a transference, but it transcends the bounds of Judith's questionable dealings concerning the assassination and moves into the evils of slavery. The maid's wild and angrily distorted face intimates an 'atmosphere of wrong-doing'.[50]

---

pp. 127-32. For a general understanding of the black African slave trade, distribution and slave life in Renaissance Europe, see Kate Lowe, 'The Stereotyping of Black Africans in Renaissance Europe', in *Black Africans in Renaissance Europe*, pp. 17-47.

44. Sergio Tognetti, 'The Trade in Black African Slaves in Fifteenth-Century Florence', in *Black Africans in Renaissance Europe*, pp. 213-24 (214).

45. Kaplan, 'Isabella d'Este and Black African Women', p. 135.

46. Kaplan, 'Isabella d'Este and Black African Women', p. 134.

47. Kaplan, 'Isabella d'Este and Black African Women', p. 137.

48. Kaplan, 'Isabella d'Este and Black African Women', pp. 146-47; Titian, *Judith with the Head of Holofernes*, 1570, oil on canvas, Detroit Institute of the Arts; Paolo Veronese, *Judith with the Head of Holofernes*, 1583–85, oil on canvas, Kunsthistorisches Museum, Vienna.

49. Antonio da Correggio, *Judith*, 1512–14, oil on panel, Musée des Beaux-Arts, Strasbourg.

50. Garrard, 'Judith', p. 298.

Fig. 12. Antonio da Correggio, *Judith,* 1512-14. Oil on panel.
Musée des Beaux-Arts, Strasbourg.

Her head, nose, mouth and eyes are all grotesquely enlarged, and her maniacal expression as the head is stuffed in the food sack, expresses wickedness in both her being and action. Judith, however, is calm and angelically illuminated in side profile; she represents innocence and good. But the maidservant's depiction as black decidedly identifies her as a slave, and so I suggest that embodied in her devilish image is the evil the enslavement of a fellow human being represents. Correggio's maidservant is emblematic of the abuse slaves endured in this system under masters such as Tobit's Sarah, who transfer misdirected anger and frustrations onto their slaves. Both Correggio's maidservant and Judith illustrate the realities of slavery in which the master remains unscathed by the atrocities of forced bondage the slave endures.

Conclusion

Throughout the book of Judith, the maidservant is shown as an active participant in Israel's salvation. She obediently and adeptly performs tasks for her mistress, and her assistance aids Judith's success in defeating Holofernes and his Assyrian forces. The maid is also a slave who remains faithful to her captor and helps protect the very society that sanctions her own enslavement. Popular depictions of the maidservant emphasize the importance of Judith's maintained chastity but may also offer a visual polemic against the institution and practice of slavery. Although she remains nameless and silent, the actions of the maidservant speak volumes; she plays a significant role in the mission to save Israel, and she, like Judith, should be praised as a hero.

French Biblical Engravings and the Education of the Spanish Woman in the Nineteenth Century

Carmen Yebra Rovira

Abstract

In the nineteenth century, Spain went through a veritable 'biblical revolution' due to the publication of different Bibles and Sacred Histories in the vernacular language. This transformation granted women access to biblical literature for the first time since the sixteenth century. Some of these editions, finely illustrated, and imported from France, Great Britain and Germany, were extensively adapted, both in text and imagery, in order to fit into the Spanish context. The work by A. Darboy, *Les femmes de la Bible*, first published in Paris in 1846, included a set of magnificent engravings by the French artist G. Staal, and by other French as well as English artists. Exclusively devoted to portrayals of biblical women, this work was translated and imported to Spain in 1846–47. It would be republished several times until the beginning of the twentieth century.

This article studies the graphic and literary origins of this type of work and shows how both texts and images were reinterpreted in the context of nineteenth-century Spain. At the same time, it analyses the different renditions published and how these images, while being Romantic interpretations that emphasize the 'frailty and sweetness' of biblical women, are in fact used as a fundamental tool for moral, familial and social education of women in terms of submission, obedience, delicacy and passivity.

1. *Introduction*

The study of the transmission of the Bible in Spain is especially rich as viewed from within the nineteenth century. This is an era of great political, social, economic and religious transformation. There is a significant increase in the publication of the Bible in Spanish and a proliferation of genres related to the Holy Scriptures, especially that of Sacred Histories. This explosion enabled ordinary Spaniards to discover the Bible for the first time.

The present study views the scenario in this era, and addresses one aspect of the times by focusing on the illustrated biblical literature aimed at women, a group that in this period is increasing in its social involvement and reading ability. Within this type of composition, the French work *Les femmes de la Bible* (Paris, 1846) is outstanding for its great impact on the configuration of biblical memory in that decade throughout Europe, but especially in Spain, where it has been published four times since 1846 with the title *Las mujeres de la Biblia*. This work should be framed in a context of national biblical renewal in which the sacred text is presented as a privileged instrument for political and social development, as the basis for the reformation of morals and as a shield against increasing secularization and the spread of Protestantism. All this is a reflection of a change of attitude in Spanish Catholicism toward the reading of the Bible that started at the end of the eighteenth century with the first translation of the Bible into Spanish, a change enhanced by the improvement of education and by the increase in the publication of books.[1] They are one of the distinctive signs of the rising bourgeoisie.

Two considerations inform the choice of this work for our study: first, *Las mujeres de la Biblia* transmits a particular conception of Sacred History because it narrates only the stories of some women and not those of the entire History of Salvation, as is usually the case in the Sacred History genre. It portrays a peculiar conception of the biblical woman and a canon of the most important biblical women in nineteenth-century Catholic piety.[2] The success of this literature was possible thanks to the increasing number of female readers who shyly began reading in Spain after the last decades of the eighteenth century.[3]

Second, closely related to the first point, is the uniqueness of this book targeted at women from the higher social ranks. This kind of work is affordable and can be read only by those belonging to the high bourgeoisie. These women were a minority, but they played a key role in defining femininity for the rest of contemporary society. Biblical women were presented as ideals

---

1. The first modern translation of the Bible into Spanish was made by the Piarist father Phelipe Scio de San Miguel with the title *La Biblia vulgata latina, traducida al español* (Valencia: Joseph y Tomás de Orga, 1790–93). Before this translation, the sacred text was available only in the Vulgate.

2. This kind of publication, in which biblical characters were proposed to a female audience as models of virtue, was typical of this context. Some examples of such publications without illustrations are José Zapatero y Ugeda, *Compendio de las mujeres de la Biblia* (Valencia: Juan Fenoll Bordonado, 1853), and Bonifacio Martín Lázaro y Garzón, *Semblanzas de las mujeres de la Biblia* (Madrid: Viuda e Hijo de Eusebio Aguado, 1883).

3. See Inmaculada Urzainqui, 'Nuevas propuestas a un público femenino' [New Proposals for a Feminine Audience], in *Historia de la edición y de la lectura en España, 1475–1914* [History of Publishing and Reading in Spain, 1475–1914] (ed. V. Infantes, F. López and J.-F. Botrel; Madrid: Fundación Germán Sánchez Ruipérez, 2003), pp. 481-91, and M. Carmen Simón Palmer, 'La mujer lectora' [The Female Reader], in *Historia de la edición y de la lectura en España, 1475–1914*, pp. 745-53.

in moral, family and social education. Domestic values and roles such as 'wife' and 'mother' are stressed and expressed through attitudes such as silence, obedience, submission, frailty and sweetness, as is expected in the Isabellan Canon.[4] It is important to take into account that all the readings and books for virtuous women are chosen by men. Fathers, husbands, teachers and confessors decide what readings are suitable for women. The books are also written by male authors, and they are used as a tool to exert control over women, specifying how they should be read and the proper attitude with which to read them.[5]

This article starts with an analysis of the illustrated literary tradition of previous centuries in which the main characters are women and texts are harmonized with illustrations. Next, it focuses on the French work that is at the origin of the Spanish tradition and of the different Spanish versions under study. The third section analyses its graphic collection, its relationship with the different Spanish editions and its influence in Spanish society. The article concludes with some salient observations from the study.

2. *Biblical Women and Biblical Literature for Women: Precedents*

Biblical literature for women illustrated with engravings has a long historical evolution. *Las mujeres de la Biblia* belongs to an old tradition that aims at transmitting—through various literary and graphic genres—virtues and values held by many biblical women. Two of these genres are worth mentioning: 'Galería de mujeres fuertes o mujeres viriles' [Gallery of strong or virile women] and 'Historias sagradas' [Sacred Histories].[6] The first kind

---

4. The expression 'Isabellan Canon' refers to the traditional cultural practices and models developed in Spain under the rule of Queen Isabella II (1833–1868), inspired especially by the Romantic movement.

5. See Pura Fernández and Marie-Linda Ortega, *La mujer de letras o la letra herida: discursos y representaciones sobre la mujer escritora en el siglo XIX* [Women of Letters or the Wounded Letter: Discourses and Representations of Women Writers in the Nineteenth Century] (Madrid: CSIC, 2008), p. 139. It is also possible to find some female writers who reinforced the patriarchal system and the submission of women with their novels and poems, such as Maria Pilar Sinués de Marco (1830–1895). See Marta del Pozo Ortega, 'La toma de conciencia feminista en las escritoras del siglo XIX: un estudio de textos y poética' [Feminist Awareness among Nineteenth-Century Women Writers: A Study of Text and Poetry], in *La imagen de la mujer y su proyección en la literatura, la sociedad y la historia,* [Images and Projections of Women in Literature, Society and History] (ed. M. González de Sande; Seville: ArCiBel, 2010), pp. 91-110.

6. The *pliegos de cordel* and the *estampas de devoción* were also forms that helped to popularize the biblical female heroine stories. The first type are short written compositions, short stories, sold in the small villages at very low prices, especially in the eighteenth century. They narrated the biography and works of biblical characters with a clear moralizing objective. An example is Joseph Manuel Martin, *La sobervia*

is a collection of narratives that describe women as main characters and as models for certain feminine virtues and abilities. Sarah, Judith, Jael and Esther are prominent here as 'strong women'. They are portrayed as saviours and hailed for their strength and commitment to their people.

Among this genre of books published in Spain, there are three works that merit special mention. The first, and most influential, was written by D. Alvaro de Luna (c. 1381–1453), *Libro de las virtuosas e claras mugeres* [Book of Virtuous and Fair Women] (1436), with 123 biographies of which 23 were of women from the Old Testament.[7] In the preface the fact is stated that when the vices or shortcomings of women are pointed out it is not with the intention of showing that these are natural in them, but only that they happen as a product of their customs. The author explains that it is possible for women also to achieve a blessed state, as the original sin was committed not only by Eve but also by Adam. When the sages of antiquity censured women they did not refer to all of them, but only to those leading *disordered* lives. This book was edited on several occasions over the following three centuries and a half.[8]

Another work is *Historia o elogios de mugeres insignes del Viejo Testamento* [History or Praises of Distinguished Women from the Old Testament], by Martin Carrillo (1565–1630), published in Huesca by Pedro Bluson in 1627, with 47 chapters that deal with 54 female characters.[9] This work, in which only the cover is illustrated, is of the type directed at women in convents, with an engraving of Juan Schorquens. The figures of Sarah, Eve, Rebekah, Judith, Jael, Esther and the Queen of Sheba appear in small rectangles with their names written at the top (Fig. 1). The preface discusses the relevance of also documenting the lives of indecent women in the Bible,

---

castigada: historia verdadera y ejemplar de Esther y Mardocheo (Madrid: Manuel Martín, 1780). They usually have a rough drawing on the cover. The devotional prints are small, very cheap pictures, for private use, which always contained some prayer, a short pious sentence or some moral maxim.

7. Don Álvaro de Luna, *Libro de las claras e virtuosas mugeres: edición crítica por Manuel Castillo* (Toledo: Rafael G. Menor, 1908; Valladolid: Maxtor, facsimile edn, 2002).

8. In the National Library of Spain (Madrid) a 1857 manuscript copy is kept (sig. MSS/19165). See J.M. Fradejas Rueda, 'Manuscritos y ediciones de las virtuosas e claras mujeres de don Álvaro de Luna', in *The Medieval Mind: Hispanic Studies in Honour of Alan Deyermond* (ed. I. Macpherson and R. Penny; Woodbridge, Suff.: Tamesis, 1999), pp. 139-52 (142-43).

9. This work was republished in the late eighteenth century: Martin Carrillo, *Historia o elogios de las mugeres insignes de que trata la Sagrada Escritura en el Viejo Testamento* (Madrid: Joseph Doblado, 1783, 1792).The preface to the 1783 edition also speaks of a missing edition printed in Lima, Peru, in the seventeenth century. For details about the author see 'Carrillo, Martin', in *Diccionario universal de historia y geografia* (Madrid: Francisco de Paula Mellado, 1846), II, p. 122.

Fig. 1. J. Schorquens, *Elogios de mugeres* (cover).
Wood engraving from Martin Carrillo, *Elogios de mugeres insignes
del Viejo Testamento* (Huesca: Pedro Blusón, 1627).

and concludes that these stories are also instructive because they provide a model of undesirable or immoral conduct.[10]

The third work is that of the French Jesuit Pierre Le Moyne, *La galerie des femmes fortes,* written and illustrated in 1647, with the purpose of 'instruction in custom', and translated into Spanish as *La galería de mugeres fuertes* [Gallery of Strong Women] (4 vols.; Madrid: Benito Cano, 1794). This edition in a compact size spread among the general public, but especially among women, in the nineteenth century when it was used as a training tool for teachers, a source of tests for the examination of female students and as a prize for the best of them.[11] The first volume is *Las fuertes judías* [Strong Jewish Women], introducing Deborah, Jael, Judith, Salomonia[12] (mother of the Maccabees) and Marina, the Jewish heroine mentioned by Flavius Josephus in the *Antiquities* (*Ant.* 15.11).[13] In each of these works, ethical questions are raised, such as woman's ability to rule, to defend the community or to perform sacrifices. The original French edition includes illustrations by Claude Vignon, engraved by Jean Mariette[14] (for example, Fig. 2).

In each of the images the main character is drawn in the foreground. In the background are represented other scenes of the same story, to the right

10. Rosilie Hernández, 'The Politics of Exemplarity: Biblical Women and the Education of the Spanish Lady in Martin Carrillo, Sebastian de Herrera Barnuevo and María de Guevara', in *Women's Literacy in Early Modern Spain and the New World* (ed. A.J. Cruz; Farnham, Surrey: Ashgate, 2011), pp. 225-42.

11. The prize for the best female students was usually 'a dowry enabling them to be taken as spouses, or a silver medal, a sewing box, a pair of scissors or a pin cushion. Normally they did not receive books but if they did the chosen ones were the catechisms of Ripalda, Fleury or Pinton, the *La galería de mujeres fuertes,* the *Biblioteca de la buena educación* [Library for a Good Education] or *El espíritu de la Biblia* [Spirit of the Bible]'; see Concha de Marco, *La mujer española del romanticismo* [Spanish Women in the Romantic Period] (León: Everest, 1969), II, p. 298.

12. With reference to the name of this character, Martín Carrillo in his *Elogios de mugeres insignes* (Huesca: Pedro Blusón, 1627), fol. 251, states, 'the sacred text endows her with no other name than *The Mother of the Seven Maccabees* and this is why Saint Thomas calls her *The Maccabean,* while others call her *Cartharia* or *Eusebia.* However Josephus, jointly with modern authors, calls her *Salomonia*'.

13. The other three volumes narrate Barbarian, Roman and Christian women's stories.

14. Claude Vignon (1593–1670) and Jean Mariette were French artists belonging to the Realistic School of the seventeenth century. See Emmanuel Bénézit y Jacques Busse, *Dictionnaire critique et documentaire des peintres, sculpteurs, dessinateurs et graveurs de tous les temps et de tous les pays* (Paris: Gründ, new edn, 1999), XIV, pp. 232-33; IX, pp. 221-22, respectively, and Alexandre Maral, 'Des Jésuites d'Aix-en-Provence au monument Sec: l'étonnante destinée des statues de la chapelle de Messieurs', *Bibliothèque de l'Ecole des chartes* 161 (2003) (= *Art et artistes en France de la renaissance á la revolution* [ed. B. Jestaz; Paris: Champion–Droz, 2003], pp. 289-321 (305). This last work mentions other specific studies.

Fig. 2. C. Vignon, *Deborah.* Wood engraving,
from Pierre Le Moyne, *La galerie de femmes fortes*
(Paris: Antoine de Sommaville, 1647), p. 2.

and left of the main figure. The illustrations in the Spanish edition retain
the key figures, but the secondary scenes are suppressed, transforming the
impression into a portrait and nullifying its narrative character.

These three works, together with *Las mujeres de la Biblia* to be analysed below, are texts with a strong biographical sense. Their essence is the
description of the life, work and virtues of the main female characters. Each
chapter is a closed and self-contained unit. No reference is made to other

biblical wisdom narratives such as Prov. 31.10-31, predominantly used in catechisms and homilies, in which women are also discussed.

The *Historias sagradas*, both in textual and graphic versions, transmit the history of salvation from its origins up to the formation of the first Christian community by way of selecting particular biblical narratives. Their diffusion was very important, constituting the only means of transmitting the sacred literature to the common populace in the nineteenth century. Use of *Historias sagradas* is particularly significant in school education.[15] These works focus not only on the most famous women of this history, as in the *Galería de mujeres fuertes,* but also deal with secondary characters, such as the woman from Thebes (Judg. 9.53), Samson's mother, the beloved woman in Songs of Solomon, and new extra-biblical characters like the mother of the Prodigal Son, who, along with the boy's father, the elder brother and a servant, awaits the return of her son (Fig. 3).

Their presence in the text reinforces the dynamism of Israel's history and the important role played by women in its development (as saviours and victims). In Spain, the collections of engravings began to be published by the end of the eighteenth century when the Bible was first translated into Spanish. These books contain an average of 250 illustrations. Worth mentioning are the works by Pedro Lozano, *Colección de estampas del Viejo y Nuevo Testamento* (Madrid: Antonio Sancha, c. 1774–78), the collection of engravings by Antonio Martínez, *Estampas que acompañan al Compendio de los libros históricos de la Santa Biblia* (Madrid: Benito Cano, 1800), and the collection by Antonio Pascual for *Historia del Antiguo y Nuevo Testamento,* written by Lemaistre Sacy (Valencia: Ventura Lluch, 1841). It is a typically Spanish trait that they all have in common the role played by women within the family structure, which is emphasized.

2. Las Mujeres de la Biblia

The work under study here, *Las mujeres de la Biblia,* is the translation and adaptation of the French work by Fr Georges Darboy, *Les femmes de la Bible*, published in Paris in two volumes with two different titles respectively in 1846 and 1850.[16] Twenty stories of Old Testament women are nar-

15. For more about this genre and its relevance in Spain, see José Manuel Sánchez Caro, *Biblia e Ilustración: Las versiones castellanas de la Biblia en el Siglo de las Luces* (Vigo: Academia del Hispanismo, 2012), pp. 31-72.

16. Their titles are *Les femmes de la Bible: Collection de portraits des femmes remarquables de l'Ancien et du Nouveau Testament, avec textes explicatifs* (Paris: H.L. Delloye, 1846), and *Les femmes de la Bible: Principaux fragments d'une histoire du peuple de Dieu avec de portraits gravés par les meilleurs artistes, d'après les dessins de G. Staal* (Paris: Garnier Frères, 1850). The first volume had a second edition in Paris: Morizot, 1858.

Fig. 3. Antonio Pascual, *The Return of the Prodigal Son.*
Wood engraving, from Maestro de Sacy, *Historia del Antiguo
y Nuevo Testamento* (Valencia: Ventura Lluch, 1841),
p. 447, 69 x 103 mm in fol. 300 x 195 mm.

rated in the first volume, 18 in the second (9 from the Old Testament and
9 from the New Testament). It was an international success in Europe and
Latin America.[17]

The first Spanish edition, *Las mujeres de la Biblia: colección de láminas preciosísimas* [Women from the Bible. Collection of the Finest Sheets],
was published in several instalments simultaneously in Madrid and Barcelona (Librería de la Sra. Vda. de Razola, and Libreria española de Llorens
Hermanos) in 1846–47.[18] It is related to the first volume by Darboy, but

17. The English version was published in two volumes. Their titles are *The Bible
Gallery: Portraits of Women Mentioned in Scripture. Engraved by the Most Eminent
Artist from Drawings by G. Staahl* [*sic*] (London: David Bogue, 1847), and *The Women
of the Bible: Portraits of Female Scripture Characters* (London: David Bogue, 1850). A
Latin American edition can be mentioned: Georges Darboy, *Las mugeres de la Biblia:
fragmentos de una historia del pueblo de Dios por el Abate G. Darboy adornados con
estampas del célebre G. Staal traducidos del francés por Agustín A. Franco* (Mexico
City: R. Rafael, 1851).

18. The full title is *Las mujeres de la Biblia: colección de láminas preciosísimas que
representan las mujeres más célebres del Antiguo y del Nuevo Testamento abiertas en*

it also introduces three notable innovations. First, a preliminary chapter about women in the Bible is added; second, the *History of the Hebrews* by Augustin Calmet is also attached;[19] and third, the *Biblical Chronology* by Fr Phelipe Scío is included as well. These innovations enhance the importance of the history of Israel and the role played by women in it. After these three introductory sections, we find 28 chapters with 27 women's stories from the Old Testament. Every chapter is a paraphrase of the biblical text, with no quotations, followed by an extensive commentary normally taken from Abate Antoine Eugène Genoude,[20] combining excerpts from the Vulgate, the Hebrew Bible, Flavius Josephus and church fathers, together with cultural elements and connections to the New Testament. Besides these references, the commentary also presents moral judgments aimed at orienting women's behaviour in the nineteenth century. Six out of the 27 biographies come from Genesis (Eve, Hagar, Rebekah, Rachel, Dinah, and the wife of Potiphar), two come from Exodus (Thermutis,[21] daughter of Pharaoh, and Zipporah, wife of Moses), one from Joshua (Rahab), three from Judges (Deborah, Jephthah's daughter, and Delilah), six from Samuel (Hannah, Abigail, Bathsheba, Rizpah, Abishag, and the Queen of Sheba), two from Kings (Jezebel and Athaliah), two from Ruth (Naomi and Ruth [Fig. 4]), one from Tobit (Sarah, wife of Tobias), Judith, Esther, Susanna and the mother of the Maccabees. The final chapter is titled 'On Moses' Law'.

Women are exemplars of both positive and negative values (Eve, Jezebel and Athaliah); some characters are mentioned about whom the Bible says hardly a word, such as Thermutis, or Zipporah (Exod. 2.21-22). The appearance of Abra[22] (Judith's maidservant) is also worth mentioning. It is

---

acero por los mejores artistas de Londres. El texto que acompaña contiene: la cronología bíblica, pruebas de la escelencia de la historia de los hebreos por el Benedictino Calmet, y explicación de los episodios sagrados a que se refieren las láminas por Genoude.

19. Antoine Augustin Calmet (1672–1757), a French Benedictine and biblical commentator and theologian. Between 1707 and 1717 he wrote his *Commentaire littéral sur tous les livres de l'Ancien et du Nouveau Testaments* in 23 volumes. In 1720 he published in Paris his *Dictionnaire historique, critique, chronologique, géographique et littéral de la Bible* (2 vols.). He also wrote *L'histoire de l'Ancien et du Nouveau Testament et des Juifs* (Paris, 1718).

20. Antoine Eugène Genoude (1792–1849), biblical scholar and a patristics specialist, was the author of the French biblical translation *La Bible, traduction nouvelle* (Paris: Imprimerie royale, 1820–24, 16 vols. in 8; and 1839–40, 5 vols. in 4). His text was more palatable than the translation by de Sacy, known as the *Bible de Port-Royal* or *Bible de Sacy* (1667–1696).

21. The daughter of Pharaoh is named Thermutis in *Las mujeres de la Biblia*, as found in Josephus, *Ant.* 2.7.224. She is not named in the book of Exodus although 1 Chron. 4.18 calls her Bithiah.

22. Abra's name refers to Judith's maid. It is used in some Spanish translations of the Vulgate from the seventeenth century. It was used by Cipriano Valera, for instance, in

RUTH.

Fig. 4. G. Staal (designer) and F. Holl (engraver), *Ruth.*
Steel engraving, from *Las mujeres de la Biblia: colección de láminas
preciosísimas* (Madrid–Barcelona: Vda. de Razola–Llorens Hnos., 1846),
165 x 124 mm. in fol. 260 x 185 mm.

especially remarkable that no mention is made of Sarah or of Miriam. In all,
generally speaking, the most relevant figures are the matriarchs who parallel the patriarchs, and the women linked to Moses, David and Solomon.

1602 when he translated, 'And Abra was called, their maid' (Jdt. 10.2). Abra is, however,
not a personal name but a Latin noun meaning 'maid' or 'servant', and thus 'Abra the
maid' is redundant.

In a way, these women represent an excuse to narrate men's stories. They 'represent different facets of the human heart, and women's role in society: wife, daughter and mother'.[23] Here we can appreciate to what extent, as is explicitly expressed in the Prologue, the work praises 'women's virtues and frailties', such as love for the family (Rachel), love for the homeland (Judith), expiation (Eve), pride (Athaliah), chastity (Susanna), obedience (Jephthah's daughter) or maternal love (the mother of the Maccabees).

The second edition of *Las mujeres de la Biblia* was published in Barcelona by Llorens Brothers in 1850,[24] under the title *Mugeres de la Biblia*. It is, in fact, a completely new work, adapted from Darboy's original by Joaquín Roca y Cornet.[25] This author from Barcelona is not so much interested in presenting Israel's history with its moral import as in using biblical narrative as an excuse to write a completely new kind of literary work. His text departs from the biblical and patristic references and introduces new elements of poetry, theatre and folk stories. It is an over-elaborated literary composition with 38 chapters (29 from the Old Testament and 9 from the New Testament) plus extensive paraphrases, always with a strong moralizing message for women.

With respect to women included in the first edition, new characters are introduced, such as Sarah, Miriam, the Levite's wife from Ephraim and the 'Pythoness' or Witch of Endor (1 Sam. 28.7). All these figures are common in the illustrated Sacred Histories, but quite unusual in stories from biblical literature. A narrative about Michal and the Shulammite is also included. Dinah, Rizpah, Abishag and Naomi are obliterated, as is the final chapter 'On Moses' Law'. New Testament women include the following: Anna (Mary's mother), the Virgin Mary, Elizabeth, the daughter of Herodias, the Canaanite woman, the Samaritan woman, the adulterous woman, Mary Magdalene and Martha. Anna is an extra-biblical character who is presented in parallel with the mother of Samuel.[26]

3. *Biblical Women and their Graphic Representation*

The link between the French work and its various Spanish versions is the graphic work attached to them. It is a collection of 38 illustrations drawn

23. Prologue, p. 1.

24. The third (1857) and fourth (1862) editions have the same title, but they include the claim that they are revised works; they were published in a single volume. Another version of Roca y Cornet was printed in París by Garnier Frères, in 1874.

25. Joaquín Roca y Cornet (1804–1873) graduated in law and was very committed to the Catalan Romanticism movement; he was a member of the Academy of Letters of Barcelona. His work was primarily religious, doctrinal and moral.

26. Mary's parents, Anna and Joachim, are presented in the *Protoevangelium of James* (*Prot. Jas.* 1–2).

Fig. 5. J. Johannot (designer) and A. Revel (engraver), *Naomi.*
Steel engraving, from *Las mujeres de la Biblia: colección de láminas preciosísimas*
(Madrid: Librería de la Sra. Vda. de Razola, and Barcelona:
Libreria española de Llorens Hermanos, 1846),
140 x 100 mm in fol. 260 x 185 mm.

by the French designer Pierre Gustave Eugene Staal (1817–1882),[27] and engraved in steel by English artists.[28] The images were used throughout the nineteenth and twentieth centuries to various biblical formats.[29] In the Spanish edition of 1846 not all of Staal's engravings are reproduced, but some compositions of the British illustrator J. Johannot are included. The designs are engraved in oval and rectangular form, size 115 x 95 mm and 130 x 90 mm respectively. The smallest of these also have one fine frame that enlarges the design (140 x 100 mm) (Fig. 5). Thus this edition has three different kinds of engravings.

These compositions, designed in Romantic style, are exclusively portraits that, according to the Spanish prologue, 'descend from or fly to the sky, but that certainly only belong to the earth for the sake of teaching and consoling us' (Prologue to the 1846 edition, p. 3). The main character usually is not portrayed as looking ahead (except for Sarah, the Queen of Sheba and the mother of the Maccabees) but appears half-side, looking downward or heavenward. A melancholic outlook is a common trait to all, achieved through gestures, the atmosphere surrounding the characters and an undefined background, usually a landscape. Delicate and graceful as they are, the figures nearly always wear some kind of jewelry or ornament and exhibit a feature that permits their clear identification (the child for Eve, cornstalks for Ruth, bread for Abigail, a cup and exuberant jewelry for the Queen of Sheba, the throne for Athaliah . . .). Their hands are drawn delicately, and are usually open, offering or pointing at something, or else close to their bodies (for example, Fig. 6).

These are images that convey tranquillity, shyness, propriety, delicacy (Jephthah's daughter, Susanna and the daughter of Pharaoh); piety (through a prayerful attitude, as in the case of Mary, the mother of Samuel, Dinah and the mother of the Maccabees); submission (remarkable in the case of Jephthah's daughter, Esther and Hagar); and candour and quietness (except

27. Emmanuel Bénézit, *Dictionary of Artists* (Paris: Gründ, 2006), XIII, p. 181. Staal was a disciple of Paul Delaroche, and he studied in the Fine Arts School of Paris. He exhibited his work in the Salon from 1839 to 1872. He was in charge of making the illustrations for the English edition of Don Quixote and was well known for his regular drawings in the *Magasin pittoresque*.

28. They are F. Holl, W.H. Mote (three engravings respectively), Heath and W.J. Edwards (two); and B. Eyles, P. Pelée, G.J. Edwards, A. Revel, J. Brown, C. Cousin, Bosselman and Mme L. Girard (one each).

29. See *La Santa Biblia traducida al español por D. Felipe Scío de San Miguel* (Paris: Garnier et Frères, 1871–72). In this edition Staal's series is mixed with some other engravings reproducing some masterworks painted by Nicolas Poussin, Horace Vernet and Le Brun. It is also published in the form of panels adapted by the great Catalonian illustrator Joan Aleu Fugarul, size 90 x 32 cm and 105 x 49 cm, edited in Barcelona: Suc. De Llorens y Hermanos, 1899.

Fig. 6. G. Staal (designer) and F. Holl (engraver), *Abigail.*
Steel engraving, from *Las mujeres de la Biblia: colección de láminas preciosísimas*
(Madrid: Librería de la Sra. Vda. de Razola, and Barcelona:
Librería española de Llorens Hermanos, 1846),
165 x 124 mm in fol. 260 x 185 mm.

Fig. 7. G. Staal, *Jephthah's Daughter.* Steel engraving, from
Las mujeres de la Biblia: colección de láminas preciosísimas
(Madrid: Librería de la Sra. Vda. de Razola, and Barcelona:
Libreria española de Llorens Hermanos, 1846),
165 x 124 mm in fol. 260 x 185 mm.

for that of Athaliah and Deborah). Negative feelings or experiences such as fear of death or outrage at injustice are not expressed; nor is any movement portrayed (see, for example, Fig. 7).

All the pictures share the same representational style; consequently, plurality is lost in the characterization of biblical characters, in many cases distorting the most salient features of the biblical protagonists and their relevance to the theme of salvation. It is a collection of great beauty and excellent artistry, in regard to both drawing and engraving.

There are significant differences between the genres mentioned earlier (Galleries of Strong Women and Sacred Histories) and this collection. Some of them are not only typological but also hermeneutical, and allow for a study of the evolution of the concept of biblical illustration and also of the biblical women proposed and their virtues. In the eighteenth century, the domestic nature of female virtues was becoming evident, suggesting an exclusive dedication to family life or to closely related functions (see Fig. 8). Such a strategy conveys a rupture with previous periods, with important and long-standing repercussions.[30] In Spain, strong women were especially relevant as models against the French invasion (1808–1809) but would now be slowly transformed, around the mid-century, into new biblical roles.[31] Accordingly, two different models of femininity coexisted at that time: faithful wives belonging to patriarchal families, and strong active women. However, the reference to the 'strong woman' in these biblical works is a rhetorical device designed to emphasize the responsibility of the Spanish woman in the fight against laicism through her educative task as wife and mother.[32] Staal's graphic work contributes to this domestication of tradition and the idealization of woman as simple wife, mother and citizen, reinforcing interpretations transmitted by the texts of de Genoude, Darboy and Roca y Cornet.

---

30. See Victoria López Cordón, 'La rueca y el huso, o el trabajo como metáfora' [The Spinning Wheel and the Spindle: Work as a Metaphor], in *El trabajo en la historia* [*Work in History*] (ed. F. Blanchard and A. Vaca Lorenzo; Salamanca: Universidad de Salamanca, 1996), p. 197.

31. See Marieta Cantos Casenave, 'Las mujeres en la prensa entre la Ilustración y el Romanticismo' [Women in the Press between the Enlightenment and Romantic Periods], in *La guerra de pluma: estudios sobre la prensa de Cádiz en el tiempo de las Cortes (1810–1814). III. Sociedad, consumo y vida cotidiana* [The Pen War: Studies on the Cadiz Press during the Constitutional Period (1810–1814). III. *Society, Patterns of Consumption and Everyday Life*] (ed. M. Cantos Casenave, F. Durán López and A. Romero Ferrer; Cádiz: Universidad de Cádiz, 2009), p. 182.

32. Cf. Iñigo Sánchez Llama, *Galería de escritoras isabelinas: la prensa periódica entre 1833 y 1895* [Gallery of Isabellan Women Writers: The Periodical Press between 1833 and 1895] (Madrid: Cátedra Instituto de la Mujer, Universitat de València, 2000), pp. 92-93.

Fig. 8. G. Staal (designer) and B. Eyles (engraver), *Hannah, Samuel's Mother.* Steel engraving, from *Las mujeres de la Biblia: colección de láminas preciosísimas* (Madrid: Librería de la Sra. Vda. de Razola, and Barcelona: Libreria española de Llorens Hermanos, 1846), 165 x 124 mm in fol. 260 x 185 mm.

4. *Conclusions*

The study of *Les femmes de la Bible* and its different Spanish illustrated editions reveals how important the trade in biblical works in Europe and Latin America was in the nineteenth century, contributing to the creation of a common biblical universe and unveiling the process of adaptation and reinterpretation of graphic and textual works and collections to the specific circumstances of each period. Just as importantly, it shows the significance of engraving as a source for the study of the biblical world and as a resource for the study of processes of Bible transmission and interpretation.

The collection of *Las mujeres de la Biblia,* both in its graphic and textual versions, is significant; it shows how the Bible was read, imagined, interpreted and used in nineteenth-century Spain.

Regarding the text, one may note the importance of stories of biblical women and the interest shown in preserving and transmitting them as models for training women. In this process, one may perceive an evolution from textual fidelity toward re-creation accompanied by a loss of the textual elements of the narrative. This is highly paradoxical since it happened in a period when it was possible, for the first time, to read the Bible in the vernacular language. The biblical story became an excuse to compose a moralizing religious work. The changes brought about by the selection or silencing of particular narratives are not accidental. They show how the Bible was being used for the social construction of women and to define their new role in Spanish society.

Through image analysis, one can appreciate the importance of updating graphic models in order to meet the tastes of the times. It speaks to a capacity to adapt, acculturate and modernize sacred representations according to the canons of the Romantic movement, and create the ideals of female imagery in this era. In this process of creative adaptation, some features in the Sacred History are distorted in order to offer a different profile of female identity. The great significance of the genre of portraiture in this period implies a departure from narrative action and, consequently, from the relevance of the saving role of the protagonist. The loss of this fundamental reality narrows the historical dimension of revelation (its realization in time, space and within the scope of human activity) and that of salvation. Passivity becomes a salient feature of femininity, 'inspired' by these representations of biblical models. Stylistic unity also reduces the multiplicity of messages and teachings on the part of these feminine characters. Portraiture as a genre denaturalizes the biblical narration by way of presenting an idealized and simplified vision of women. The female model promoted in the Victorian and Isabellan canon is passive and submissive, contradicting, in many cases, the biblical text and its message. A comparative approach to the graphic work shows how the descriptions of biblical females changed over time in order to emphasize increasingly domestic values and virtues and dismiss their dynamism, social participation, public duties and political import.

The illustrated work gains significance in this century as an ideal channel for establishing standards of biblical identity and memory, linked to female figures in biblical texts, with great power to configure social identity. The dissemination of this work and its graphic collection created a common image—with respect to these figures—in France, Italy, Spain, England and Latin America. Repercussions, however, changed from place to place due to contextual, religious, political and cultural circumstances. The images also show a specific selection of texts, characters and passages that created a canon of biblical reading that needs to be studied further.

It is clear from all the foregoing that biblical illustrations are not value-neutral, but contain and transmit a set of interpretations and biases, some-times discordant with the original text and its message; they need to be unveiled and critically analysed.

A PLACE FOR PUSHY MOTHERS?
VISUALIZATIONS OF CHRIST BLESSING THE CHILDREN

Christine E. Joynes

ABSTRACT

This article examines some visual interpretations of Mk 10.13-16 where Christ blesses the children. I highlight the narrative's changing fortunes in art, focusing in particular on possible reasons for its sudden prominence in the sixteenth century. Using some examples of *Christ Blessing the Children* from the workshop of Lucas Cranach the Elder (1472–1553), I explore the role of the 'pushy mothers' in his images. I then compare Cranach's visual interpretations of the Markan narrative with other, later, paintings by Giovanni Tinti, Anthony van Dyck, Nicolas Maes and William Blake.

Cranach's paintings offer the viewer significant exegetical insights into the biblical text, drawing attention in particular to the important role played by the women who bring their children to Jesus. Cranach's recurrent motif of a resisting child in his images also challenges interpretations of 'receiving the kingdom of God like a child' (Mk 10.15) that have portrayed children in idealized and unrealistic ways. I therefore argue that Cranach should be taken seriously as a biblical interpreter, and that his work should not be regarded simply as a response to the Anabaptist controversy.

Mark 10.13-16, where Christ blesses the children who are brought to him, has had a chequered history in visual art.[1] Despite the episode's familiarity through stained-glass windows and panel design, prior to the sixteenth century the narrative was rarely depicted. Its sudden rise in popularity is often linked to Martin Luther's use of the text in his controversy with the Anabaptists. However, as is evident in representations of *Christ Blessing the Children* by Lucas Cranach the Elder (1472–1553) and his workshop, this context provides only a partial explanation for the narrative's broader appeal. The distinctiveness of Cranach's 'pushy mothers' becomes clear when his pictures are compared with other, later, depictions of the same

---

1. I focus on the Markan text, since I assume Markan priority (cf. Mt. 19.13-15; Lk. 18.15-17); in addition, the Cranach images discussed explicitly cite the Markan text as their basis. We should not, however, overlook the common practice of harmonizing elements from the different Gospels in images, as artists seek to engage with the biblical text imaginatively, rather than seeking to 'copy' it visually.

biblical passage. By focusing on Cranach's portrayal of those who brought children to Jesus, I endeavour to offer what Exum (2012: 473) describes as a 'genuine dialogue' between the Bible and art: that is, a dialogue whereby the biblical text and biblical art are equal partners in the task of interpretation. In contrast to those who interpret Cranach's images purely in the light of historical events at the time he was working, I suggest that by taking the artist seriously as biblical interpreter one discovers significant insights into the biblical text.

1. *Locating Mark 10.13-16 in its Literary Context*

Mark 10.13-16 appears in a section of teaching in the Gospel. It is immediately preceded by teaching on marriage (10.2-12) and is followed by the account of the rich man (10.17-22) whose wealth prevents him from entering the kingdom of God. Mark 10.13-16 bears many hallmarks of themes found elsewhere in Mark's Gospel. An obvious example is the evangelist's emphasis on the disciples' misunderstanding of Jesus' mission, as shown here in their refusal to allow children access to him.[2] Mark highlights the disciples' obtuseness by placing this event in close proximity to Jesus' earlier teaching (9.36-37), where they had been explicitly directed to receive children.

Mark's positive portrayal of children in 10.13-16 corresponds to material elsewhere in his Gospel. He narrates Jesus' healing of children and, strikingly, often portrays the parent interceding with Jesus on behalf of the child: Jairus asks Jesus to help his daughter at the point of death (5.23); the Syrophoenician woman seeks Jesus out on account of her demon-possessed child (7.25); and the epileptic boy's father beseeches Jesus on behalf of his sick son (9.17).[3] Given the passive roles played by the children in these narratives, we might well ask whether in fact it is the *parent's* faith that is actually being commended. (The exception to the positive emphasis on children is, of course, the narrative of Herodias's daughter in 6.22-29, though even here the close connection between mother and daughter is highlighted.[4])

A further feature of the Markan text to note is its emphasis on touch. As Yarbro Collins (2007: 471) observes, 10.13 is the only instance in Mark where the verb *haptomai* is used in a context other than healing. I have argued elsewhere that Mark's emphasis on touch is often radically subversive, as, for example, in his narrative of the hemorrhaging woman who is

---

2. On the theme of the disciples' misunderstanding in Mark, contrast Best (1981) with Telford (1999).

3. Note also the Markan account of the paralytic's healing, where the faith of those who bring the sick man is explicitly commended (Mk 2.5).

4. This episode differs from the aforementioned examples in that the daughter, though nameless, does in fact speak in the narrative. She is therefore not a passive character. See further Joynes 2007.

healed by touching Jesus without his prior consent.[5] As we shall see, the theme of touch is a prominent feature in some visual representations of the Mark 10 narrative.

Another characteristic Markan feature is his use of tautology. His somewhat cumbersome conclusion to the narrative (where Jesus took the children in his arms, blessed them and laid his hands upon them) is therefore, understandably, abbreviated by Matthew and Luke. But interestingly, many visual representations of the narrative include all three elements mentioned in Mark.[6] Thus while commentators have been quick to dismiss Mark's laborious style, artists have been more ready to explore imaginatively the breadth of ideas contained in his text.

2. *Cranach's Pushy Mothers*

Having briefly introduced our passage within its Markan framework, we turn now to examine some artistic interpretations of the narrative. The title for my article ('A Place for Pushy Mothers?') emerged as a result of encountering Lucas Cranach's painting *Christ Blessing the Children*. Cranach and his workshop produced more than twenty versions of this biblical text.[7] The version reproduced in Fig. 1 can be found in the Städel Museum in Frankfurt, and dates from the mid-1530s. The painting adopts a horizontal format, with half-length figures, a type of composition that was characteristic of northern Italian art in the early sixteenth century.[8]

The image shows Christ surrounded by a crowd of women, densely grouped together against a black background. As Kibish notes, 'the frame cuts very low above the heads of the figures thus increasing the effect of closeness and density' (1955: 197). In his left hand, Christ, somewhat precariously, cradles a child (presumably belonging to the woman with praying hands). Simultaneously he stretches out his right hand to bless a child lying on a cushion. Its mother, however, is distracted by her other child, to whom her gaze is directed. All the babies in the picture are portrayed naked,

---

5. Joynes 2012: 118-19.

6. See, for example, the Metropolitan Museum version of Cranach's *Christ Blessing the Children*, where with one hand he takes a child in his arms, his other hand is laid upon another child, and he adopts a kissing gesture—perhaps indicating a further act of blessing. The image is reproduced in Fig. 4 below.

7. Andersson (1981: 59 n. 57) lists 23 versions, though she does not include those at Wawel Royal Castle, Poland, or at Larvik kirke, Norway. She also incorrectly lists a version as still being in the possession of Henry Schniewind, which is in the Metropolitan Museum of Art, New York.

8. In contrast, some of Cranach's images include full-length characters. See, for example, the image *Let the Children Come to Me* at the Angermuseum, Erfurt, reproduced at www.artothek.de.

Fig. 1. Lucas Cranach the Elder, *Christ Blessing the Children*, 1535–40.
Städel Museum, Frankfurt. Photo credit: © Artothek.

in contrast to the older (clothed) children present.[9] On the right, a baby
suckles at its mother's breast, while behind Jesus another baby attempts to
clamber onto his back. One of the less pushy mothers (at the back) draws
the viewer into the picture by looking straight at us. Meanwhile, the woman
on the left of the picture touches Jesus' garment, evoking the image of the
aforementioned hemorrhaging woman. Her child clutches an apple, symbolizing fallen humanity.

The image engages the viewer with its agitated movements and gestures.
I would therefore challenge Steven Ozment's suggestion that the 'scene
depicts a throng of infants and their older siblings *as they wait patiently in
line* to be taken from the arms of their mothers and placed in those of their
Savior [my italics]' (2011: 171). As I see it, the scene is more chaotic, with
figures clamouring to get near to Jesus for him to touch their children, as
they encircle him.

The male disciples are marginalized in the image, confined to the left-
hand corner in contrast to the women and children, who dominate the painting. The apostles are physically squeezed out of the picture, with only three

9. The babies are not naked in all the Cranach versions. A version currently in
a private collection but available online at www.wga.hu portrays a mother carrying a
clothed baby on her back and gazing directly at the viewer.

faces being visible (one of which bears a striking resemblance to the young Luther).

Perhaps it was the densely crowded nature of the image, with its promi-nent gaggle of women, that brought to mind the label 'pushy mothers'. The artist certainly succeeded in drawing my attention as viewer to the iden-tity of those who brought the children to Jesus. In contrast, we might note, the Markan text does not specify who brought the children to Jesus, using the impersonal third-person plural verb *prosepheron* to simply state, 'they were bringing children to him'. Later visual representations of the text have variations in the audience depicted: some include many women; others only one or two. The visual impact of Cranach's image suggests a stark contrast between the women as models of discipleship and their male counterparts. His painting therefore suggests that 'pushy mothers' deserve a place in any discussion of women disciples in Mark's Gospel.[10]

By way of comparison, I have selected three further examples from Cranach's workshop to set alongside the Frankfurt version.

The Cranach painting now found in the Hamburg Kunsthalle (Fig. 2) is clearly dated to 1538. Again we are drawn into the picture through the gaze of a woman at the back in the top, right-hand corner. On the left, the woman who touches Jesus' garment does so with a more exaggerated movement, pinching the tunic with her right hand while clutching her baby with her left. Once more in the foreground we see a mother distracted by her child, to whom her gaze is turned. This recurrent motif in Cranach's images is, I sug-gest, particularly significant when it comes to understanding what it might mean to 'receive the kingdom of God like a child' (Mk 10.15).

Familiar motifs again appear in the image from the Gemäldegalerie, Dresden (Fig. 3), which is also dated to 1538. In comparison to the previ-ous examples, the male disciples assume a more prominent position, on the right-hand side of the picture. A larger number of them appear in this ver-sion, and their pronounced hand gestures clearly highlight their opposition to the children's access to Jesus. Indeed, the two male disciples at the front both point at the child distracting its mother (whose arm is firmly gripped by the woman approaching Jesus with her back to the viewer).

Our final example (Fig. 4) is of disputed origin, still attributed in some circles to Lucas Cranach the Elder, though more recently assigned to Lucas Cranach the Younger (1515–1586).[11] It is significant for several reasons:

10. Despite extensive research on female characters in Mark's Gospel, the women who brought their children to be blessed have been overlooked. See, for example, Miller 2004.

11. The Bridgeman Art Library and Art Resource, New York, still assign this image to Lucas Cranach the Elder. However, the Metropolitan Museum of Art, New York, website entry indicates that it should rather be assigned to his son, Cranach the Younger. See further www.metmuseum.org/Collections/search-the-collections/110000469.

Fig. 2. Lucas Cranach the Elder, *Christ Blessing the Children*, 1538.
Kunsthalle, Hamburg. Photo credit: © bpk images.

first, on account of its continuation of the motifs established by Lucas Cranach the Elder.[12] Second, it introduces a new dimension as it is one of a pair, with its accompanying panel, *Christ and the Adulteress*, also belonging to the Metropolitan Museum of Art, New York.[13] The pair of paintings are notably smaller than most other Cranach versions of *Christ Blessing the Children*, suggesting that they were probably used for private devotion.[14] This highlights the varied functions for which Cranach's paintings were produced.

The similarities in composition between the versions of *Christ Blessing the Children* referred to above are striking. A rather feminine-looking Jesus blesses two different children using both his hands; in three of the versions

12. The ongoing debates about attribution indicate the close similarities between Cranach the Elder and Cranach the Younger.

13. It is beyond the scope of the present article to discuss in detail the relationship between Cranach's *Christ Blessing the Children* and *Christ and the Adulteress,* though clearly the pairing of the two episodes establishes notable intertextual and intervisual resonances. Indeed, our 'pushy mothers' become even more striking when juxtaposed with the crowd of men in the *Christ and the Adulteress* painting.

14. Each panel measures 16.5 x 22.2 cm, in contrast to the much larger Städel Museum panel, which measures 83.8 x 121.5 cm. The panels illustrated in Figs. 2 and 3 are a similar size to the one in the Städel Museum.

Fig. 3. Lucas Cranach the Elder, *Christ Blessing the Children*, 1538.
Gemäldegalerie, Dresden. Photo credit: © Artothek.

a baby attempts to clamber onto his back. Meanwhile, all include a woman who grips a less-than-compliant child in the foreground. Attention is drawn to this action by the direction of the woman's face, which turns toward the resisting child rather than toward Jesus. Another feature to appear frequently is a woman tugging at Jesus' sleeve for attention. Meanwhile the male disciples appear disgruntled, with hands raised in gestures of disapproval.

Despite the similarities between these compositions, Cranach includes different inscriptions at the top of the pictures (all from Mark's Gospel): thus in the Metropolitan Museum of Art painting, we find a German translation of Mk 10.14: *Lasset die kindlin zu mir komen und weret inen nicht. Denn solcher ist das reich Gottes* ('Let the children come to me and do not hinder them, for to such belongs the kingdom of God'). Here the text's emphasis is upon Jesus' rebuke to the disciples. In contrast, in the Hamburg version we find (again in German) a caption from Mk 10.13, *Und sie brachten Kindlein zu im das[s] er sie anrurete* ('They were bringing children to him that he might touch them'). This citation emphasizes the positive initiative taken by those seeking to gain access to Jesus. Despite the different implications of these two references, there is no marked difference between the images to correspond to the change of text. This in itself raises interesting questions about the relationship between text and image.

Fig. 4. Lucas Cranach the Younger, *Christ Blessing the Children*,
mid-1540s. Metropolitan Museum of Art, New York. Photo credit:
© Metropolitan Museum / Art Resource, New York.

3. *The Changing Fortunes of the Narrative*

To appreciate the significance of Cranach's focus on the episode, we should note that prior to Cranach the story had not been used in panel design—at least no predecessors have been found.[15] Indeed Cranach's *Christ Blessing the Children* is often described as a catalyst for the scene's subsequent prominence.[16] So what are the reasons for its change of fortune?[17]

The commonest explanation for the sudden popularity of *Christ Blessing the Children* is that it was the result of Martin Luther's appeal to the Markan text in his controversy with the Anabaptists.[18] Since Anabaptists rejected infant baptism, Luther was challenged to provide a biblical rationale for the

15. Both Kibish (1955: 196) and Schiller (1971: 157) note the rarity of the scene in mediaeval art.

16. Schiller 1971: 157; Andersson 1981: 53.

17. There is not space here to offer a full survey of the text's reception history. For an excellent survey of the use of Mk 10.13-16 in the context of infant baptism, see D.F. Wright's article (2002). He points out that the text is cited in the order for infant baptism in all versions of the Anglican *Book of Common Prayer* from 1549 to 1928 (2002: 189).

18. This interpretation is advocated by Kibish (1955: 199) and Noble (2009: 118).

doctrine. In this context he appealed to Mk 10.13-16 by way of support.[19] From his first *Taufbüchlein* of 1523, Luther incorporated the Markan passage as a clear example of the Lord's mandate to baptize infants.[20]

Luther and Cranach

The close relationship between Luther and Cranach is, of course, significant. Cranach entered the service of the elector at Wittenberg in 1504.[21] Shortly afterward, Martin Luther was appointed as Professor in Theology at the University of Wittenberg. The two men became good friends, acting as godparents to each other's children. Beyond the ties of friendship, we know that their paths also crossed professionally. Cranach supplied Luther with illustrations for the title pages of his books and supported Luther's polemics against the papacy by providing satirical illustrations, as in Luther's 1522 edition of the *Apocalypse*. On the basis of the evident close links between the two men, it is plausible that Cranach illustrated Luther's ideas in his paintings.

However, Luther's controversy with the Anabaptists does not necessarily provide the sole explanation for the image's popularity in Cranach's workshop. Thus, Dieter Koepplin attaches it to a less polemical background, while still acknowledging Luther's influence on Cranach. He describes Luther's attraction to Mk 10.13-16 as due to his positive appreciation of children more generally, with their 'simple, just faith which should not be complicated'.[22] Similarly, Bodo Brinkmann argues for the image's broader significance, asserting,

> The warning contained in the picture illustrates a central Lutheran position: only an unspoiled childish belief in God, as revealed in Christ, can prepare the way for sinful mankind to achieve redemption. In its emphasis

19. Kibish (1955: 200) notes Luther's use of Mk 10.13-16 in support of infant baptism in *Kirchenpostille: Taufbüchlein verdeutscht* (1523); 'Vom Anbeten des Sacraments des heiligen Leichnams Christi' (1523); 'Sermon am 11 Sonntag nach Trinitatis' (August 7, 1524); 'Von der Wiedertaufe an zwei Pfarrherrn' (1528); 'Von der kinder Tauff, und frembden glauben' (1529); 'Auslegung des ersten und zweiten Kapitel Johannis' (1537 and 1538).

20. See further Wright 2002. The significance of Mk 10.13-16 in the debate about infant baptism during this period is also evident in Anabaptist writers. For example, Menno Simons (1496–1561) clearly rejects the suggestion that the text provides any justification for infant baptism. See here Wenger 1956: 280. I am grateful to Alan Kreider for alerting me to this discussion.

21. From that time on he was court painter and on intimate terms with elector Frederick the Wise of Saxony and his two succeeding electors, John the Constant and John Frederick.

22. Koepplin 2008: 70.

on family values it also relates closely to basic Reformist views, giving a Protestant thrust to the picture.[23]

Instead of explaining the image as a response to the emergence of the Ana-baptists, Brinkmann argues, 'The true message of this painting . . . is rather to be found in general statements of belief. . . . It would be more appropriate to compare its didactic character with that of a sermon.'[24]

One further significant factor to consider when assessing the sudden popularity of the episode is patronage. Kibish notes that 'no records of the commission for the first picture have been found, although it is known that several pictures of the same subject were purchased by the Elector of Saxony, as is evidenced by records of payments dated 1539, 1543 and 1550'.[25] So it is clear that Cranach produced at least three copies of the episode for his patrons. We should not overlook the importance of patronage when discussing the popularity of certain themes, although it is probable that many of Cranach's patrons were also swayed by Luther's propaganda.

4. *Cranach and his Successors*

We can appreciate the distinctiveness of Cranach's composition further if we briefly compare it with subsequent representations of the same biblical scene. So, for example, Giovanni Tinti's version (now in the Art Museum of Chicago) offers the viewer a much less intense image, with its presentation of women and children sprawled around Jesus, not clustered together in a crowd.[26] Jesus is here encircled by women and children, but the ambience is more one of a relaxed playtime. Jesus is not engaged in taking up children in his arms, blessing or laying hands on them. Nor is resistance from male disciples suggested by the artist.

Another contrasting approach is evident in the painting by Anthony van Dyck (1599–1641), with its group of male disciples whose space has been invaded by a solitary woman, her husband and her four children.[27] Here

---

23. http://www.royalacademy.org.uk/exhibitions/cranach/the-pictorial-world-of-the-protestants,566,AR.html. Accessed March 26, 2013.

24. Ozment (2011: 25) also emphasizes the painting's focus on family values.

25. Kibish (1955: 198).

26. See www.artic.edu/aic/collections/artwork/84961. Accessed March 27, 2013. Tinti (1558–1604) was an Italian painter, about whom scant information survives. It is known that he had connections with Parma, where he painted an *Assumption* for the cathedral. His image *Suffer the Little Children to Come unto Me* has no date, and it measures 36.2 x 44.9 cm. Although Tinti is not a particularly influential artist, his work is nevertheless illustrative of a very different interpretation of Mk 10.13-16 compared to Cranach's.

27. www.artstor.org. The painting is currently in the National Gallery of Canada, Ottawa.

again there is no suggestion of mothers clamouring to see Jesus but being prevented from gaining access. Rather, an intimate scene is presented in which Jesus blesses a small number of children who have been brought to him. Dating from 1618, this image, it has been suggested, may have been commissioned to celebrate the elder son's Communion. This can only be guesswork, as the family portrayed is unidentified, but the image reminds us of the important role that patronage and commissioning played in the production of paintings.

Nicolas Maes's image (1652–53)[28]—now in the National Gallery, London—adopts a particularly distinctive interpretation by depicting the episode shrouded in darkness.[29] His composition focuses on Christ's act of blessing, with his hand extended over the head of the girl in the centre, who clutches an apple. I was tempted to label this image 'pushy fathers' on account of the male figure in the background who thrusts his child over the heads of those in front of him, so that his child can be blessed by Jesus. Maes's inclusion of male parents bringing their children to Jesus contrasts with Cranach's focus on the mothers.

Further contrasts are apparent when we introduce William Blake's later depiction of the narrative (Fig. 5). This painting is one of a group of biblical illustrations commissioned by Blake's patron, Thomas Butts. Christ sits beneath a spreading tree, blessing the children brought to him.[30] The woman on the right kneels, gesturing with her left hand to the children to advance to see Christ. The woman on the left is hidden from view, locked in conversation with a stern-looking male disciple who raises his hand in reproach. In the centre, Christ is flanked by two children with hands clasped in prayer, looking heavenward, while he holds two babies to his bosom. It may be that Blake positions these two babies, together with the child who is oddly placed between Christ's legs, to symbolize male and female, thereby calling to mind Victor of Antioch's response to the Mark 10 text:[31]

> Fitly does he take them up into his arms to bless them, as it were, lifting them into his own bosom and reconciling himself to his creation, which in the beginning fell from him and was separated from him.

In contrast to Cranach's painting, Blake's scene is serene, despite the large number of children (11) and the sparse number of adults (4). As is common elsewhere in Blake, the children are portrayed as small adults.

---

28. The painting was originally attributed to Rembrandt, but subsequently assigned to Maes, who was a pupil of Rembrandt during his time in Amsterdam.

29. www.nationalgallery.org.uk/paintings/nicolaes-maes-christ-blessing-the-children.

30. The image has similarities with Blake's Job illustration, Plate 1 ('Thus Job did continually'), where Job is also seated under a tree.

31. Cited by Aquinas in his *Catena aurea* (1997: 198). See also Marcus 2009: 719.

Fig. 5. William Blake (1757–1827),
Christ Blessing the Little Children, 1799.
Tate. Photo credit: © Tate, London 2013.

Christopher Rowland (2010: 222) notes that Christ appears detached rather than involved in this image. He proposes that Blake may have Isa. 40.11 in mind ('He shall feed his flock like a shepherd: he shall gather the lambs with his arm and carry them in his bosom, and shall gently lead those that are with young').

Some insight into Blake's understanding of children can be found in his Letter to Dr Trusler, who wanted Blake to explain his pictures:[32]

> But I am happy to find a Great Majority of Fellow Mortals who can Elucidate My Visions, & Particularly they have been Elucidated by Children, who have taken a greater delight in contemplating my Pictures than I even hoped. Neither Youth nor Childhood is Folly or Incapacity. Some Children are Fools & so are some Old Men. But There is a vast Majority on the side of Imagination or Spiritual Sensation.

Blake's comments here lead us to reflect further on what the Markan text might mean where Jesus urges his disciples to 'receive the kingdom of God *like a child*' (Mk 10.15).

---

32. Cited by Rowland 2010: 7. See further http://www.blakearchive.org/exist/blake/archive/erdman.xq?term=trusler&id=b15.5#702.

5. *'Receiving the kingdom of God like a child':*
Revisiting the Markan Text

In our exploration of artistic representations of *Christ Blessing the Children* we have already encountered several suggestions about what it might mean to 'receive the kingdom of God like a child'. Brinkmann, for example, referred to 'unspoiled childish belief in God'. Across the centuries commentators have sought to pinpoint the quintessential childlike quality that Jesus is commending in Mk 10.15, most frequently identifying their innocence or integrity. Thus John Chrysostom writes, 'For indeed the mind of a child is *pure from all passions*, for which reason we ought by free choice to do those works which children have by nature'.[33]

Bede (673–735) develops further the idea of childlike innocence, suggesting that children display exemplary behaviour. He writes,

> We are ordered to receive the kingdom of God, that is the doctrine of the Gospel, as a little child, because as a child, when he is taught does not contradict his teachers, nor put together reasonings and words against them, but receives with faith what they teach, and obeys them with awe, so we also are to receive the word of the Lord with simple obedience, and without any gainsaying.[34]

Similarly, Erasmus, in his *Paraphrase on Mark* (1523), suggests particular qualities children possess when he writes:

> In them [the children] we have an example of the innocence and the simplicity according to which a proud and wicked man must be forged anew if he wants to be admitted to the kingdom of heaven. Let no one think that they are contemptible because they are physically weak or simple. Verily I say to you: Unless a man is reborn and casts off all cleverness, avarice, ambition, hatred, wrath, vindictiveness and spite, and is made like these young ones, he will not be received into the kingdom of heaven.[35]

Interestingly, in his final comment on our Markan passage, Erasmus draws attention to the need to *ask* Jesus to touch little ones, commending the actions of those who brought children to Jesus.[36]

At this point it is helpful to bring our artistic interpretations of Mk 10.13-16 into conversation with these commentators to consider if they offer any

---

33. My italics. PG 57.600-601. Cited by Aquinas in his *Catena aurea* on Mk 10.13-16. See further Wright 2002: 200 n. 42.

34. PL 92.230. Cf. similarities to Basil, *Baptism* 2.4.2: 'It is necessary and salutary to believe [the Lord] as infants believe their parents and children their teachers, according to the word of our Lord Jesus Christ himself, "Whoever does not receive the kingdom of God as a little child shall never enter it"'.

35. Rummel 1988: 123.

36. Theophylact (1025–1125) also highlights the faith of those who brought their children to be blessed by Jesus. Cited by Aquinas in his *Catena aurea* (1997: 198).

new insights into the meaning of 'receiving the kingdom of God like a child'. In particular, I would draw attention to Cranach's repeated inclusion of the resisting child in his painting of the biblical scene. This suggests to me that the artist does not have an idealized notion of 'being a child', and he certainly does not portray children as models of exemplary obedience![37] Furthermore, I would highlight again Blake's own reflections on the nature of children, where he asserted that children do not inherently possess a single characteristic that Jesus is commending. Thus Blake writes, 'Some Children are Fools & so are some Old Men'.[38]

In contrast to the vexed quest for an inherent quality of children that adults are to emulate, more recently our Markan text has been interpreted as illustrating, rather, the process of role reversal, where the marginalized are prioritized. Thus, Joel Marcus writes: 'In antiquity . . . the dominant features of the image of the child were its vulnerability, dependence and social marginality' (2009: 718).[39] Marcus then points out that the role reversal Jesus pronounces 'is not because the children . . . possess hidden virtues, but because of the peculiar dynamic associated with God's action in the world, which is epitomized by the mind-boggling conundrum that one cannot enter the dominion of God unless one first receives it (10.15)'.[40] Thus, he concludes, the image of entering the Kingdom 'combines passivity (*being carried*) with activity (moving in)' (my italics). Marcus thus highlights the significant role played by those who brought their children to be blessed by Jesus, while also noting the position of children as nonentities in the ancient world. This shift in interpretative approach is particularly illuminating and brings a new dimension to our debate about the place of pushy mothers. Marcus, Blake and Cranach all highlight (in their different ways) that attempts to find a distinctive childlike virtue are misguided, missing the point of the Markan narrative.

5. *Conclusions: The Politics of Biblical Interpretation*

Charting the changing fortunes of our biblical text in art and reflecting upon the reasons for its fluctuation in popularity alert us to the polemical use of biblical texts. Cranach's close links to Luther and the emergence of Mk 10.13-16 as a prominent artistic subject at around the same time as Luther's

37. Interestingly, Steven Ozment (2011: 25) suggests that Cranach's *Christ Blessing the Children* reminds the viewer to 'build the kingdom of God in and through *disciplined* children and loving families' (my italics).
38. Cited by Rowland 2010: 7.
39. Similarly Myers 1988: 267.
40. Marcus (2009: 718) links the emphasis on role reversal in Mk 10.13-16 with a similar approach in other parts of Jesus' ministry, such as his calling of the sick and unrighteous.

conflict with the Anabaptists are, I have suggested, hardly a coincidence. However, I have also hinted that the popularity of the text goes beyond this particular controversy, relating to a broader Lutheran message of divine grace.

I have also argued that Cranach's paintings of *Christ Blessing the Children* offer significant, but overlooked, exegetical insights into our understanding of discipleship—particularly the place of women disciples—in Mark's Gospel. The dominant visual presence of the 'pushy mothers' in his paintings prompts us to return to the biblical text and reconsider the role of those who brought their children to Jesus. This striking feature of Cranach's paintings seems to be unrelated to the Anabaptist controversy, with which the paintings are so frequently associated. Instead of focusing solely on the role of the child in the episode, we are encouraged to contemplate the place of the pushy mothers, fervent disciples who leave the male apostles in the shadows.

Finally, I have suggested that Blake's comment that 'Some Children are Fools & so are some Old Men' alerts us to the false polarization that has persisted across the centuries in commentators' vain attempts to find a single defining characteristic of a child that adults should emulate. The variety of ways in which the children Jesus blessed are portrayed in art also supports this position.

By taking artists seriously as biblical interpreters some conventional interpretations have been scrutinized and found inadequate. Equally, I have argued that to explain artists' work only in terms of their immediate historical contexts misses the wider contribution that their paintings make. New Testament scholars can learn much from an encounter with Cranach's 'pushy mothers'. Gaps in the Markan narrative are fully exploited, offering fresh exegetical insights, as he and his successors deal imaginatively with the episode where Christ blesses the children. I therefore suggest that Cranach's 'pushy mothers' provide clear evidence to support the need for visual criticism within biblical studies.

Bibliography

Andersson, Christiane D.
  1981   'Religiöse Bilder Cranachs im Dienste der Reformation', in *Humanismus und Reformation als kulturelle Kräfte in der deutschen Geschichte* (Berlin: Walter de Gruyter), pp. 43-79.
Aquinas, Thomas
  1997   *Catena aurea* (ed. John Henry Newman; London: Saint Austin Press).
Best, Ernest
  1981   *Following Jesus* (Sheffield: Sheffield Academic Press).
Brinkmann, Bodo
  2007   *Cranach* (London: Royal Academy of Arts).

Collins, Adela Yarbro
2007   *Mark* (Minneapolis, MN: Fortress Press).
Exum, J. Cheryl
2012   'Toward a Genuine Dialogue between the Bible and Art', in *Congress Volume Helsinki 2010* (ed. Martti Nissinen; VTSup, 148; Leiden: Brill), pp. 473-503.
Gnilka, Joachim
1999   *Das Evangelium nach Markus (Mk 8,27–16,20)* (Zurich: Benzinger; Neu-kirchen–Vluyn: Neukirchener Verlag).
Joynes, Christine E.
2007   'Visualizing Salome's Dance of Death: The Contribution of Art to Biblical Exegesis', in *Between the Text and the Canvas: The Bible and Art in Dialogue* (ed. J. Cheryl Exum and Ela Nutu; The Bible in the Modern World, 13; Shef-field: Sheffield Phoenix Press), pp. 145-63.
2012   'Still at the Margins? Gospel Women and their Afterlives', in *Radical Chris-tian Voices and Practice: Essays in Honour of Christopher Rowland* (ed. Z. Bennett and D. Gowler; Oxford: Oxford University Press), pp. 117-35.
Kibish, Christine Ozarowska
1955   'Lucas Cranach's *Christ Blessing the Children*: A Problem of Lutheran Ico-nography', *The Art Bulletin* 37.3, pp. 196-203.
Koepplin, Dieter
2008   'Cranach's Paintings of Charity in the Theological and Humanist Spirit of Luther and Melanchthon', in *Cranach* (ed. Bodo Brinkmann; London: Royal Academy of Arts), pp. 63-79.
Kolb, Karin
2005   'Bestandskatalog der Staatlichen Kunstsammlungen Dresden—Cranach-Werke in der Gemäldergalerie Alte Meister und der Rüstkammer', in *Cranach* (ed. Harald Marx and Ingrid Mössinger; Cologne: Wienand).
Marcus, Joel
2009   *Mark 8–16* (New Haven, CT: Yale University Press).
Miller, Susan D.
2004   *Women in Mark's Gospel* (London: T. & T. Clark International).
Myers, Ched
1988   *Binding the Strong Man: A Political Reading of Mark's Story of Jesus* (Mary-knoll, NY: Orbis Books).
Noble, Bonnie
2009   *Lucas Cranach the Elder: Art and Devotion of the German Reformation* (Lan-ham, MD: University Press of America).
Ozment, Steven
2011   *The Serpent and the Lamb: Cranach, Luther and the Making of the Reforma-tion* (New Haven, CT: Yale University Press).
Rowland, Christopher
2010   *Blake and the Bible* (New Haven, CT: Yale University Press).
Rummel, E.
1988   *Collected Works of Erasmus: Paraphrase on Mark* (Toronto: University of Toronto Press).
Schiller, Gertrud
1971   *Iconography of Christian Art*, I (London: Lund Humphries).

Telford, William
    1999   *The Theology of the Gospel of Mark* (Cambridge: Cambridge University Press).
Wenger, J.C. (ed.)
    1956   'Christian Baptism (1539)', in *The Complete Writings of Menno Simons* (Scottdale, PA: Herald Press).
Wright, D.F.
    2002   'Out, In, Out: Jesus' Blessing of the Children and Infant Baptism', in *Dimensions of Baptism: Biblical and Theological Studies* (ed. S.E. Porter; Sheffield: Sheffield Academic Press), pp. 188-206.

MARY AND JESUS IN THE GARDEN:
BAN AND BLESSING

Deirdre Good

ABSTRACT

In this essay I describe two contrasting strands of interpretation in text, art and music in order to ask how the encounter between Mary and Jesus in the garden generates and sustains both readings of ban (in the command 'Do not touch me') and blessing (in a meeting between a woman and the beloved she sought beyond death).

Introduction

Jesus' resurrection is central to Christian faith. In the Gospels and in Christian art of the East and West, the resurrection is first proclaimed not seen. And at the heart of the resurrection is the witness of women disciples: to the empty tomb and then to an encounter with Jesus. So when Christian art begins later to depict these events in the fifth century CE, we see renditions of the empty tomb and women disciples meeting angels and Jesus. Mary Magdalene, with other women or alone, is in all Gospel accounts of the empty tomb and resurrection appearances of Jesus. Still later, the encounter between Mary Magdalene and Jesus in the garden becomes stylized on the basis of Jesus' words to Mary in the garden, *Noli me tangere*, the Latin translation of the words Jesus spoke to Mary. In the scene, Mary reaches toward a resurrected Jesus while he extends a hand toward her speaking words modern translations render as 'Do not hold on to me'.

Well-known renditions of this scene, such as that by Titian in 1594, might reflect earlier translations of the Bible, such as Tyndale's in 1526, 'touche me not'. Yet prohibition seems an odd way to describe the scene since Titian's picture centers on the interaction of the two figures. Mary's hand reaches toward Christ. The curve of Christ's body leans toward Mary as one hand holds back the clothing.[1] A gardening implement frames and curtails an upward movement of ascension repeated by the tree that hems

1. David Brown, Sylvia Ferrino Pagden and Jaynie Anderson, *Bellini, Giorgione, Titian and the Renaissance of Venetian Painting* (New Haven, CT: Yale University

in the two figures. Why should these particular words name the meeting of Mary and Jesus, eclipsing all other aspects of their encounter?

There is another perhaps less well-known interpretation of their meeting in the hymn 'Come to the Garden'.[2] The hymn verses describe first someone alone in a garden and then the joy of meeting, recognition and finally ongoing companionship in a shared walk. All who sing or hear the song become the woman meeting Jesus in the garden. C. Austin Miles, author of the hymn, wrote it in March 1912 while meditating on the meeting between Jesus and Mary Magdalene in the garden. 'As the light faded', he said, 'I seemed to be standing at the entrance of a garden, looking down a gently winding path, shaded by olive branches. A woman in white, with head bowed, hand clasping her throat, as if to choke back her sobs, walked slowly into the shadows. It was Mary.' He continues, 'As she leaned her head upon her arm at the tomb, she wept. Turning herself, she saw Jesus standing, so did I. I knew it was He. She knelt before Him, with arms outstretched and looking into His face cried "Rabboni!"'

While some may find the hymn mawkish and sentimental, the idea behind it is not in fact new. It derives from a second-century literary trope in which interpreters elaborated the scene of Mary at the empty tomb to portray her search in the garden as the woman of the Song of Songs inquiring for and eventually finding her beloved. In this interpretation, the woman's experience of search, encounter with Jesus, and walk together with him in the garden is the polar opposite of 'Do not hold on to me'. Taking both interpretative streams into account, this article identifies reports of the meeting between Mary and Jesus in the garden as both ban and blessing. Then the article asks how and in what ways these parallel and sometimes contradictory streams existed side by side. On at least two occasions we can identify blended interpretations of ban and blessing. These interpretations from the mediaeval and modern periods interest me most, and I conclude by reflecting on their possible implications and meanings.

Gathering the Traditions

We know that Mary Magdalene exists in interpretative traditions in which she is witness, apostle, penitent and contemplative, expanding far beyond the biblical text.[3] A recent writer, for example, discusses her as apostle,

---

Press, 2006), p. 128, report that X-rays of the painting show that the figure of Christ changed from moving left stiffly to the present dynamic spiral motion.

2. http://www.youtube.com/watch?v=_2eSfKqMRbA. The link is to the version by Mahalia Jackson.

3. Diane Apostolos-Cappadona, *In Search of Mary Magdalene: Images and Traditions* (New York: American Bible Society, 2002); Kevin J. Coyle, 'Mary Magdalene in Manichaeism?', *Le muséon* 104 (1991), pp. 39-55, reprinted as 'Twelve Years Later:

beloved and archetype of divine wisdom.[4] In Christian tradition, her witness to the resurrected Jesus is followed by Jesus' commission to her to preach the good news of the resurrection to apostles. In patristic writings, she merges with Mary of Bethany or an anonymous woman who anoints Jesus (in Luke 7) and becomes a model penitent from whom Jesus casts out seven demons.[5] In Ethiopic tradition, 'Mary of the perfume' anoints Jesus. Syriac traditions identify the Mary figure at the empty tomb and in the garden as Jesus' mother. One challenge is not so much to classify these images as to support their co-existence.

Another challenge is to look beyond literary texts to other material forms of John 20. In this essay I use art (an illustration from the Rabbula Gospels of 586, a twelfth-century ivory plaque, a plate from the mediaeval *Biblia pauperum*, 'Bible of the Poor', and Titian's *Noli me tangere*, 1510–11) and music (the hymn 'Into the Garden' and Easter motets by Abelard and Chiara Marguerita Cozzolani). Taking art and music into account presents another way of analysing the generative influence and effects of John 20. I take Mary and Jesus in the garden as a starting point because of my training as a biblical scholar, knowing that this trope is not fixed. I ask how an artist or a musician might have actualized the encounter in particular interpretations in terms of style, history and iconography or musical form. How do artistic and musical renditions change and deepen an understanding of the meeting in the garden? How do they enrich applications of the text?

'Understanding through the eyes' is not a new approach. Now called 'reception history', it has many advocates, among them feminist scholars.[6]

Revisiting the "Marys" of Manichaeism', in *Mariam, the Magdalen, and the Mother* (ed. Deirdre Good; Bloomington, IN: Indiana University Press, 2004), pp. 197-211; Katherine Jansen, *The Making of the Magdalene: Preaching and Popular Devotion in the Later Middle Ages* (Princeton, NJ: Princeton University Press, 2000); Karen King, *The Gospel of Mary of Magdala: Jesus and the First Woman Apostle* (Sonoma, CA: Polebridge Press, 2003); Antti Marjanen, *The Woman Jesus Loved: Mary Magdalene in the Nag Hammadi Library and Related Documents* (Leiden: Brill, 1996).

4. Cynthia Bourgeault, *The Meaning of Mary Magdalene: Discovering the Woman at the Heart of Christianity* (Boston: Shambhala Publications, 2010). Scholarship on Mary Magdalene is immense: see www.sbl-site.org/publications/article.aspx?articleId=215 for an overview. Accessed May 17, 2013.

5. F. Stanley Jones (ed.), *Which Mary? The Marys of Early Christian Tradition* (Atlanta, GA: Society of Biblical Literature, 2002).

6. Margaret Miles, *Image as Insight: Visual Understanding in Western Christianity and Secular Culture* (Boston: Beacon Press 1985). Chapter 4, 'Women in Fourteenth-Century Tuscan Painting', is a nuanced discussion of the reception images of Mary and Mary Magdalene may have had on women in fourteenth-century Tuscany without linguistic training and men with it. For a recent discussion, see Timothy Beal, 'Reception History and Beyond: Toward the Cultural History of Scriptures', *Biblical Interpretation* 19 (2011), pp. 357-72. He sees 'biblical literary history not as the history of the influence

To art, we can now add music.[7] Since I am not an art historian or music critic I take comfort from Erwin Panofsky's remark that 'synthetic intuition [a sense of the meaning of the whole picture] may be better developed in a talented layman than in an erudite scholar'.[8] In trying to understand the way an artist or musician renders a text, I see in the rendering an expansion of the text, influenced by factors including the composer's social, political and religious contexts and by sources contributing to the artist's work. The work itself may also be independent of the text.

Mary in the Garden

In traditions of both ban and blessing, the garden is the place of meeting. How is it that Mary and Jesus meet there? All four Gospels of the New Testament record that desolate and despairing women go to Jesus' tomb two days after the crucifixion to anoint the body. They are astonished not just to find it empty and the body gone but to see and hear interpreting angels at the empty tomb declare, 'He is not here, he has been raised, as he said' (Mt. 28.6). In every New Testament Gospel except Mark's, a resurrected Jesus then appears, first to women and then to others.

It is the version in John's Gospel that features a garden and a gardener. After Jesus' death, Mary weeps alone outside the tomb in a setting John identifies as a garden.[9] When two angels ask why she weeps, she explains that she does not know where the body has been taken. Turning, she sees someone whom she takes for the gardener who also asks why she is weeping. 'Tell me where you have taken him and I will remove the body', she says. In perhaps the most famous meeting scene of the New Testament, Jesus (the gardener) says 'Mary!' Recognizing him she responds, 'Rabbouni! (Teacher)!' Then Jesus commands and commissions her, 'Do not

of an original "classic" text, but as the ongoing, culturally specific process of relationship between texts and readers'. However, he thinks the approach 'privileges scriptural content', downplays the materiality of scripture and assumes a fixed origination. He wants to move to a cultural history of the Bible.

7. Wendy J. Porter, 'The Composer of Sacred Music as an Interpreter of the Bible', in *Borders, Boundaries and the Bible* (ed. Martin O'Kane; JSOTSup, 313; London: Sheffield Academic Press, 2002), pp. 126-53; Charles H. Cosgrove, *An Ancient Christian Hymn with Musical Notation* (Studien und Texte zu Antike und Christentum, 65; Tübingen: Mohr Siebeck, 2011).

8. Erwin Panofsky, 'Iconography and Iconology: An Introduction to the Study of Renaissance Art', in his *Meaning in the Visual Arts* (Chicago: University of Chicago Press, 1955), pp. 26-54, cited in Heidi Hornik and Mikeal Parsons, *Illuminating Luke: The Infancy Narrative in Italian Renaissance Painting* (Harrisburg, PA: Trinity Press International, 2003), p. 7.

9. 'Now there was a garden in the place where he was crucified, and in the garden there was a new tomb in which no one had ever been laid' (Jn 19.41).

hold on to me, for I have not yet ascended to my Father but go, say to my brothers that I am ascending to my Father and your Father, to my God and your God' (Jn 20.11-17).

John's garden location passes into tradition. Paintings like those of Fra Angelico and Titian are located in the garden while others render Jesus as a gardener, complete with gardening hat and gardening implements.[10]

The Prohibition

The words of Jesus to Mary in the garden, 'Do not touch me', or the more recent translation, 'Do not hold on to me', were understood for a long time as a prohibition occasioned by something Mary did. In the fourth century, Codex Sinaiticus preserved a corrector's addition to the text of Jn 20.16 after Mary's address to Jesus, 'Rabboni!', namely, 'and she ran to touch him'.[11] The addition does not belong in the text, but it does clarify Jesus' warning words in the next verse. Augustine of Hippo in the fourth century explained that the experience of physical touch limited Mary Magdalene's experience of the divine.[12] Jerome thought that Mary was unworthy since she did not believe in the divinity of Jesus.[13] And a marginal gloss in the much later Geneva Bible (1560) clarifies, 'because she was to[o] much addicted to the corporeal presence, Christ teaches her to lift her mind by faith into heaven where onlie after his ascension he remaineth'.

All of these readings not only introduce explanations for Mary's reach toward Jesus on the basis of ideas imported into the text but also give pre-judicial weight to Jesus' opening words in Jn 20.17. Maybe equal weight should be given to the remaining words in the sentence spoken to Mary: 'Do not hold on to me, *because I have not yet ascended to the Father.* But go to my brothers and say to them, "I am ascending to my Father and your Father, to my God and your God."' If equal weight were given to both parts of Jesus' sentence, the issue might not lie so much with Mary as with the transitional state of Jesus' body, as explained in the subsequent reference to its ascending. If Mary is not to continue holding, it is because Jesus' physical body is liminal, which is why he explains, 'because I have not yet ascended to my Father'.

For this reason, some interpreters and modern translations soften the prohibition by rendering the present tense of the verb as 'Do not cling to

10. Albrecht Dürer, *Noli me tangere*, 1511, woodcut.
11. Codex Sinaiticus at Jn 20.16, codexsinaiticus.org/en/manuscript.aspx?book=36 &chapter=20&lid=en&side=r&verse=16&zoomSlider=0 (accessed February 26, 2013).
12. Augustine, *Sermons* 244.2-3.
13. Jerome, *Epistle* 59.

me'.[14] While in a temporary state, Jesus would then prohibit not touch but clinging. This illuminates the imperative verb both in John 20 and the wider context of New Testament Gospels that characterize Jesus' ministry during his life as one of touching or being touched by people so as to hold and heal.

Touch in the Gospels

Touch is a hallmark of Jesus' ministry in New Testament Synoptic Gospels in distinction to John's Gospel. Mark's Gospel, for example, explores ways Jesus is tangible. Jesus reaches for and grasps people to heal them by the power of God. This makes Jesus accessible and vulnerable.

At the beginning of Jesus' ministry in Mark, Jesus holds Simon Peter's mother-in-law by the hand, raising her up from a bed of fever. He then extends his hand (either in anger or compassion, the text is not clear) and touches a leper who requests healing (1.41). Sometime later, a woman in a state of impurity lays a hand on his garment and is healed. In the same episode, Jesus touches a corpse and raises a young girl thought to have died. But the actions and force with which he reaches out to heal are reversed in the course of the narrative. Those around Jesus, his family, perhaps his disciples, seek to restrain him early in his ministry, thinking him unbalanced (3.21). A crowd presses against him, restricting movement (5.31). His healing ability is inhibited by the skepticism of those in his hometown (6.5). In the latter half of the gospel, opponents seize people Jesus knows: John the Baptist, the naked young man in the garden, and finally Jesus too. The pendulum of Mark's Gospel is that until an arrest, Jesus raises people up and heals them from sickness and death in the face of some opposition and disbelief. Then he is seized and arrested, tried and killed. After crucifixion, he is raised by God to new life.

Mark's Jesus can heal the daughter of the Syrophoenician woman from a distance (Mark 7) but he heals people more frequently by touching, laying on of hands and holding them firmly. In describing an angry and compassionate Jesus, in showing Jesus being inhibited from healing by doubts of others and having others take healing from him, and in being tortured and crucified, Mark seems to be meditating on the wonder of Jesus' physical body from which power seems to ebb and flow. To Mark's presentation of a tangible, even porous, body of Jesus, John's portrait of Jesus' resurrected body in transition (Jn 20.17) is complementary.

Matthew's Gospel is a bridge between Mark and John. While Matthew's Gospel takes over from Mark the portrait of a Jesus who heals by touching (*haptomai*) and holding firmly (*krateō*), uses of the latter verb decrease in

---

14. Thus CEV (Contemporary English Version) and CEB (Common English Bible) 'Don't hold on to me!' Cf. *The Voice* (2012), 'Mary, you cannot hold Me'.

relation to Mark. But the verb is more prominent in the narrative of Jesus' arrest and trial (26.4, 48, 50, 55, 57), in other violent actions such as the arrest of John (14.3) and the violent seizure of one slave by another (18.28; 22.6). And it also occurs in Matthew's resurrection account, where it has no parallel in Mark, since there is no resurrection account in Mark's Gospel. In Matthew, Mary Magdalene and the other Mary are commissioned by the angel at the empty tomb to tell Jesus' disciples 'he has been raised', and then encounter Jesus. Jesus greets them, and they in turn come toward him, grasp his feet and worship him (Mt. 28.9).

Holly Hearon believes Mt. 28.9-10 draws on an oral source, which is indicated by the presence of non-Matthean phrases, including the use of the verb 'to grasp' with 'his feet' as the object.[15] But she recognizes that the whole verse in its present form is Matthean in its use of the two verbs 'come toward' (*proserchomai*) and 'worship' (*proskuneo*). In fact, Matthew uses the former as an adverbial participle quite often, for example, 'Jesus came and said to them' (28.18). So Matthew reports that the women hold the feet of the resurrected Jesus. To understand this aspect of Jesus' physical presence makes a reading of Jesus' words to Mary in John's Gospel as 'Do not cling to me' and thus not as outright ban more likely.

In John's Gospel, Jesus' healing ministry is not carried out through physical contact. What about the hands of others? Although adversaries desire to seize him, they are unable: 'Then they tried to seize him, but no one laid a hand on him, because his hour had not yet come' (7.30, my translation). He announces when 'the hour has come' (17.1) and, at the point of arrest, takes the initiative: he 'comes forward' and asks, 'Whom do you seek?' (Jn 18.4). Touch continues to be avoided even in death: the soldiers, seeing that he is dead, do not break his legs to hasten the process (Jn 19.32-3). Thus, forestalling clinging in the resurrection narrative is of a piece with the Gospel in which only skeptics like Thomas are invited to reach out with a finger and a hand to put into Jesus' permeable resurrected body (20.27).

Women at the Tomb

Images of two or more holy women at the tomb of Christ exist from the early fifth century onward. In the Rabbula Gospels from the Biblioteca Laurentiana in Florence, dated to 586, a resurrected Christ in the lower right corner greets the two Marys with hands extended while they reach hands out toward him. Similarly, in a ninth-century diptych from the Cathedral Museum in Milan, Jesus appears to two kneeling women whose hands are

---

15. Holly Hearon, *The Mary Magdalene Tradition: Witness and Counter-Witness in Early Christian Communities* (Collegeville, MN: Liturgical Press, 2004), pp. 70-71.

outstretched toward him. One of his hands extends in blessing over them, behind which is a tree reaching upwards.

A more individualized encounter can be seen somewhat later in an ivory plaque dated 1115–1120 in the Metropolitan Museum of Art in New York City. The upper scene is the appearance of Christ to two disciples on the road to Emmaus while the lower scene shows an encounter between Jesus and Mary. With head averted, his right hand points toward her head while both her arms and hands extend toward him beneath his. The inscription reads *Dominus loquitur Mariae*, 'the Lord speaks to Mary', which could simply be a title; but the Metropolitan Museum, perhaps taken by the dramatic gestures of both figures, entitles the image *Noli me tangere*. We are meant to take this ivory as a transition to the later *Noli me tangere* type, of which the Titian painting mentioned at the beginning of this essay is an example.

The Search for Jesus

Descriptions of a prolonged search by women for Jesus after death go back to the second century. A commentary on the Song of Songs (attributed to Hippolytus [170–235], though some scholars regard its authorship as unattributed and date the commentary to the second century CE) describes a nocturnal search for the lover using the text of Song of Songs 3 as an analogy to the search of Martha and Mary for Jesus. The commentary is based on John 20 but seems also to know other traditions of two women at the tomb as bearers of myrrh since it specifically identifies Martha and Mary, neither of whom is identified together in any Gospel account of a search for Jesus. And since the commentary mentions 'Martha and Mary' without specifying which Mary, the Mary of the commentary may well be Mary of Bethany, the woman who anointed Jesus (John 12). Some regard this figure not as Mary Magdalene, but other scholars posit that she may well have already been identified with Mary Magdalene.

The commentary describes the woman's search to include looking, questioning the night watchman and finally finding, holding and refusing to let the loved one go. In fact it is the earliest text to call the women myrrh-bearers 'apostles to the apostles'. But there is a double analogy made by the commentary for it sees in the search of the women for the beloved a search by the synagogue and also by believers for Christ. And because the commentary uses the first-person singular voice of the text of the Song of Songs, the women's search is also articulated in the first-person singular and plural, 'Have you not seen him whom my soul loves?', in contrast to the Gospel narratives, which use the third person. In the ongoing narrative of the commentary, the search is successful, and the lovers' hold of each other replaces what other church fathers such as Ambrose, Augustine and Jerome read as a prohibition to Mary Magdalene not much later:

> The Savior therefore answered and said, 'Martha, Mary'. And they said, 'Rabbi', which means 'My Lord'. 'I found him whom I have loved and would not let him go.' For it was then that she took hold of his feet, hold-ing them tightly. And crying out he says to her, 'Do not touch me for I have not yet ascended to my Father'. And she (the spouse) held on and said, 'I will not let you go until I bring you into my heart. I will lead you into the treasures of my mother's house and the treasuries of the one who conceived me.' The love of Christ was gathered in her breast and she did not wish to be moved. Because of this she cries out and says, 'I have found him and do not wish to let him go'.

Yancy Smith interprets the intensified search and the women's grasp of Jesus' feet as Hippolytus's portrait of a desire for union with Christ. We see here, he thinks, early Christian desire for Christ in which the fault of Eve is transformed by the ardent desire of Mary and Martha. Hippolytus describes Eve, in the person of the *myrrhophores*, taking the fruit of the tree of life and giving it to the male disciples, who represent Adam.

> From now on she will no longer either crave or proffer to men food that corrupts; she has received incorruptibility; from now on she is in unity and [is] a helper, for Adam leads Eve. O good helper, with the gospel offering (or sacrificing) [it] to her husband! This is why the women evangelized the Disciples.[16]

Smith thinks that the commentary gives prominence to Martha and Mary to downplay the significance of Mary Magdalene in noncanonical texts. But by the second century, I think the composite identity of Mary Magdalene is already evident[17]; and, if this is so, it is reasonable to see in depictions of the myrrh-bearing women who cling to the feet of the resurrected Jesus not only the ardent desire of early (Jewish and Gentile) believers for union with Christ but also the women apostles themselves—including the Magda-lene—who longed for and would not let him go.

The determined clinging of Mary and Martha is not just that of figures in the text but is an action to be emulated by believers, according to religious leaders of the time. Cyril of Jerusalem (313–386) gave several baptismal

---

16. Hippolytus, *Cant.* 25.8; cited in Yancy W. Smith, *The Mystery of the Anointing: Hippolytus' Commentary on the Song of Songs in Social and Critical Contexts* (PhD diss., Brite Divinity School, Fort Worth, TX, 2008). This book includes a translation of the Georgian text, the most complete text of the commentary on the Song of Songs, a translation of the Greek epitome and surviving fragments in paleo-Slavonic.

17. Clement (150–215 CE), *Excerpta* 50.1; *Paidagogus* 2.8. A different and composite Mary (Magdalene) figure can be seen in texts also dated to the second century: the *Dialogue of the Savior*, the *Gospel of Thomas* and the *Sophia of Jesus Christ*. A more widely recognized and acknowledged conflation occurs in the fourth century and later.

lectures to candidates for Christian baptism. In the fourteenth baptismal lecture, Cyril clearly understands Mary Magdalene to embrace Jesus and assumes that candidates for baptism should want to do the same.[18] Cyril puts quotations from the Song of Songs in the mind and mouth of the women. In Cyril's account, the women of Matthew's Gospel appear along-side Mary Magdalene in John:

> The Bridegroom and Suitor of souls was sought by those noble and brave women. They came, those blessed ones, to the sepulchre, and sought Him Who had been raised, and the tears were still dropping from their eyes, when they ought rather to have been dancing with joy for Him that had risen. Mary came seeking Him, according to the Gospel, and found Him not: and presently she heard from the Angels, and afterwards saw the Christ. Are then these things also written? He says in the Song of Songs, On my bed I sought Him whom my soul loved. At what season? By night on my bed I sought Him Whom my soul loved: Mary, it says, came while it was yet dark. On my bed I sought Him by night, I sought Him, and I found Him not. And in the Gospels Mary says, They have taken away my Lord, and I know not where they have laid Him.[19]

When the angels asked the women why they sought the living among the dead, Cyril adds, 'But she knew not, and in her person the Song of Songs said to the Angels, Saw ye Him Whom my soul loved? It was but a little that I passed from them [that is, from the two Angels], until I found Him Whom my soul loved. I held Him, and would not let Him go.'[20]

Although Cyril follows Hippolytus in using the Song of Songs as a prism through which to view the visit of the women to the tomb, Cyril has a distinct reading. It is he who sees Mary as the first witness to the resurrection. Yancy supposes that Hippolytus writes catechetical instruction for elite women in Rome new to the faith, and for such women the women apostles at the tomb might have provided a model of ardent devotion. But what of Cyril of Jerusalem writing for a different audience of catechumens at a different time and place about women holding Jesus' feet and, in the same context, Mary of John's Gospel who, when she found him whom she sought, clung to him with fervor? Cyril does not mention the ban *Noli me tangere*.

Mary's search for Jesus continues in the so-called *Biblia pauperum* or *Bible of the Poor*. The origins of this book are unknown, but by the late Middle Ages, there are many examples of it. Reflecting a widespread method of interpreting the Bible by means of typology, in the *Bible of the Poor* persons, objects and episodes from the Old Testament are seen to prefigure

18. Cyril of Jerusalem, *Catechetical Lectures* 23.3.

19. Cyril, *Cat.* 14.12. Hippolytus's commentary on the Song of Songs is the likely source.

20. Cyril, *Cat.* 14.13.

aspects of Christ's ministry. The book is a book-block with pictures and text produced by impressions from carved wooden blocks. Between 1460 and 1490, the book-block was a transitional form of publication leading to book printing by moveable type. Whether the book was really designed to educate the poor or whether it was intended to instruct clergy in their preaching is uncertain. However, printing undoubtedly facilitated spread of the book.

Three panels on a single page depict scenes thought to be typologically interrelated. In one example we see Christ appearing to Mary Magdalene in the garden, in the central panel.[21] This is an interpretation of John 20. Christ holds a garden implement in a garden setting. In the panel to the left we see the king of Babylon visiting Daniel the morning after Daniel had been cast into the lion's den. Discovering Daniel alive brought the king great joy. The Latin above the panel continues, 'Indeed the king prefigures Mary Magdalene when she went to the tomb. After she saw the Lord, she also rejoiced exceedingly because he rose from the dead.'

The panel on the right is entitled 'The Daughter of Sion Discovers her Spouse'. It shows the bride and bridegroom embracing each other. It is a reference to chap. 3 of the Song of Songs. The Latin inscription declares, 'We read in the Canticle of Canticles, chapter 3, that when the bride had found her beloved, she said, "I have found him whom my soul loves; I will hold him and I will not let him go". This bride prefigures Mary Magdalene who seeing her spouse, that is Christ, wanted to touch Him. Christ responded, "Do not touch me; I have not yet ascended to my Father".'

In this panel we see the juxtaposition of the two themes of this essay: the ban and the blessing of John 20. The central panel shows Jesus and Mary Magdalene encountering each other in the garden (John 20). The cruciform nimbus identifies Jesus. The same figure occurs in the panel on the right, in which the bride of the Song of Songs has wrapped her arms around the bridegroom Jesus while the scroll above her head (mediaeval equivalent of bubble speak) shows her speaking the words of the bride in Song of Songs 3: *Tenui eum nec dimittam*, 'I held him and I will not let him go'.

Two inscriptions under the panel, 'The beloved bride now enjoys the much sought spouse', and 'Showing yourself, O Christ, you console the holy Mary', seem to indicate that, while the scene renders both 'Do not cling to me' and 'I held him and I will not let him go', the emphasis of the scene is on the encounter in the garden and the solace Jesus offers Mary, not the prohibition of clinging. This balance allows us to see how later depictions

---

21. Plate 1, 'Christ Appears to Mary Magdalene in the Garden', in Albert C. Labriola and John W. Smeltz, *The Bible of the Poor: A Facsimile and Edition of the British Library Bookblock C.9 d.2* (Pittsburg, PA: Duquesne University Press, 1990), p. 45 (the Latin transcriptions are on p. 87).

of the scene proscribing further touch, like that of Titian, can nevertheless imply exactly the opposite: an ongoing encounter.

Musical Settings of Women at the Empty Tomb

From the tenth century onward, for six hundred years, liturgical use of the visit of women to the empty tomb (*Visitatio sepulchri*) at Easter, although formally stable, changed in style and function.[22] Liturgical ceremony itself is stable: in the core element of the procession of Mary and Martha to the tomb where they met an angel, material is reused and, over a longer period, there are additions. In style, this trope changed from prose to metrical texts. Musically, the form changed from chant modes to tones using octaves, corresponding to general musical changes. In function the ceremonies changed from cult ritual to didactic ceremony and eventually to popular performance. The core metrical element seems to be the Latin text rendered as an antiphon: 'Tell us, Mary, say what you saw on the way', with the response, 'The tomb the Living did enclose; I saw Christ's glory as He rose!'[23]

This is the collective voice of chant. In such examples we find representations of the women's search for and meeting with the risen Jesus. Later additions from the twelfth and thirteenth centuries and subsequently include the visit of Mary Magdalene alone to the tomb, where she met the risen Christ. These additions included a prohibition and a new preface rendering the Vulgate of Jn 20.11 as Mary's lament. Susan Rankin says that through the addition of lament, 'Mary's role is emotively developed', and that this element is connected to the eleventh-century expansion of interest in her and the specific portrait of Mary now understood as Mary of Bethany, the woman sinner, and Mary who encountered the risen Christ.[24] Thus in the earlier *Victimae paschali laudes* there is no rendition of any prohibition.

An example of this is the *Epithalamica* or 'Bridal Song' sung in the Easter Sequence of the twelfth century and attributed to Peter Abelard, although it may derive from Heloise:

> Bride, sing a wedding song, and proclaim out loud inner joy!
> Make us glad by the proclamation of your bridegroom whose presence
>   always renews.

22. Susan K. Rankin, 'The Mary Magdalene Scene in the *Visitatio sepulchri* Ceremonies', in *Early Music History: Studies in Medieval and Early Modern Music* (ed. Iain Fenlon; New York: Cambridge University Press, 1981; digital version, 2009).

23. *Victimae pascali laudes*, in which the antiphon is found, is the Sequence for Easter Sunday, thought to originate in the tenth century.

24. Rankin, 'Mary Magdalene Scene', p. 255.

You young maidens, lead the dance and join in the song which you began.
The friends of the bridegroom have invited you to the wedding feast and
      we wish for a song from the new Lady.
See how he comes from the mountains in giant steps.
Through the window he looks in at me.
Through the lattices he speaks presciently:
Get up! Female friends and hurry!
White dove, fly by!
Since the terrible winter is over and the violent rain has receded,
Lovely Spring has opened up the land: the flowers bloom and the turtle
      dove coos.
Arise! female friends and hurry!
White dove, fly by.
The king has already endowed the banquet and my sweet-smelling nard is
      poured out;
I came into the garden in which he had arisen but missed him in passing
      on the way.
So I went out and sought him throughout the night, now here, now there,
      and full of worry
I run around searching everywhere.
The guards encounter me but in burning desire I leave them behind.
I find my future husband. Already I see what I have longed for.
Already I hold my beloved in my arms!
Already I laugh about what I had previously wailed—joy outweighing the
      pain.
Night created sleepless pain, it became intense out of love
From the lack grew the longing until the beloved sees the beloved.
Joy in the day and weeping at night, by day joy, by night weeping.
On now, companions and daughters of Zion
Add psalms to the songs of the bride in which all sadness meets the
      renewed presence of the bridegroom and transforms our mourning
      songs into songs of joy!
What the Lord has made! This is the day![25]

Now the first-person singular voice of searching women that we saw in
the second-century commentary on the Song of Songs attributed to Hippolytus and the forms of the *Visitatio sepulchri* with its eleventh-century additions continue in the much later compositions of Easter music by women
musicians and composers who were nuns: Sulpitia Cesis and Chiara Margarita Cozzolani. Chiara Margarita Cozzolani (1602–1677), a nun of the
community of St Radegonda in Milan, was a prolific composer. In 1650
she wrote a motet, *Maria Magdalene stabat*, which describes the search of
Mary Magdalene at the empty tomb. By giving long phrases to the singer of
Magdalene's lament with texts from the Song of Songs, Cozzolani extends

25. Chrysogonus Waddell, 'Epithalamica: An Easter Sequence by Peter Abelard',
The Musical Quarterly 72 (1986), pp. 239-71.

not only the lament but also the encounter between the woman and the angel and the specific description of the resurrected Jesus as the bridegroom in the Song of Songs. It is a creative expansion of the encounter between Jesus and Mary in the garden to extend a text well beyond the question and answer of John's Gospel. And yet, it is not free form: the expansion uses biblical text that has already from the second century been used to interpret the encounter of Mary and Jesus in the garden. In this rendition of the motet the material in bold highlights inclusion of texts from the Song of Songs:

> Mary Magdalene stood at the tomb, weeping; while she mourned, she turned to the tomb and saw two angels in white sitting there, and said to them:
>
> *Num quem diligit anima mea vidistis?*
> **1. Have you seen him whom my soul seeks?**
>
> *Mulier, quid ploras? Quem quaeris?*
> Woman, why do you weep? Whom do you seek?
>
> They have taken away my Lord and I do not know where they have put him. **I searched for him in the night and did not find him.**
>
> *Qualis est dilectus tuus ex dilecto,*
> *O pulcherrima mulierum?*
> **2. Who is your beloved among beloveds?**
> **O most beautiful of women?**
>
> *Dilectus meus candidus et rubicundus, electus ex millibus; totus amabilis, totus desiderabilis.*
> **My beloved is white and ruddy, chosen among thousands; completely loveable, completely desirable.**
>
> *Dic nobis Maria, quis est dilectus tuus?*
> **3. Tell us, Mary, who is your beloved?**
>
> *Dilectus meus, amor meus speciosus forma prae filiis hominum. Crucifixus Jesus est.*
> **My beloved is beautiful among the sons of men, he is the crucified Jesus.**
>
> *O mea lux, ubi es? O amor meus, ubi es? O vita mea, ubi es? Veni, dilecti mi, amore tuo langueo, amore tuo morior.*
> **O my light, where are you? O my love, where are you? O my life, where are you? Come, my beloved, for I languish for your love. I am dying for your love.**
>
> *Quid quaeris vivendum cum mortuis?*
> *Surrexit; non est hic! Precedet vos in Galileam, alleluia, Maria. Noli amplius plorare, gaude, laetare.*

> Why do you seek the living among the dead? He is risen; he is not here! He will go before you to Galilee. Weep no more but rejoice and be glad.[26]

Thus, expansive musical traditions about the women's search for the risen Jesus, using texts from the Song of Songs, continue in seventeenth-century motets and the twentieth-century hymn 'Come to the Garden', with which this essay began. However, the final piece of evidence in this history of Mary's encounter with Jesus as blessing and ban emerges in another modern reading of *Noli me tangere*.

Titian's Noli me tangere *as Blessing*

A national reading of Titian's *Noli me tangere* painting as blessing emerges in the middle of the twentieth century. During the Second World War, to keep them safe without removing them from the United Kingdom, paintings from London's National Gallery were hidden in Welsh mines. Two years later, the public complained that contemporary art and concerts were taking place in the National Gallery, but there were no great paintings to see. After considerable deliberation the trustees decided that each month one treasured great work of art could return to hang in the National Gallery even at great risk. After canvassing the nation to discover which picture should be brought back first to be seen, Kenneth Clarke, the director, discovered to his astonishment that everyone requested Titian's *Noli me tangere*.

Neil MacGregor, recent director of the National Gallery, speculates that what drew the public to Titian's painting within the context of nightly bombings and air raids on London is the encounter between the living and the dead.[27] MacGregor's reading of the painting seems to center on the hands of Jesus and Mary, which are often the center of artistic depiction and implied but not described in the text. Titian depicts the moment when Mary Magdalene reaches out to touch Christ, and as he draws away, he leans over and blesses her. The painting is an investigation of what happens to physical love after death, of how physical love and spiritual love meet or don't meet, but can be reconciled. MacGregor sees it as an incomparable meditation on love continuing without physical contact, without physical proximity, as Christ protects, blesses and loves without allowing physical touch.

---

26. Chiara Margarita Cozzolani, *Maria Magdalene stabat*, dialogue motet from *Dialogues with Heaven* (Musica Secreta, Linn Records, 2001). The Cozzolani project at www.cozzolani.com is a website with links to recordings of Cozzolani's compositions as streaming audio and digital downloads.

27. Neil MacGregor, 'A Pentecost in Trafalgar Square', in *Whose Muse? Art Museums and the Public Trust* (ed. James Cuno; Princeton, NJ: Princeton University Press; Cambridge, MA: Harvard University Art Museums, 2004), pp. 27-49.

Conclusion: Seeing and Hearing the Garden
Encounter as Ban and Blessing

MacGregor's reading of Titian's *Noli me tangere* brings us to a place where 'Do not cling to me' is informed by the experience of World War II as an encounter in which enforced separation of death is overcome by a painting showing the connection between the living and the (resurrected) dead. To overcome separation, all senses are invoked. Sound (of voice), sight (of eye) and reach (of hand) listen, seek and stretch out to transcend prohibition, separation and even death itself. Such a reading may be seen as specific to a particular circumstance and place, where in the face of death, survivors sought to maintain severed connections. But it may also be seen as an evocation of earlier versions of the same encounter between Jesus and Mary in the garden before the *Noli me tangere* type came into existence. These extend from early interpretations of Mary at the tomb searching for the beloved (for example, by Cyril of Jerusalem) through the mediaeval illustrations of the *Bible of the Poor,* wherein the encounter in the garden is shown both as *Noli me tangere* and, at the same time, 'I held him and would not let him go'. Then music lengthens and expands layers of interpretation from art to sound in later Easter motets and the hymn 'Come to the Garden', wherein the gaze and reach of the bride in the Song of Songs looks for, finds and refuses to let her lover and bridegroom go. X-rays of Titian's painting show that 'Christ was originally painted wearing a gardener's hat and turning away from the Magdalen'.[28] But clearly, Titian reconsidered. In the end, Titian's painting in the garden shows two figures whose posture and demeanor opens up a long tradition of reading, hearing and seeing Jesus' encounter with Mary where the ban 'Do not cling to me' is, in fact, blessing.

---

28. www.nationalgallery.org.uk/paintings/titian-noli-me-tangere (accessed May 19, 2012).

AFTERLIVES OF THE AFTERLIFE: THE DEVELOPMENT OF HELL IN ITS JEWISH AND CHRISTIAN CONTEXTS

Mark Finney

ABSTRACT

The singular construct of afterlife within the Hebrew Bible is Sheol, a desolate place where, to the lament of many, the souls of both the righteous and the wicked reside. Yet there are striking developments within the periods of Second Temple Judaism, the New Testament and the post-apostolic Christian era. Within Second Temple Judaism, Sheol is transformed into a place of differentiation: the souls of the righteous depart to a place of blessing, the wicked to a place of torment. For the New Testament writers, this concept remains, but the soul is now conjoined to the physical body, and in the later post-apostolic period there is accentuated terror for the wicked in vivid descriptions of the eternal fires of hell. The modern understanding of a tortuous afterlife is drawn from the imagery of the church fathers, which was further accentuated within mediaeval Christendom.

Yet the polemical and apologetic context of this development needs to be recognized. Within Judaism, changes were made to defend the Jewish faithful and castigate apostates in the context of encroaching Hellenism. For the early Christ-movement, further development was related to the need to define and defend itself both against first-century Judaism and Graeco-Roman paganism from without and apostasy from within. For the church fathers, the fear of hell was employed for ideological purposes in asserting ethical priorities in the early church. As such, the development of the afterlife can be seen as a social construct, the repercussions of which in the modern period have, for many people, had a lasting, destructive influence.

Afterlife in the Hebrew Bible[29]

Hell, as a place of eternal suffering and punishment, does not exist in the Hebrew Bible. Early Israelite thought on death simply assumed that it

---

1. On the following section see E. Schürer, *The History of the Jewish People in the Age of Jesus Christ* (4 vols.; London: T. & T. Clark, rev. edn, 1979–87), II, pp. 539-46 (and bibliography, II, p. 539 n. 90); H.C.C. Cavallin, *Life after Death: Paul's Argument for the Resurrection of the Dead in 1 Cor 15* (ConBNT, 7; Lund: Gleerup, 1974); A.J.M. Wedderburn, *Baptism and Resurrection: Studies in Pauline Theology against its Graeco-*

marked, for all people, the end of worthwhile existence. From a *physical* perspective, death led both to the destruction of the flesh (for example, by decomposition, fire, or being ravaged[2]) and to the dissipation of the blood (by draining away, drying up, or by less delicate means[3]). The bones, being more resilient, may remain for some time.[4] Typically, Hebrew texts reiterate that the body is formed from dust (עפר; LXX, χοῦς),[5] and on death will return to dust,[6] in the sense that those who are said to 'dwell' in the dust are the dead.[7] And as the body returns to dust, in the words of Job, hope and youthful vigour are dragged down also.[8] Similar expressions are found in the Apocrypha.[9]

From a *nonphysical* perspective however, things look very different. The soul (ψυχή), sometimes called the spirit (πνεῦμα), is considered the essence of the human being.[10] This is articulated in Genesis 2, where the divine breath breathed into the body brings life; its removal brings death.[11] For the

---

Roman Background (Tübingen: J.C.B. Mohr, 1987); M.C. de Boer, *The Defeat of Death: Apocalyptic Eschatology in 1 Corinthians 15 and Romans 5* (JSNTSup, 22; Sheffield: JSOT Press, 1988); R. Bauckham, *The Fate of the Dead: Studies on the Jewish and Christian Apocalypses* (Leiden: Brill, 1998); R.N. Longenecker, *Life in the Face of Death: The Resurrection Message of the New Testament* (Grand Rapids, MI: Eerdmans, 1998); N.T. Wright, *The Resurrection of the Son of God* (London: SPCK, 2003).

2. Gen. 40.19; Lev. 26.29; 2 Macc. 9.9; *4 Macc.* 9.17; Ps. 26.2; Prov. 5.11; Job 33.21; 34.15; Lam. 3.4; Jer. 7.33; Isa. 34.3.

3. Gen. 4.10; Zeph. 1.17; Ezek. 32.5-6; 1 Macc. 7.17; *4 Macc.* 10.8; Isa. 49.26 (where the blood is, hopefully metaphorically, drunk).

4. Ezekiel 37, of course, details the procedure in reverse.

5. E.g., Gen. 2.7; Ps. 103.14; Eccl. 3.20.

6. Pss. 22.29; 30.9; 104.29; Eccl. 3.20; 12.7; 4 Kgdms 13.7; 1 Macc. 2.63. Cf. Ps. 22.15, the 'dust of death'. The NRSV rendition of Ps. 7.6 ('then let the enemy pursue me and overtake me, trample my life to the ground, and lay my soul in the dust'), is misleading. Δόξα may have a wide semantic range, but is never translated 'soul' (LSJ, BAGD *s.v.*). Better is 'glory' (so, NASU), or 'honour' (so, NKJV). See Walter Brueggemann, 'From Dust to Kingship', *ZAW* 84 (1972), pp. 1-18. G.F. Moore, *Judaism in the First Centuries of the Christian Era: The Age of the Tannaim* (3 vols.; Cambridge, MA: Harvard University Press, 1946–1948), sees such ideas as 'common notions . . . which are found among various peoples on comparable planes of civilization' (II, p. 287). On 'dust', see also Nicholas J. Tromp, *Primitive Conceptions of Death and the Nether World in the Old Testament* (Rome: Pontifical Biblical Institute, 1969), pp. 85-91.

7. Gen. 3.19; Pss. 90.3; 104.29; Dan. 12.2; Job 20.11.

8. Job 17.16; 20.11; cf. 21.26.

9. E.g., Sir. 17.1 ('the Lord created human beings out of earth, and makes them return to it again'); Wis. 2.3 ('When it is extinguished, the body will turn to ashes').

10. See Sir. 51.6, 'My soul drew near to death, and my life was on the brink of Hades below' (where, in Hebrew parallelism, 'soul' is contiguous with 'life').

11. Moore (*Judaism*, II, p. 287) notes, 'Death is the departure from the body of the life, or, as we say, souls, concretely imagined as the vital breath (Gen. 2.7) or as the blood, or *in* the blood (Lev. 17.14)'. Cf. Lev. 17.11; Gen. 9.4.

Psalmist, 'when you take away their breath [πνεῦμα], they die and return to their dust. When you send forth your spirit [πνεῦμα], they are created' (104.29-30). So, too, Tobit laments, 'my spirit is taken from me so that I may be released from the face of the earth and become dust' (3.6).[12] Interestingly, as the flesh can be said to return to the dust, the same is also said of the soul, although the context of 'dust' is quite distinct and is contiguous with the underworld realm of Sheol (שְׁאוֹל; LXX ᾅδης),[13] also known as the Pit (λάκκος),[14] and synonymous with 'death' (θάνατος),[15] and with the 'grave',[16] or the 'places of the dead' (such as the 'earth', or Abaddon).[17] So, the soul survives the demise of the body and departs to Sheol, 'an undesirable abode of wretched shades',[18] where it knows nothing and sees nothing.[19]

In Hebrew thought, Sheol was an extensive underground area: dark, dusty and gloomy.[20] It was also a place of no return, a vast prison with its

---

12. Cf. Ps. 7.5, 'The enemy pursue and overtake me, trample my life to the ground, and lay my soul in the dust'.

13. Job 17.16 ('Will [my hope] go down to the bars of Sheol? Shall we descend together into the dust?'); Ps. 7.5; Isa. 29.4; *4 Ezra* 7.32 ('The earth shall give up those who are asleep in it, and the dust those who rest there in silence; and the chambers shall give up the souls that have been committed to them'). S.G.F. Brandon notes that in Mesopotamian thought the underworld was called the 'House of Dust'; see *The Judgement of the Dead: An Historical and Comparative Study of the Idea of a Post-Mortem Judgement in the Major Religions* (London: Weidenfeld & Nicolson, 1967), p. 51. See also Tromp, *Primitive Conceptions*, pp. 85-91.

14. Job 33.18-30; Pss. 16.10; 30.3, 9; 29.4; 49.9-14; 87.4-5; Ezek. 31.16. See E. Yamauchi, 'Life, Death and the Afterlife in the Ancient Near East', in R.N. Longenecker (ed.), *Life in the Face of Death: The Resurrection Message of the New Testament* (Grand Rapids, MI: Eerdmans, 1998), pp. 21-50 (43-45).

15. Nearly thirty-times throughout the LXX (e.g., Job 17.13-14; Pss. 6.6; 17.5-6; 88.5-10; 89.48; Prov. 7.27; Isa. 28.15, 18; Hos. 13.14; Dan. 3.88; Sir. 51.6; Wis. 1.12-16; 16.13; *Pss. Sol.* 16.2; Rev. 6.8; 20.13.

16. Job 10.19-22; 17.1-7; Ps. 88.5-6, 11; Ezek. 32.23.

17. *1 En.* 51.3; *4 Ezra* 7.32; *Ps.-Philo* 3.10; *2 Bar.* 42.8; 50.2. On Abaddon, see Job 26.6; 28.22; 31.12; Ps. 88.11; Prov. 15.11; 27.20.

18. C.K. Barrett, 'Immortality and Resurrection', in C.S. Duthie (ed.), *Resurrection and Immortality* (London: Bagster, 1979), pp. 68-88 (70).

19. Eccl. 9.5; Ps. 88.3-7, 10-12; Isa. 26.14; see also Gen. 3.5; Ps. 6.5; 16.10; 30.9; 115.17; Isa. 38.10f., 18f.; 2 Sam. 14.14; Job 3.13f., 17-19; Pss. 29.4; 48.15-16; 85.13; 88.49; 93.17; 116.3-7; Job 33.22; Wis. 16.13-14; *Pss. Sol.* 16.2; Isa. 14.9; Bar. 2.17. Cf. Sir. 51.6 (n. 10 above). See Yamauchi, 'Life, Death and the Afterlife', pp. 43-44.

20. Gen. 37.35; 42.38; 44.29, 31; 1 Sam. 2.6; 1 Kgs 2.6, 9; Tob. 3.10; 4.19; 13.2; Ps. 54.16; 87.5 [LXX]/88.4; *Odes* 3.6; Prov. 2.18; 5.5; 7.27; 15.24; Job 7.9; 17.16; 21.13; Wis. 16.13; Isa. 14.11, 15; 38.18; 57.9; Bar. 3.19; Ezek. 31.15-17; 32.27; *Pss. Sol.* 15.10. Num. 16.30, 33 notes a descent alive into Sheol, which, in the context, is considered extraordinary. See Tromp, *Primitive Conceptions*, pp. 91, 145-47.

own gates, bars and guards.[21] However, in both Hebrew and Greek thought, Sheol/Hades was not a place of punishment for the wicked; it was the place where the souls of *all* the dead go.[22] Here, all hope is gone (Ps. 143.3; cf. Wis. 13.10), and God has no more dealings with the departed, who are forgotten forever (Ps. 88.10ff.; Eccl. 2.16). On the rare occasions that a soul is said to leave Sheol, it is said to *rise up*. So, Saul's enquiry of the witch of Endor in 1 Samuel 28 was that the spirit or soul of Samuel be brought *up* out of Sheol (ἀνάγω, v. 11; ἀναβαίνω, vv. 13, 15).[23]

In Sheol, souls exist as shades, *rephaim*, in a dark world;[24] and although they have some kind of 'existence', and could even be 'conscious' enough to speak (so, Samuel to Saul), they are certainly considered the *dead*.[25] This is found in a wide range of texts from the Hebrew Bible and Apocrypha (for example, Psalms, Proverbs, Job, Isaiah, Daniel, Hosea, Sirach, Baruch).[26] Hence, the common term for the ψυχή in Sheol is νεκρός (Ps. 88.10).[27] Most writers of the Hebrew Bible appear to deliberately avoid any discussion

21. Isa. 38.10; Job 38.17; Pss. 9.14; 107.18; Eccl. 9.10. See Robert Martin-Achard, 'Resurrection: Old Testament', *ABD*, V, pp. 680-84; Richard Bauckham, 'Hades, Hell', *ABD*, III, pp. 14-15; Moore, *Judaism*, II, p. 289. Sheol is imagined as a monster with gaping jaws that greedily swallows men down and is never sated (Isa. 5.14; Hab. 2.5; Prov. 27.20; 30.15f.).

22. 2 Macc. 6.23; *1 En.* 102.5; 103.7; *Sib. Or.* 1.81-84; *Ps.-Phoc.* 112-13; *2 Bar.* 23.4; *T. Ab.* resc. A 8.9; 19.7.

23. Cf. Ps. 30.3 [29.4 LXX]; 88.10 [87.11 LXX]; Isa. 26.19). Moore, *Judaism*, II, p. 289, notes, 'From Sheol there is no exit; compare the Babylonian Aralu, the Land without Return'.

24. See 1 Sam. 28; Ps. 88.10; Prov. 2.18; 5.5; 7.27; 9.18; Isa. 14.9; 26.14, 19; R.N. Longenecker, 'Introduction', in *Life in the Face of Death: The Resurrection Message of the New Testament* (Grand Rapids, MI: Eerdmans, 1998), pp. 1-17 (8).

25. For Homer, too, souls in Hades are always defined as *dead*. See Dag Øistein Endsjø, 'Immortal Bodies, before Christ: Bodily Continuity in Ancient Greece and 1 Corinthians', *JSNT* 30 (2008), pp. 417-36 (428).

26. Ps. 17.6 (the cords of Sheol entangled me; the snares of death confronted me); Pss. 48.14; 54.15; 88.48; 116.3; Prov. 2.18; 5.5; 7.27; 9.18; Job 33.22; 38.17; Sir. 14.12; Hos. 13.14 ('Shall I ransom them from the power of Sheol? Shall I redeem them from Death?'); Isa. 14.19; 28.15-18; 38.18; Bar. 2.17 ('Open your eyes, O Lord, and see, for the dead who are in Hades, whose spirit has been taken from their bodies, will not ascribe glory or justice to the Lord'); Dan. 3.88. In the Apocrypha, Sirach has much to say on Sheol and the state of the dead. The author asks, 'Who will sing praises to the Most High in Hades, in place of the living who gives thanks? From the dead (νεκρός), as from one who does not exist, thanksgiving has ceased'. So, those in ᾅδης are the νεκροί as opposed to the ζῶντες, and the answer to the question is, of course, no one (17.27-28; cf. 51.6; 38.23; 48.5).

27. Deut. 18.11 speaks of 'a medium, or a spiritist, or one who enquires of the dead'; and for Isaiah too, the *dead* are the νεκροί (Isa. 26.14; cf. 8.19). Νεκρός is also used of the dead physical body, as in Gen. 23.6, 9.

of the subject, but some do reflect on the afterlife and with it the apparent injustice of death for the righteous, for it was assumed that both the righteous and the wicked were destined for this same place of misery and desolation (texts in Ecclesiastes, Psalms, Proverbs, Isaiah).[28] Such was the anticipated horror of Sheol that, in the words of Qohelet, 'a living dog is better than a dead lion',[29] that is, the poorest living wretch was considered better even than the king who abides in Sheol.[30]

Interestingly, the evidence of the Hebrew Bible suggests that Sheol was not necessarily considered unclean in early Israel: there are no regulations against kissing a corpse (Gen. 50.1); bodies could be interred in the home after death (1 Sam. 25.1; 1 Kgs 2.34);[31] and, according to Ezekiel, departed kings were buried close to the temple until the exile (Ezek. 43.7).[32] Hence, the sphere of death, as demarcated 'unclean', either socially or legally, is not an ancient concept for the early Israelite community. (Interestingly, too, is that the early church, in recognizing the assertion of the Hebrew Bible that everyone, righteous and wicked, goes to Sheol,[33] taught that the Old Testament saints went to an upper level of Sheol from which Christ would later deliver them.[34])

Second-Temple Judaism:
Resurrection and the Myths of Israel

The reception history of the 'afterlife' texts of the Hebrew Bible within the Maccabean period shows an interesting development. There is continuity in that, on death, the soul/spirit is released from the body to Hades, a place in

---

28. Eccl. 3.16-21; 9.2-3, 9-10; 12.7; Job 7.9-10; 14.7-22; 30.23; Ps. 6.5; 90.3, 10-12; Prov. 5.11; Isa. 26.14.

29. Eccl. 9.4.

30. Cf. Bauckham, *Fate of the Dead*, pp. 80-81, who writes that the dead, in Hebrew thought, 'were cut off from God, the source of all life. It is this view, which is not peculiar to Israel but was common to many ancient peoples that most of the Hebrew Scriptures take for granted'. He concludes, 'evidence for a belief in life after death in the Old Testament is, at best, minimal' (p. 81). Cf. Longenecker, *Life in the Face of Death*, pp. 10-11.

31. Theoretically, 'house' could stand for 'grave', but archaeological evidence has established the practice of interring in the house.

32. See Rachel S. Hallote, *Death, Burial and Afterlife in the Biblical World: How the Israelites and their Neighbors Treated the Dead* (Chicago: Ivan R. Dee, 2001); Tromp, *Primitive Conceptions*, p. 207.

33. Gen. 37.35; Isa. 38.10; Ps. 30, 3, 9; Num. 16.30, 33.

34. J. Lunde, 'Heaven and Hell', in Joel B. Green, Scott McKnight and I.H. Marshall (eds.), *Dictionary of Jesus and the Gospels* (Leicester: InterVarsity Press, 1992), pp. 307-12 (309).

the lowest regions of the earth, the place of the dead,[35] where it remained for a while or forever.[36] Yet there is also sharp discontinuity. One of the earliest, and clearest, expressions of this change is found in Dan. 12.1-3. (Discussion of the antecedents to the Danielic text, particularly the metaphorical imagery of Isa. 26.19 and Ezek. 37.1-14, will be passed over and left to a future work.[37]) I concur with the consensus of scholarly opinion that Daniel 12 is one of the earliest explicit references to some form of afterlife in the Hebrew Bible:

> At that time Michael, the great prince, the protector of your people, shall arise [ἀναστήσεται] . . . at that time your people shall be delivered [מלט;[38] ὑψόω], everyone who is found written in the book.[39] Many of those who sleep in the dust of the earth shall awake [קיץ; ἐξεγείρω], some to everlasting life,[40] and some to shame and everlasting contempt. Those who are wise shall shine like the brightness of the sky, and those who lead many to righteousness, like the stars forever and ever.[41]

The various crises of the period generated ideological reflection on an afterlife that, to the lament of the Hebrew Bible, saw no distinction between the righteous and the wicked. How could the righteous, heroic Jew, put to death for refusal to compromise Torah, comport with those who were all too willing to Hellenize and forsake the traditions of Israel?[42] The texts of

35. Tob. 3.6, 10; 5.12; 13.2; Wis. 1.14.

36. Wis. 12.1; Sir. 38.16-23; Bar. 2.17; *4 Ezra* 2.45; *4 Macc.* 17.2; 18.23.

37. On the imagery of Ezekiel 37, see de Boer, *Defeat of Death*, p. 44, 'symbolizing the miracle of national revival by God after the annihilation of His people by foreign powers'.

38. BDB, 'Slip away; escape; be delivered'. See the striking parallels (thematic and linguistic) with Isa. 49.24-25 and also see Ps. 89.48.

39. The 'Book of Life'; see Exod. 32.32-33; Ps. 69.28.

40. Most likely *physical* life; Wedderburn, *Baptism and Resurrection*, p. 169; although see Cavallin, *Life after Death*, p. 28 n. 1.

41. On this text, see esp. G.W.E. Nickelsburg, *Resurrection, Immortality and Eternal Life in Intertestamental Judaism* (Cambridge: Cambridge University Press, 1972); Cavallin, *Life after Death*, pp. 26-27; J.J. Collins, *The Apocalyptic Vision of the Book of Daniel* (Missoula, MT: Scholars Press, 1977), pp. 191-218; P.R. Davies, *Daniel* (Old Testament Guides; Sheffield: JSOT Press, 1985), pp. 109-20; Wright, *Resurrection*, pp. 109-15. Davies (*Daniel*, p. 113) notes, 'The description in these verses is extremely sketchy . . . a series of brief statements which hardly amount to a coherent description'. Alexander DiLella claims that Dan. 12.2 is an 'inspired midrash' on the Isaiah text (Louis F. Hartman and Alexander A. DiLella, *The Book of Daniel* (AB; New York: Doubleday, 1978), p. 307.

42. C.K. Barrett, *New Testament Background: Selected Documents* (San Francisco: Harper & Row, rev. edn, 1987), writes of the literature of the Maccabees, 'In these circumstances, martyrdoms took place, perhaps for the first time in religious history' (p. 306).

this period (of which Daniel is a part) demonstrate a conceptual shift to take cognizance of the deaths of these righteous martyrs and, henceforth, for the apocryphal and pseudepigraphical literature, the soul of the righteous would head in a very different direction to that of the wicked.

In the Apocrypha, we find the author of Sirach noting, 'It is easy for the Lord on the day of death to reward individuals according to their conduct' (Sir. 11.26), and for Tobit, the (righteous) spirit is released to an eternal home (in a positive sense, 3.6). *First Enoch* 1–36 (second century BCE) is perhaps the earliest text within Judaism that provides an expression of the concept of explicit divisions *within* Sheol for the righteous and the wicked.[43] The author asserts, 'You, souls of the righteous . . . Be not sad that your souls have gone down into Sheol in sorrow', for there is the promise of restoration (*1 En.* 102.4f.). This is further accentuated in the Wisdom of Solomon (first century BCE), 'The souls of the righteous are in the hand of God . . . they are at peace . . . their hope is full of immortality . . . they will govern nations and rule over peoples . . . the Lord will reign over them forever . . . they will stand with confidence [and] will receive a glorious crown' (Wis. 3.1, 7; 5.1, 15). For the wicked, however, their spirits will wander about in torments (*4 Ezra* 7.80-99). For them, 'there will be no resurrection to life!' (2 Macc. 7.14). Elsewhere, Pseudo-Philo (first century CE) even quotes God himself to confirm the same, 'At the end of the lot of each one of you will be life eternal, for you and your seed, and I will take your souls and store them in peace until the time allotted the world be complete' (*LAB* 22.13). So, all souls are held in Hades until the day of judgment, and the souls of the righteous are kept in what are called 'chambers', where they are guarded by angels, and where they rejoice that they have now escaped what is mortal.

If *1 Enoch*, cited above, notes that the soul of the righteous goes *down* into Sheol, other texts speak of the righteous soul rising *upward* to heaven. The doctrine of the Essenes affirms that when they are set free from the bonds of the flesh they then rejoice and mount upward (1QM 2.155). In the *Apocalypse of Adam and Eve,* the soul of Adam is taken *up* to heaven (13.3-6, 37ff.). The same is said of Abraham in the *Testament of Abraham,* and Job in the *Testament of Job.* Interestingly, these (and other) texts omit entirely the descent into Sheol, and note that the righteous soul ascends immediately into heavenly paradise (although whether such a purview is simply temporal compression, that is, omitting *mention* of the intermediate stage of a descent into Sheol, or actually rejecting it altogether, is difficult to ascertain).

From the perspective of Josephus, once the righteous soul is released from the treasury it then undergoes a transformation into the glorified splendour of angels. For the wicked, however, things are very different. Josephus

---

43. T. Francis Glasson, *Greek Influence in Jewish Eschatology* (London: SPCK, 1961), p. 12, suggests that such an idea came from the Greeks.

notes that they are to be detained in an everlasting prison where their souls are subject to eternal punishment (*War* 2.163; *Ant.* 18.14). *Second Baruch* confirms the same, 'After the appointed day, the wicked will be changed into startling visions and horrible shapes; and they will waste away even more. Then they will go away to be tormented' (cf. 51.1-6). That this section of *2 Baruch* speaks of the afterlife of the soul and not the body comports with 49.1-3, where the author looks forward to the soul's release from its evil chained members (that is, the body).

For some authors, at this point in the resurrection scenario the righteous souls are glorified and are made manifest to the *living*. Typically there is no overlap between the present order and that of the end-time, but (as has been seen elsewhere), certain texts appear to demonstrate temporal compression: the death of the wicked is omitted and the narrative moves directly to a scenario of the judgment of the souls of the wicked and their sending to a place of torment. Here, it is as if the author cannot resist articulating a grand display of divine one-upmanship when the wicked, *while still alive,* will recognize the error of their ways![44]

The concept of eschatological judgment and voyeurism is found in other texts of the period. *Fourth Ezra* 7.75-101, for example, notes that after death, souls have seven days of freedom, during which they see the rewards awaiting the righteous and the torments awaiting the wicked. As the righteous rejoice, the wicked despair. After the seven days, the righteous enter their chambers where they rest in quietness, guarded by angels (7.85, 95), and the wicked wander around in tormented awareness of their doom (7.80, 93).[45] The two locations are in sight of each other (see *4 Ezra* 7.85, 93), but this need not necessarily imply that both are in the underworld, since even after the last judgment paradise and Gehenna are said to be visible to each other (*4 Ezra* 7.36-38; *1 En.* 108.14-15; *Apoc. Elij.* 5.27-28).[46]

For some authors, the souls of the righteous will be given garments of glory, as noted in *1 Enoch,* where the righteous will shine like the lights of heaven.[47] Other texts concur with Josephus above, that resurrected souls

---

44. On the idea of voyeurism, eschatological judgment and the dynamics of power, see Kimberly B. Stratton, 'The Eschatological Arena: Reinscribing Roman Violence in Fantasies of the End Times', in *Violence, Scripture, and Textual Practice in Early Judaism and Christianity* (ed. Ra'anan S. Boustan, Alex P. Jassen and Calvin J. Roetzel; Leiden: Brill, 2010), pp. 45-75 (66-71). This display of one-upmanship is also noted in later Rabbinic literature; see C.G. Montefiore and H. Loewe, *A Rabbinic Anthology* (London: Macmillan, 1938), p. 601.

45. Bauckham, 'Hades', pp. 14-15.

46. See Stratton, 'Eschatological Arena', pp. 45-75, noting *1 Enoch* 27, the *Similitudes of Enoch,* the *Apocalypse of Peter* and the *Apocalypse of John.*

47. *1 En.* 51.1-2 (italics, mine); cf. 22; 62.13-16; 103.3-4; 104.2.

will become like angels.[48] For Philo, Abraham left the mortal realm to be 'added to the people of God . . . having received immortality, and having become equal to the angels . . . for the angels are incorporeal and happy souls' (*Sacr.* 1.5). In the *Ascension of Isaiah*, the writer describes the seventh heaven where he saw 'Enoch and all who were with him in their robes of the above, and they were like the angels who stand there in great glory' (9.7-8). For *1 Enoch* too, 'the righteous and the holy ones from among (the risen dead) will all become angels in heaven. . . . The righteous will shine like the lights of heaven' (*1 En.* 51.1-2; cf. 104.2).

Elsewhere, there is the claim that the resurrected soul will become as stars or a heavenly body. Philo writes that the stars are embodied, intelligent souls, describing the (resurrected) patriarchs as stars or constellations and noting that the rewards of the righteous soul are immortality and being inscribed 'in the records of God, sharing the eternal life of the sun and moon and the whole universe'.[49] Pseudo-Philo claims the same.[50] So, too, *4 Ezra* notes that 'the righteous souls rejoice that they have now escaped what is mortal, they are to be made like the stars'.[51] *Second Baruch* notes the same (51.1-6). Finally, as noted above, Pseudo-Phocylides (103–15) asserts that the resurrected souls become gods (ὀπίσω δὲ θεοὶ τελέθονται, 102).

In summary, the reception of the Hebrew Bible's concept of afterlife within Second Temple Jewish texts demonstrates both continuity and discontinuity. There is continuity in the sense that the afterlife experience is for the soul alone, not the body. The body, as many comparative texts of the ancient Near East recognize, simply decomposes.[52] The dramatic change within Second Temple Judaism rests in the demarcation of righteous and wicked souls after death and their final place of abode. The righteous soul goes to a place of blessing, the wicked to a place of torment. This sharp disjuncture emerges within a context of ideological reflection within the Maccabean crisis and is made for a number of polemical or apologetic reasons.

Afterlife in Paul

So how does all this comport with the concept of afterlife in the New Testament? Within the earliest writings of the New Testament, which are the genuine letters of the apostle Paul, there is no Hades, no Gehenna, no 'pit',

---

48. Cavallin, *Life after Death*, pp. 203-205; David C. Sim, *Apocalyptic Eschatology in the Gospel of Matthew* (Cambridge: Cambridge University Press, 1996), pp. 142-45.

49. *Opif.* 144; cf. *Somn.* 1.135-45; *Gig.* 7; *Quaest. in Exod.* 2.114; *Mos.* 2.108.

50. *LAB* 23.13; 28.10; 15.5; 16.3; 23.6; 51.5; 63.4; and see also *4 Ezra* 4.35, 41; 7.95-96 (and see wider, 7.75-101).

51. *4 Ezra* 7.97. Cf. *LAB* 33.5, 'Then your likeness shall be seen as the stars of the heaven'.

52. See, Brandon, *Judgement of the Dead*; Tromp, *Primitive Conceptions*.

and no 'hell'. There will certainly be a day of wrath (Rom. 2.5, 8; 3.5; 5.9; 9.22), when vengeance will be inflicted on the *unbelieving*, but there is no concept of eternal suffering in the fires of hell.[53] As argued elsewhere,[54] in the Corinthian correspondence (1 Cor. 15; 2 Cor. 4–5), we find Paul in continuity with the Second Temple Jewish texts noted above, envisioning an afterlife comprised of the soul even though he can confusingly employ *body* language. Here, he does not mean flesh and blood (1 Cor. 15.50) but a type of anthropomorphic entity capable of housing the spirit. What he experienced on the Damascus road was the new postmortem existence of Christ in a form of christophanic glory similar to theophanies noted of Yahweh in the Hebrew Bible of which no author uses the term 'body'.[55] What Paul appears to mean in terms of the glorified Christ is actually a new entity stripped of its natural flesh and blood.

Along with the weight of Second Temple Jewish texts discussed, and particularly the writings of Josephus, Paul most likely construes Jesus' death being followed by his soul raised from Sheol (that is, from the dead); and, as Josephus, being taken up to heaven. From there the now-glorified Christ comes out of heaven to reveal himself in successive christophanies. Whereas, for Josephus, the soul will 'at the end of the ages' enter a new habitation, for Paul, his Damascus road experience is a proleptic experience, a depiction of the firstfruits and an image of the splendour awaiting believers. At the end of the age, when there is a new or re-creation, the righteous will be transformed to have some kind of new existence, which Paul describes (in 1 Corinthians 15) as a *resurrection 'body'*, or, later (2 Corinthians 5), as a dwelling from heaven, a house/building from God eternal in the heavens. So, the 'chaste body/new habitation' of Josephus can be seen to stand in correlation to the new 'form' that Paul experienced on the Damascus road.

In sum, the reception of the afterlife scenarios of the Hebrew Bible within the Pauline corpus, like those of other Second Temple Jewish texts, demonstrates both continuity and discontinuity. Paul is in continuity with the emphasis on the afterlife of the soul/spirit and not a resurrected physical earthly body (and so is consistent with other Second Temple texts), and yet he stands in discontinuity with the Hebrew Bible in his affirmation of a day of wrath and distinctions of afterlife scenarios for the souls of the righteous as opposed to the wicked. He stands in continuity with other Second Tem-

---

53. See 2 Thess. 1.7-8, 'when the Lord Jesus is revealed from heaven with his mighty angels in flaming fire, inflicting vengeance on those who do not know God and on those who do not obey the gospel of our Lord Jesus'.

54. Mark T. Finney, *Resurrection, Hell, and the Afterlife: Body and Soul in Antiquity, Judaism and Early Christianity* (Durham: Acumen, forthcoming).

55. Although theophanies in the Hebrew Bible can be described in anthropomorphic terms (Gen. 32.28-30), they are normally described in terms of the supra-natural (Exod. 13.21-22; 24.9-11; Judg. 13.21-22; Isa. 6.1).

ple Jewish texts when they speak of a positive afterlife for the soul of the righteous, but not where they speak of *eternal* punishment for the wicked.[56]

Afterlife in the Gospels

It is only in the Synoptic Gospels (and Jas 3.6) that, for the first time in biblical literature, we see the construct of what is normally understood as hell (the translation of the Greek *Gehenna*).[57] In Mk 9.43 it is placed on the lips of Jesus: 'If your hand causes you to stumble, cut it off; it is better to enter life maimed than to have two hands and go to hell'. It is repeated in 9.45 (If your foot causes you to stumble . . .), and 9.47 (If your eye causes you to stumble . . .). In this section of the Markan text, there are numerous textual variants. Verses 44 and 46 ('where their worm does not die and the fire is not quenched') are omitted by a large number of significant manuscripts and should not be read.[58] At Mk 9.45 the textual apparatus of the United Bible Societies' *Greek New Testament* (4th edn) details the textual variants found alongside the Greek phrase εἰς γέενναν (into hell), which is also found at 9.43. These include:

εἰς γέενναν (without the definite article)
εἰς τὴν γέενναν, τοῦ πυρός (into the hell of fire)
εἰς τὸ πῦρ τὸ ἄσβεστον (into the unquenchable fire)
εἰς τὴν γέενναν, εἰς τὸ πῦρ τὸ ἄσβεστον (into hell, into the
unquenchable fire)

A likely textual scenario would be that the original text was simply 'it is better for you to enter life crippled than with two feet to be thrown into hell', which would then parallel vv. 43 and 47. Yet such a reading gives no sense of either the type of punishment to be administered in hell or the temporal aspect of that punishment (how long it would last). The various textual variants, through scribal additions, then determine and accentuate the nature of Gehenna: it is now the 'fire of hell' or the 'unquenchable fire', where 'their worm does not die, and the fire is not quenched' (v. 44). These various additions assert unambiguously that Gehenna will be a place of *eternal* punishment!

---

56. 2 Thess. 1.9, a later pseudepigraphical text, does assert that the wicked 'will pay the penalty of *eternal destruction*, away from the presence of the Lord' (italics mine). As such, the text stands in continuity with other texts of the later New Testament (see below).

57. 'Gehenna' occurs in the Gospels in Matthew (7); Mark (3); Luke (1); but not in John.

58. So, Bruce M. Metzger, *A Textual Commentary on the Greek New Testament* (Stuttgart: German Bible Society, 1994), pp. 86-87; William L. Lane, *The Gospel of Mark* (NICNT; Grand Rapids, MI: Eerdmans, 1974), p. 346.

Further, Mk 9.49 is found in three major textual forms: 'For everyone will be salted with fire'; 'For every sacrifice will be salted with fire'; and 'For everyone will be salted with fire and every sacrifice will be salted with salt'. The various additional minor textual variants on these phrases are even more diverse and are not found in the Synoptic parallels of Matthew or Luke.[59] Especially interesting is that Matthew, who employs γέενναν more extensively than Mark or Luke, omits Mark's εἰς τὴν γέενναν in his parallel of Mk 9.43. It would thus appear that the various scribal additions to Mark appeared in the later textual history of the Gospel with the sole purpose of accentuating the horror of Gehenna.

In a similar way, the extensive use of Gehenna in Matthew may be for apologetic or polemical reasons where he follows the (original) Markan tradition, yet extends and intensifies it as part of a sustained anti-Jewish polemic.[60] This is certainly clear in Mt. 23.15, 33 (and possibly 5.22 and 10.28) where he employs *gehenna* in the context of a sharp attack on the Pharisees. Indeed, throughout his Gospel, Matthew repeatedly undermines the authority of the Pharisees and criticizes their behaviour:

- 5.11-12. God's favour rests with a faithful minority 'persecuted for righteousness' sake' who are contrasted (5.20) with the unrighteous Pharisees.
- Chapter 6 highlights the hypocrisy of the Pharisees and scribes.
- 8.5-13, the faith of the centurion and the messianic banquet at which the Jews are rejected.
- The parable of the vineyard (21.33-46). The kingdom of God will be taken away and handed over to other tenants/nation (*ethnos*). The Pharisees realize that he is referring to them. Both of these points are Matthean additions or alterations to Mark.
- Chapter 23 contains the most sustained polemic: the sustained denunciation of the Pharisees; attribution to them of the death of prophets, wise men and scribes.
- Matthew's use of 'Jews' indicates an ideological break (28.15). This is also evident in Matthew's use of 'their' synagogues (4.23; 9.35; 10.17; 12.9; 13.54). In the last two texts, Matthew has added these to his Markan source (and cf. 'your' synagogues in 23.35).

Elsewhere in the Gospels, Gehenna is used consistently to refer to a place of punishment prepared for the wicked—who consist of the devil and his

---

59. See Metzger, *Textual Commentary*, p. 87; Lane, *Gospel of Mark*, pp. 346-47.

60. See Graham N. Stanton, *A Gospel for a New People: Studies in Matthew* (Edinburgh: T. & T. Clark, 1992).

angels,[61] the hypocrites and disobedient[62] and those who reject Jesus, or God, or the prophets.[63] Gehenna may be pre-existent (Mt. 25.41, where it has been 'prepared' beforehand), and its punishment is eternal (Mt. 25.41, 46); it stands as both the place of judgment for the soul of the wicked immediately after death (Lk. 12.5) and for the judgment of the wicked in a reunited body and soul after resurrection and judgment (Mt. 10.28).[64] Predictably, its location is understood by Jesus to be in the depths of the earth,[65] and, as noted, there is an emphasis that individuals sent to Hades will be in the body.[66] Finally, it seems that Jesus taught that hell would involve an eternal, conscious punishment, with such images as the 'undying worm', the 'fire that is not put out', and the emotive picture of 'weeping and gnashing of teeth'.[67]

So, the language of the afterlife placed on the lips of Jesus in the Gospels vis-à-vis the demarcation of the righteous and the wicked stands in continuity with Second Temple Judaism but not with the Hebrew Bible. Yet such language also stands in discontinuity with Second Temple Judaism in its assertion that postmortem judgment will be made in a bodily afterlife. This appears to have been part of a trend toward the end of the first century CE and into the second century, where discussion took place over the punishment of the wicked and the necessity of a bodily presence, for it was thought that the immortal soul could not feel pain and so a physical aspect to postmortem existence was necessary in order for suitable punishment to take place.[68]

The textual history of the Gospel of Mark also shows the editorial activity of various later scribes in order to accentuate the horrors of the afterlife for the wicked. As before, this may be part of a polemical or apologetic move over the late first and early second centuries as the Christ movement

---

61. Mt. 25.41; Lk. 8.31.

62. Mt. 5.22; 7.19; 13.40, 42, 50; 25.30; 18.8-9 // Mk 9.43-47; Mt. 24.45-51//Lk. 12.41-46; 23.15, 33; Jn 15.6; 5.28-30.

63. Mt. 11.20-24 // Lk. 10.12-15; cf. also Mt. 8.8-12 // Lk. 7.6-9 with 13.28-29; Mt. 22.1-14; 25.41-46; Mt. 23.31-33; Lk. 16.29-31.

64. Interestingly, while Lk. 16.23, 26 and Rev. 20.13f. note that all of the dead will be in Hades, 1 Pet. 3.19 has only the spirits of the wicked there.

65. Mt. 11.23 // Lk. 10.15.

66. Cf. Mt. 5.29-30; 10.28; 18.8-9; Mk 9.43-47 (unquenchable fire); see also Lk. 12.4-5.

67. Mt. 25.46; Mk 9.48; cf. Isa. 66.24; Mt. 8.12 // Lk. 13.28; Mt. 13.42, 50; 22.13; 24.51; 25.30; cf. *Sib. Or.* 2.305; Mk 9.48; Mt. 25.41. However, the use of the verb 'destroy' (ἀπόλλυμι, Mt. 10.28) and the frequent image of 'burning' has been understood by some to imply annihilation (e.g., Mt. 7.19; 13.40, 42, 50; Jn 15.6; cf. *4 Ezra* 7.61; *1 En.* 10.13-14; 38.3-6; 90.26-27; 91.9; 108.3).

68. Gregory J. Riley, *Resurrection Reconsidered: Thomas and John in Controversy* (Minneapolis, MN: Fortress Press, 1995), p. 161; Athenagoras, *De resurrectione* 21.4.

came into increasing conflict with Judaism and Roman imperialism (particularly with regard to the Roman imperial cult[69]), and even intra Christian conflict(s) regarding various schismatic groups.[70]

Afterlife in the Later New Testament and Post-apostolic Literature[71]

Descriptions of the afterlife in the later New Testament and post-apostolic literature continue the trend established in the Gospels. Hell is now a place of eternal punishment for the wicked, and it is described in language that becomes increasingly horrific.

For Jude and 2 Peter the end of the wicked is 'destruction' (2 Pet. 1.12; 2.1, 3; 3.16), where the destruction of Sodom is an example of fiery judgment (Jude 7; 2 Pet. 2.6-10; cf. Mt. 10.15; *1 Clem.* 11.1-2). God will rescue the righteous from the fire as he did Lot, whereupon he will then destroy both heaven and earth in a fiery conflagration (2 Pet. 3.7-12). The later New Testament also offers a picture of Christ descending into hell during the time between his death and resurrection to preach to the spirits in prison (1 Pet. 3.19; 4.6; Eph. 4.9-10). This doctrine was firmly established by the second century in the works of Justin Martyr, Irenaeus and the apocryphal *Gospel of Nicodemus.*[72]

The most sustained and graphic picture of the horrors of the afterlife in the later New Testament is found in the book of Revelation. Here, the final abode of both the wicked angels and the unrighteous is the 'lake of fire'. This or burning sulphur is common in apocalyptic literature, where it is equivalent to 'gehenna'. The beast and false prophet, followed by the devil, death and Hades, join the wicked in being cast into the lake (20.10, 14-15, 20; 21.8). The book of Revelation also employs the language of the Abyss, a bottomless pit, from which emerges the beast to make war on the saints (9.1-2; 11.7; 14.18; 17.8; 20.1-3, 7).[73] Like Matthew, the emphasis on the

---

69. A topic of increasing recent interest, see Steven J. Friesen, *Imperial Cults and the Apocalypse of John: Reading Revelation in the Ruins* (New York: Oxford University Press, 2001); J. Nelson Kraybill, *Apocalypse and Allegiance: Worship, Politics and Devotion in the Book of Revelation* (Grand Rapids, MI: Brazos, 2010).

70. E.g., the 'Jews' of the Fourth Gospel and secessionist group of 1 and 2 John.

71. See especially, G.S. Shogren, 'Hell, Abyss, Eternal Punishment', in Ralph P. Martin and Peter H. Davids (eds.), *Dictionary of the Later New Testament and its Developments* (Downers Grove, IL: InterVarsity Press, 2000), pp. 459-62.

72. L. Goppelt, *A Commentary on 1 Peter* (Grand Rapids, MI: Eerdmans, 1993), pp. 260-63.

73. The *Apocalypse of Zephaniah* (6.15, first century CE) connects the abyss to Hades.

punishment of the unbeliever in Revelation may also be for an anti-Jewish or anti-Roman imperial polemic.[74]

The picture of hell in the later New Testament is continued into the post-apostolic age with the language of 'unquenchable fire' in Ignatius (35/50–98/115),[75] 'burning hell' and 'eternal destruction' in the Shepherd of Hermas (95/100) (*Vis.* 3.7.2; *Sim.* 6.2.4), and, in Polycarp (69–155 CE), the fire of coming judgment and eternal punishment reserved for the ungodly—an eternal fire that is never extinguished (*Mart. Pol.* 11.2 ; 2.3). Justin Martyr (100–165 CE) uses the language of 'fires of hell' for apologetic purposes in that if Christians believe wickedness leads to the eternal fires of hell, they are highly motivated to live as good citizens (*Apol.* 1.12, 17). Interestingly, he also makes a polemic against the imperial cult and asserts that eternal punishment awaits those not offering worship to God (1.17). In the writings of Justin Martyr, 'eternal fire' was certainly intended to intimate everlasting suffering (*Apol.* 1.8.52).

Between the late second and mid-third century CE, the descriptive language of hell becomes more acute. For Hippolytus (212 CE),

> the lovers of evil shall be given eternal punishment. The unquenchable and unending fire awaits these latter, and a certain fiery worm which does not die and which does not waste the body but continually bursts forth from the body with unceasing pain. No sleep will give them rest; no night will soothe them; no death will deliver them from punishment; no appeal of interceding friends will profit them (*Against the Greek* 3).

And for Minucius Felix (226 CE), 'clever fire burns the limbs and restores them, wears them away and yet sustains them, just as fiery thunderbolts strike bodies but do not consume them'. They would prefer to be annihilated rather than be restored for punishment (*Octavius* 34.12–35.3). Finally, for Cyprian of Carthage (252),

> An ever-burning Gehenna and the punishment of being devoured by living flames will consume the condemned; nor will there be any way in which the tormented can ever have respite or be at an end. Souls along with their bodies will be preserved for suffering in unlimited agonies. . . . The grief at punishment will then be without the fruit of repentance; weeping will be useless, and prayer ineffectual. Too late will they believe in eternal punishment, who would not believe in eternal life (*To Demetrian* 24).

---

74. Rev. 2.9-10, 14, 20; 3.9; Friesen, *Imperial Cults*; Elaine Pagels, *Revelations: Visions, Prophecy and Politics in the Book of Revelation* (New York: Viking Books, 2012).

75. Ignatius, *Eph.* 16.1-2; see also *2 Clem.* 5.4, 'fear him who, after you are dead, has power to cast soul and body into the flames of hell'.

The Development of Hell in the Middle Ages

The conceptions of hell described by the writers of the second- and third-century church continued to be embellished into the Middle Ages. Roman Catholic thinkers in the period developed a series of levels in hell, all with no biblical basis:

- *Infernus*, the place of torment for the unrighteous damned and the demons. This is, in popular imagination, the place most often associated with the concept of hell.
- Purgatory, where the saved souls go to be purged of the temporal effects of their sins.
- *Limbus infantium* (Limbo of the Infants), a place of perfect, natural, subjective happiness to which those who died before Baptism but who have not committed personal sins (so do not warrant punishment) go.
- *Limbus patrum* (Limbo of the Patriarchs), where the righteous who lived before Jesus came to earth went. It is this part of hell that Christ descended into. In Catholic theology it no longer exists.

The artistic representations of hell in the late mediaeval and early Renaissance periods enhanced and gave suitable expression to a theology of the afterlife within Catholicism. Three of the key artistic works of the period are the *Hortus deliciarum*, Dante's *Divine Comedy* and the later Renaissance fresco, the *Last Judgment*, by Michelangelo. As a preface to a discussion of the influence of any form of art in the late mediaeval to high Renaissance periods, it must be remembered that a singular truth bound together almost everyone alive in late mediaeval Europe: unconditional and total belief in Christianity and with it concepts of heaven and an eternal torment in hell. The *Hortus deliciarum* (Garden of Delights) provided visual expression to the latter. Compiled by the Abbess Herrad of Landsberg between 1167 and 1185 it is an illuminated manuscript designed as a pedagogical tool for young nuns at Hohenburg Abbey in Alsace. It was one of the most celebrated illuminated manuscripts of the period for it stood as a compendium of twelfth-century knowledge, containing poems, music, and 336 illustrations, the best known of which is a depiction of hell (folio 155; see Fig. 1).[76]

The image is strikingly graphic with a jagged border, black background (unique in the period), and accented by red tongues of fire and rivers of flame that divide the four registers of the scene into distinct levels of hell. The demons are a bluish-grey colour, which serves to highlight them from the black and red of their surroundings.[77] The people represented suffer a

---

76. The image is in the public domain, http://en.wikipedia.org/wiki/File:Hortus_ Deliciarum_-_Hell.jpg.

77. See Fiona Griffiths, *The Garden of Delights: Reform and Renaissance for Women in the Twelfth Century* (Philadelphia, PA: University of Pennsylvania Press, 2007);

Fig. 1

variety of torments: some are strung up and tortured in various ways; others are force-fed coins; while still others are boiled in large cauldrons (these are clearly identified as Jews and knights). In the deepest register, the lowest level of hell, Satan (chained at the neck, Rev. 20.1-3) is seated upon a

Theodore Spencer, 'Chaucer's Hell: A Study in Mediaeval Convention', *Speculum* 2 (1927), pp. 177-200.

Fig. 2

throne of beasts with a human Antichrist in his lap. In this level stands a
fully clothed clergyman (in colour), being led toward Satan by a devil.

Herrad's concept of hell developed into the refined literary visions that
we read of in Chaucer as well as in the works of the poet Dante (1265-
1321). Indeed, from the period, the primary images of hell we have today
come from Dante's *Divine Comedy,* in which the reader is taken through
three realms of the afterlife: Hell, Purgatory and Paradise. The poet has
developed places for every type of person, allowing him to editorialize
about people's actions in the world of his day. In the process, he creates
vivid scenes of all three realms. These, then, became the basis for virtually all of the artistic depictions of hell in the Middle Ages and our modern
conceptions of afterlife with demons, eternal torment and fire. All of it is
literary imagination; none derives from the biblical texts (see Fig. 2).[78]

78. The most extensive illustrations made of Dante's text are those by Gustave
Doré (1832–83); see *The Doré Illustrations for Dante's Divine Comedy: 136 Plates by
Gustave Doré* (New York: Dover Publications, 1976); *Dante's Inferno, Illustrated by
Gustave Doré* (New York: Paddington Press, 1976). The above illustration by Doré is of
the ferryman Charon herding sinners onto his boat, taking them to be judged. The image

Fig. 3

In Michelangelo's, *The Last Judgment*[79] (1536-41), the well-known fresco spanning the entire altar wall of the Sistine Chapel (Fig. 3), the artist provides a fitting summary of reflection upon death, resurrection and the afterlife in the high period of the Renaissance. Christ, centred, with Mary on his right, is surrounded by the saints, while a group of angels (centred below him) announce, with trumpets and open books, the judgment of all

is in the public domain, http://en.wikipedia.org/wiki/File:Gustave_Dor%C3%A9_-_Dante_Alighieri_-_Inferno_-_Plate_10_%28Canto_III_-_Charon_herds_the_sinners_onto_his_boat%29.jpg.

79. The image is in the public domain, http://maitaly.wordpress.com/2011/04/04/michelangelo-sistine-chapel-the-last-judgement/

people. From the viewer's perspective scenes on the bottom left show the righteous leaving their graves and, some with the help of angels, rising to join the elect with Christ. Other righteous souls return to physical bodies and some, shrouded in burial cloths or as ghostly skeletons, sit between the forces of heaven and hell.

In contrast, scenes of hell on the bottom right show the influence of Dante's *Divine Comedy*, with Charon, the ferryman of the underworld, beating and casting the wicked from his boat, who are then dragged down by demons into the depths of hell.[80] Another figure from Dante is Minos, the mythological king of hell, seen as the most prominent figure in the bottom right, and painted in the likeness of one of Michelangelo's fiercest critics, the Pope's master of ceremonies, Biagio da Cesena. It is said that when Cesena complained to the Pope of the image, the pontiff joked that his jurisdiction did not extend to hell, so the portrait would have to remain.

The commissioning of the work was done by Pope Clement VII (1523– 34), the second of the Medici popes, the ruling family of Florence, who abused their power and in some senses were thought to have 'bought' the papacy. The first Medici pope, Leo X (1513–21), is best remembered for granting indulgences to those who donated to the reconstruction of St Peter's Basilica, a papal offer that was critically challenged as part of Martin Luther's 95 Theses in 1517. The turmoil of the Reformation during Clement's papacy saw Protestant armies fuelled by religious hatred of the Catholic Church sacking Rome in 1527, and engaging in a spree of killing, burning and looting. It was in this context that Clement commissioned the *Last Judgment* in order to reassure Catholics of papal authority and of the Roman Catholic Church as the only faith that could assure eternal salvation.[81] Those considered to be outside the church, indicated vividly in the fresco, were doomed to an eternity in hell.

Conclusion

The reception history of the Hebrew Bible's concept of the afterlife can be seen to have been multivalent. Within Second Temple Judaism an emphasis on the afterlife of the soul remains, yet this is transformed for various apologetic and polemical reasons into scenarios in which the righteous soul departs to a place of blessing and the wicked soul to a place of torment. The rising influence of Hellenism within the period and particularly the conflict

---

80. For fuller details, see Fabrizio Mancinelli, *The Sistine Chapel* (Vatican City: Ufficio Vendita Pubblicazioni e Riproduzioni, 2000).

81. A clear and unambiguous depiction of the white-haired and bearded St Peter stands on Christ's left, looking over to the saviour and holding out the keys (to heaven and earth) in his left hand.

under Antiochus Epiphanes and the ensuing struggles of the Maccabees fomented a conceptual change wherein the faithful Jew would be rewarded and the apostate Jew condemned. In the period of the New Testament, the earliest writings, those of the apostle Paul, demonstrate continuity with Second Temple Jewish texts but which, along with postbiblical Judaism in general, place him in tension with the Hebrew Bible.

Significant changes begin within the Gospels and later New Testament for not only is there development away from an emphasis on an afterlife for the soul alone, toward an afterlife that included body and soul together, but the concept of Gehenna, the underworld place of torment and fire, takes precedence. This was begun in the Maccabean period but is now accentuated in the later New Testament, a trend that continues into the post-apostolic age with further emphasis on the horrors of hell. These changes, too, can be seen as deriving from apologetic or polemical impetus as the early Christ movement attempted to define and defend itself against both first-century Judaism and Greco-Roman paganism. The church fathers, in particular, employed the fear of hell for ideological purposes in asserting ethical priorities in the early church.

Finally, further literary emphasis in the late mediaeval period was compounded by visual modes of expression. In the case of the *Hortus deliciarum,* this was done for pedagogical purposes, and for the *Last Judgment,* for apologetic reasons within the religious and socio-political turmoil of the early Reformation.

Overall, the development of Sheol/Hades/hell can be construed as an ideological construct stemming from notions of religious authority: it was the Jewish religious hierarchy in Second Temple Judaism who demarcated the righteous from the wicked and asserted the victory and blessing of the faithful righteous Jew in the face of encroaching Hellenism; the religious leaders of the early Christ movement or the post-apostolic ecclesiastical church who held the keys to heaven and hell and who, similarly, were able to differentiate the wicked from the righteous; and within a mediaeval framework that believed fundamentally in the truth of Christianity, it was the papal office alone that held the keys to heaven and the certainty of a blessed afterlife.

The theological afterlife of an eternal fiery pit of hell persists into the modern period, with modern concerns and worries now labeled hadephobia and with the Internet full of discussion boards and threads prompted by those with deep anxiety and fear over thoughts of a tortuous afterlife.[82] A traditional Christian reading of such a framework is defended and indeed

---

82. See, for example, http://www.christianforums.com/t7605491/; http://recovering fundamentalists.com/fear-of-hell.html; http://www.ex-christian.net/topic/7197-fear-of-hell.

insisted upon by those who undertake fundamentalist literal readings of the biblical texts, and yet the study here has hopefully demonstrated the ideological impetus behind such discourse. Perhaps the time is right for a (socio-theological) review of the social construction of hell together with a salient reminder that the texts *are* polemically and apologetically driven, and that understanding the social context(s) is vital. Holding such texts a little more lightly could help to alleviate the anxiety of hadephobes and may be a cause of suitable pastoral reflection by those who can all too easily employ 'hell' as a tool with which to assert authority and to instill fear into nonbelievers, and even believers, of many religious traditions. At the very least, profound reflection and debate on how and why the picture of the afterlife placed upon the lips of Jesus in the Gospels places him in tension with the Hebrew Bible is worthy of serious discussion.

MUSIC

Musical Paths to Experiencing Job

Helen Leneman

Abstract

The intellectually demanding text of the book of Job seems an odd choice to set to music. The characters are largely mouthpieces for lengthy poems, and the only journey is an intellectual one: from blind faith in the doctrine of retribution to acceptance that innocent suffering is possible. There are about thirty known oratorios, dating from the earliest Italian works of the seventeenth century up to the late twentieth century, and only four known operas, all twentieth century, that deal with the book of Job. This essay focuses on two significant British *Job* oratorios (those of C.H. Hubert Parry and Peter Maxwell Davies) and one Italian 'sacred drama' (Luigi Dallapiccola). The music of these oratorios highlights the biblical text in amazing ways, with musical techniques conveying despair, anger, indignation and resignation. Through this music, the listener is able to grasp the text on a deep and emotional level.

There are over two dozen oratorios and a handful of operas based on the book of Job, and countless settings of particular verses.[1] The text, arguably the most consistently theological and intellectually demanding of the Hebrew Bible, seems an odd choice to set to music. It consists largely of poetry or dialogue and has little plot or action. The characters are basically mouthpieces for lengthy poems, and the only journey is an intellectual one: from blind faith in the doctrine of retribution to acceptance that innocent suffering is possible. The text seems to have drawn composers who were grappling with these concepts.

The book of Job is about a good and very prosperous man afflicted by the Satan/Adversary, who makes a wager with God that Job would turn against God if he suffered material losses. Job continues to praise God through hor-

---

1. A complete bibliography of musical works based on *Job* can be found in David J.A. Clines, *Job 38–42* (Word Biblical Commentary, 18B; Nashville, TN: Thomas Nelson, 2011), pp. 1443-50.

rible afflictions, even though he laments his fate and protests God's injustice. He also speaks out against the commonly accepted doctrine of retribution, insisting that his suffering is undeserved because he is righteous. His friends come to comfort him but also insist his suffering must be due to a sin on his part. God finally addresses Job 'out of the whirlwind' and ultimately restores all his fortunes. Job never receives an explanation or justification from God.

Why music? My thesis is that music can be considered *midrash* because it retells the story in a different language. Text alone can describe emotions but does not *contain* emotions the way music does. The story of Job evokes sympathy in the reader, but musical renditions of his story can create an emotionally empathic response. Music has the power to enable us to read between the lines of a text and fill in the gaps, while creating an inner world of the heart and mind.

Music is completely abstract yet also deeply emotional. There is known to be a closer relation between hearing and emotional arousal than seeing. This is why movies always have background music—to stimulate the viewer's emotions. The most important technical musical devices that I will be referring to in this article are the following:[2]

- *Vocal range*: High notes indicate excitement and also elicit that response in the listener. A lower range of pitch stands for calm. Soprano is the highest female voice, while alto is the lowest. Bass is the lowest male voice, tenor the highest, and baritone between the two.
- *Key* (see Glossary): Major keys are upbeat, while shifts between major and minor keys evoke a mood change even when it is not explicit in the text.
- *Tempo/rhythm* (see Glossary): Fast tempos establish a positive mood, while slower tempos evoke calm. Different moods are established by alterations in tempo and rhythm.

The large bulk of works based on the book of Job are settings of specific verses. Those most often set are 14.1-2; 19.25-27; and 1.20-21, all of which are regularly read at funerals and are standard texts for state funerals in the United Kingdom. Other verses often set are 7.16-21; 2.10; and 19.25 ('I know that my Redeemer liveth', best known from Handel's *Messiah*). These solos or short choral settings far outnumber settings of the full book of Job. The book of Job, therefore, has been selectively used to project a theological and moral message that is not clearly present.

The interest of such works lies in their use of the Job text to put forth an affirming theological message. This could only be done, of course, by

---

2. Definitions of musical terms can be found in the Glossary at the end of this article on p. 201.

selectively utilizing very few chapters and verses from the whole book, out of context. The book of Job in these works is only a handle on which to hang a religious message. This is an important part of the history of Job in music. But the more interesting works are those that set the full book, or at least a large part of it.

This article will focus on three *Job* oratorios, one from the nineteenth and two from the twentieth century. My choices are based on the high quality of the music, the interesting contrasts between the settings, and the availability of scores and/or recordings. The composers are Sir Charles H. Hubert Parry (British, 1848–1918), Luigi Dallapiccola (Italian, 1904–1975) and Sir Peter Maxwell Davies (British, 1934–). The two British oratorios were written a century apart.

These are not lengthy works, all being under or around an hour long. The composers and their librettists were selective about which parts of the full book of Job they set. Since my discussion of the biblical book will focus primarily on those parts that are used in the musical settings, I will list these now.

Chapters and Verses Found in the Oratorios

Charles Hubert H. Parry, *Job, An Oratorio* (1892)[3]

Job 1.1, 3-14, 20-22
    2.1
    3.1-3, 5, 9, 11, 13, 17-22
    9.1-11
    10.1-3, 8, 20-22
    14.1-2, 11-12
    29.2-5, 14, 21-22, 25
    30.16-17, 19-21, 23
    38.2-13, 16-18, 25-30
    39.19, 21-25
    40.7-14
    42.1-3, 5-6, 10, 12, 17

The verses from chapter 1 do not appear in the right sequence in this oratorio. Many verses from various chapters are interspersed in the chap. 3 lament. Parry also wrote many verses himself, which he blended into the biblical text (KJV).

---

3. Sir Charles Hubert H. Parry, *Job, An Oratorio* (London: Novello, 1892).

Luigi Dallapiccola, *Job, una sacra rappresentazione* (Mystery Play; 1950)[4]

Job 1.1-4, 6-12, 14-21
  2.2-7
  3.3-7
  4.12-15
  5.17
  7.5
  8.3
  11
  29.2-4
  31.1, 19-21, 24-28
  38.2-14
  40.9
  42.5-6, 10-13, 15

This list is somewhat misleading, as Dallapiccola scrambled or deleted many of the verses, blended his own text with the biblical text, and often summarized or paraphrased verses. Even with the shortened verses, though, his is the only libretto that includes parts of the speeches of Eliphaz, Bildad and Zophar. This work is not actually an oratorio but a chamber opera (a 'sacred drama'), meant to be staged but also performed in concert.

Peter Maxwell Davies, *Job, an Oratorio* (1997)[5]

Job 1.4-9, 12, 20
  2.2-6
  3
  4.6-7
  5.6-7, 17-21, 26
  6.1-4
  7.1-7
  13.23-24
  10.8-22
  15.9-13
  9.2-3, 14-16, 22-24
  29.2-10, 22-25
  25.4-6
  27.1-6
  38.2-15, 39-41
  40.8
  39.2-4, 26-30
  42.1-6

---

4. Luigi Dallapiccola, *Giobbe, una sacra rappresentazione* (Milan: Suvini Zerboni, 1950).
5. Peter Maxwell Davies, *Job* (London: Chester Music, 1999).

It is clear from this list that Davies not only scrambles verses, he also alters the order of the chapters. This is largely because his libretto utilizes the unusual poetic translation of *Job* by Stephen Mitchell (1992), which makes these alterations.

The only chapters to appear in all three works are chaps. 1, 2, 3, 29, 38 and 42. Which parts of these chapters are used—particularly the con-clusion—is significant and will be discussed. The standardized cycles of speech that follow Job's initial lamentation in chap. 3 appear in chaps. 4–14, 15–21 and 22–27; these are mostly eliminated in these oratorios. Chapters left out of all the works are 12–13 and 15–26, so clearly the second two cycles are mostly eliminated in these oratorios. Parry himself explained why he omitted these parts of the book:

> I failed to see how to make the friends musical. . . . To introduce the friends into the scheme would necessitate an absolutely different plan and . . . principle of treatment.[6]

The music of these oratorios highlights and underlines the biblical text in amazing ways, from instrumental imitations of animals (chaps. 38–39) to musical techniques conveying despair, anger, indignation and resignation. Even the most powerful text does not have the ability to convey such emo-tions. The part of Job is taken by a baritone in Parry and Dallapiccola, while it is sung by both solo and multiple voices in Davies. The voice of God was always an issue for composers of oratorio. In these Job oratorios, all three composers chose to represent God by a chorus, usually of only one voice type (that is, tenor or soprano). It was felt that no solo voice could represent a deity, because it would sound too weak. The music in these three oratorios allows the listener to grasp this difficult text on a deep and emotional level, and this article will attempt to explain how this is accomplished.

General Comments on the Book of Job

The book opens with a six-scene prose prologue, the scenes alternating between earth and heaven. This prologue is an example of narration through dialogue. The structure is stylized and tends toward the naïve and simple.[7] It has often been noted that the poetic sections of the book are in tension with the seemingly complacent character of Job within the framework of the folktale. These two representations seem so disharmonious that there is a hypothesis that two different characters have been fused. One is Job 'the patient', the hero of the prose sections of the book; the other is Job 'the

---

6. Quoted in Jeremy Dibble, liner notes, p. 7; CD of Charles H. Hubert Parry, *Job* (Hyperion Label, with Guildford Choral Society and the Royal Philharmonic, 1997).

7. David J.A. Clines, *Job 1–20* (Word Biblical Commentary, 17; Dallas, TX: Word Books, 1989), p. 6.

impatient', central in the poetic sections. In a different hypothesis, there are really two books: the fable of Job, a simple folktale of faith maintained and rewarded (chaps. 1, 2, 42), and the poem, which is far longer and more complicated. Not only are the first two chapters in prose, they are also in simple language, while the poem's language is extremely complex.[8] The music in all three oratorios differentiates between these contrasting parts of the book.

Job is convinced of his innocence (as is the reader). Since he knows his misfortune is not the result of a particular sin, he 'senses that his misfortune is symptomatic of a grave and general disorder of the universe'. Job's numerous attacks against God are certainly among the most powerful in the Bible. God is depicted as a 'demonic deity' and a 'cosmic bully'.[9]

The arguments of the friends are lengthy but also repetitive (probably why most of them were not included in librettos). The main themes appear in Eliphaz's first speech: that people are worthless before God and that we are all ephemeral and consequently ignorant. His speech includes a call to turn to God in penitence and praise, and highlights both the disciplinary purpose of misfortune and the happiness of the penitent.

The rhetoric of debate on these themes permeates Eliphaz's and the other friends' speeches. Job's rejection of the patriarchal model of God as inadequate was a radical notion.[10] Perhaps Job's case is a warning never to infer sin from suffering (the friends' error) or God's enmity toward sufferers (Job's error). There is much irony and unresolved tension throughout the book. It remains the classic expression of 'the irrepressible yearning for divine order, baffled but never stifled by the disarray of reality'.[11] Another important theme of the book is the significance of personal experience as a source of religious insight.[12]

The concern of the book is not only the problem of suffering, but how people experience and endure it. As Mitchell states, 'Ultimately the dialogue is not about theological positions but human reactions'.[13] Music is the best medium for projecting the experience of suffering, which is well demonstrated by the musical settings of Job. This explains why particular verses dealing with suffering have been singled out to appear in so many musical settings.

---

8. Harold S Kushner, *The Book of Job: When Bad Things Happened to a Good Person* (New York: Schocken Books, 2012), p. 15

9. J. William Whedbee, *The Bible and the Comic Vision* (Minneapolis, MN: Fortress Press, 2002), p. 237.

10. Carol Newsom, 'Job', in *The Women's Biblical Commentary* (ed. Carol Newsom and Sharon Ringe; London: SPCK, 1992), p. 130.

11. Moshe Greenberg, 'Job', in *The Literary Guide to the Bible* (ed. Robert Alter and Frank Kermode; Cambridge, MA: Belknap Press, 1987), p. 301.

12. Newsom, 'Job', p. 130.

13. Stephen Mitchell, *The Book of Job* (New York: HarperPerennial, 1992), p. xiv.

The poetry in Job is amazingly powerful and inventive, allowing multiple possible interpretations. This is evident from the wide range of translations. Its difficulty may correspond to the unresolved tensions in the author's vision of reality. This author is forcing us to see things in new ways.

In the opening scenes, the characters of Yhwh (this name for God is only found in chaps. 1–2 and 42) and the Satan are contrasted by means of their speech. Yhwh sounds brusque, while the Satan inserts folk sayings, and generally depicts a mastery of conscious rhetoric. Yhwh seems plainspoken in contrast. This distinction is highlighted in musical settings with various techniques.

Is the book about Job or 'Everyman'?[14] Clines believes that the indeterminacy and vagueness of the opening verses suggest the book is to be read as wisdom literature rather than as biography: that there is a 'transformation of an individual into an everyman'.[15] The music makes it more personal—Job comes across as a real person crying about his pain—even though the story is certainly more effective when read as a universal one. We can never know the writer's intent, of course.

The Composers

Charles H. Hubert Parry completed a Bachelor of Music degree at Oxford in 1867 and continued to study music privately. His earliest works, in the 1880s, were primarily symphonies. Later, he turned to writing oratorios, of which he wrote three: *Judith* in 1888, *Job* in 1892, and *King Saul* in 1894. His esteem and popularity during the 1890s were so great that he was considered the nation's 'unofficial composer laureate'.[16] He was knighted in 1898 and became Professor of Music at Oxford in 1900.

When he was commissioned to write a new oratorio for the Gloucester (Three Choirs) Festival of 1892, Parry turned to the book of Job. Job struck a deep chord of sympathy in Parry, an agnostic struggling with uncertainty and dissatisfaction.[17] Parry included his own original text in addition to *Job* verses. In spite of its unusual and almost experimental nature, this oratorio was enormously successful in its day.

One of the more unusual aspects of the oratorio's general structure is its use of leitmotifs (see Glossary). There are two motifs for Job, used very

---

14. The word 'everyman' has come to be a common noun, defined by the OED as 'An ordinary or typical human being'. The origin of the term is believed to derive from a late-fifteenth-century morality play by that name. It is not known if the definition preceded the play in usage, or the common definition was coined by the play.

15. Clines, *Job 1–20*, p.17.

16. Jeremy Dibble, in *The New Grove Dictionary of Music and Musicians* (ed. Stanley Sadie; 29 vols.; New York: Grove, 2nd edn, 2001), XIX, p. 153.

17. Jeremy Dibble, CD liner notes, p. 5.

effectively to frame his scenes, and less frequent motifs identified with God, the Satan, and the shepherd boy (an invented character). The solo vocal writing is largely in a declamatory style, a significant change in English oratorio.[18]

Besides the unusually lengthy solo setting for Job's lament, the most unconventional feature of this oratorio is that it ends with a solo rather than the expected chorus, which traditionally concludes an oratorio. Performances of *Job* declined after World War I, when so much Victorian and Edwardian music went rapidly out of fashion.[19]

Peter Maxwell Davies began composing at an early age. He studied composition in England, Italy, the United States and Australia. He has also conducted many prominent orchestras. Davies was made CBE in 1981, was knighted in 1987, and in 1997 became president of the Society for the Promotion of New Music. He has been 'Master of the Queen's Music' since 2004. His music has both Classical and Romantic traits, yet his harmony avoids any suggestion of either neo-classicism or neo-romanticism. His approach is individual and unique even as it renews some traditional forms.[20]

Davies's oratorio *Job* premiered in Vancouver in 1997. This work is a manifestation of the religious sensibility that has pervaded Davies's work, particularly his use of plainchant (see Glossary). Davies writes that he had been interested in the book of Job since he was 18, especially in its unresolvable moral questions. He welcomed the chance to 'investigate the work with abstract music rather than concrete words'. He views the work as an internal drama taking place inside Job's head.[21]

There are interesting differences, both musical and textual, between these two British works written one hundred years apart. Parry uses the KJV while Davies uses the modern Stephen Mitchell translation. Parry adds a character, a shepherd boy sung by a boy soprano, but does not include any of Job's friends, which Davies does. Both composers utilize a chorus for the voice of God. Davies ends the oratorio with Job quietly murmuring, 'I am dust', while Parry includes a short postlude sung by the Narrator relating the happy ending of the biblical story.

---

18. Howard E. Smither, *A History of the Oratorio*. IV. *The Oratorio in the Nineteenth and Twentieth Centuries* (Chapel Hill, NC: University of North Carolina Press, 2000), p. 358.

19. Jeremy Dibble, personal communication.

20. John Warnaby, in *The New Grove Dictionary of Music and Musicians*, VII, pp. 64, 69.

21. David Nice, CD liner notes in Peter Maxwell Davies, *Job* (Collins Classic CD, with Canadian Broadcasting Corporation. Vancouver Orchestra, live recording of the 1997 world premiere).

Luigi Dallapiccola was a pioneer of twelve-tone music (see Glossary) in Italy. After studying piano and harmony in Trieste in 1919, he spent several years studying Debussy's music. From 1929 to 1931 he studied in Florence and was first exposed to both Schoenberg's and Berg's music, other major influences. He was professor of piano at the Florence Conservatory from 1934 to 1967. *Job* was his first large-scale twelve-tone work, showing Webern's influence. Like his other music, it is avant-garde, featuring mixed meter and virtually atonal.[22]

This work was commissioned by the Anfiparnaso association of Rome and composed in the summer of 1950. It has received little musicological attention, overshadowed by the composer's more famous work, *Il Prigioniero* (1949). The dramatic and musical value of *Job*, Dallapiccola's first twelve-tone theatre work, has been somewhat underrated. The idiom he aimed to give the biblical story was a rhythmic prose in which 'symmetries and sonorities impart a mythical and ritual aura to the text. . . . Dallapiccola animates the psychological development of his characters by employing dramatic and musical strategies that exploit very particular timbres and sonorities and specific rhythmic and harmonic formulas'. These combined elements underpin the work's structure.[23]

The remainder of this article will be a chapter-by-chapter discussion of the biblical text and its musical interpretations in these three works. Since the composers frequently scramble chapters and verses, this will not be completely linear in form.

Job 1–6

Job 1.6-12

Parry's very stately opening music in C-major is suited to the text. This orchestral opening introduces several leitmotifs that will recur throughout the oratorio. The narrator's opening phrases continue in C-major, but there is an unexpected shift to B-flat major as the voice reaches *d'* on the word 'God' (2, top),[24] musically underlining its importance.

When the narrator announces the 'divine beings' presenting themselves before God, (JPS; also translated 'sons of God', 1.6), the music speeds up and becomes more dramatic, with prominent brass, before the Satan (Satan in this libretto, based on the KJV) is announced. 'The Satan' is more correct

---

22. John C. Waterhouse, in *The New Grove Dictionary of Music and Musicians*, V, pp. 854, 856.

23. Simone Ciolfi, 'Idea e strategia del dramma in "Job" di Luigi Dallapiccola', *Rivista italiana di musicologia* 37 (2002), pp. 109-30.

24. These are page references in the scores.

than Satan because it is a job description more than a name. Satan may be connected to the Hebrew word meaning to obstruct, or from the verb *shat-tat* (שׁטט), meaning 'to roam' or 'go back and forth'. In that case, the Satan would be like God's spy. When the Satan first appears, God asks him where he has been, and he says he's been roaming all over the world.[25]

God's voice is represented by a male chorus. His words, 'Whence comest thou?' (1.7), so prosaic on paper, sound ominous when sung very softly in unison (5, 3rd staff, m. 4). Satan is sung by a tenor, in music with much less gravitas than God's. Though the tenor voice is usually heroic or romantic, here it has a menacing, strident tone. He sings his opening phrases unaccompanied, but the orchestra plays suspenseful passages between his verses (6, top). Winds and strings predominate, contrasted with more brass in the music sung by God. These are all examples of musical characterization.

In 1.9, the Satan questions the link between Job's piety and his prosperity. Which came first, and which caused which? Clines proposes that this question had never been asked before in antiquity. The underlying notion is that not only Job's behavior in particular is being questioned, but rather the whole validity of the notion of divine retribution. As Clines puts it, at stake is 'the causal nexus between ethics and success' . . . which is linked to the nexus between suffering and guilt.[26]

When the Satan throws down his challenge, excited triplets and chromatic ascending passages create drama (9, bottom). These rapid passages stop abruptly, and loud accented chords create a dramatic pause before the Satan concludes his challenge (8, 4th staff). A steady ostinato (see Glossary) is the only music accompanying God's response, evoking a sense of dread (9-10). A short orchestral interlude follows this dialogue. Its major key and sweeping sound depict Job's life and contentment (11).

Parry next inserts a scene for an invented character, a shepherd boy. The combination of a rustic melody played on clarinet and a drone bass create a pastoral atmosphere (12). The shepherd boy, sung by a boy soprano, extolls Job's flocks and his wonderful, trouble-free life in a lovely, lilting melody. This musical depiction of happiness and simplicity is vaguely clouded by dark harmonies in the strings.

Davies's work is in enormous contrast with Parry's. It opens with a virtually unaccompanied chorus, which has the character of plainsong, in the composer's words.[27] Davies chooses to open with v. 4 rather than the very opening of the book. Verses 4-5 are sung by an *a cappella* (unaccompanied) women's chorus; for v. 6, a male chorus announces the 'Accusing Angel'. Just before they whisper those two words, an ominous drum roll is heard.

---

25. Kushner, *The Book of Job*, pp. 28-29.
26. Clines, *Job 1–20*, p. 28.
27. As quoted in David Nice, CD liner notes, p. 6.

The shrill and bombastic voice of God is sung by mixed chorus, with harsh winds and brass augmenting the dissonance. The Accuser is represented by two soloists, a mezzo and a soprano, in much gentler music. This in itself is an interesting and unusual choice. As the Accuser continues challenging God, the tone of the voices becomes more taunting.

Both these composers, writing a century apart, insert a note of dread in the opening scenes. Davies's music may be more suggestive or evocative for the modern listener, due in part to the more familiar musical idiom.

Dallapiccola's work is of another era and style entirely. The opening verses are spoken in a very dramatic manner by an actor, in a very deep bass voice (though no tones are indicated in the score). Initially there is no accompaniment, but when he recounts the number of Job's possessions, an oboe plays sinuous, ostinato-like phrases (9). These passages include the tritone, known as the devil's interval, historically a musical representation of the diabolical. When the Angels are mentioned, effective harp and celesta passages are heard. The narrator pronounces the name 'Satan' (Satana) in almost a whisper over a drum roll (the name is also whispered in Davies's work).

In the dialogue, both God and the Satan are represented by the chorus, alternating between whispering and speaking. Only low drum beats can be heard under their voices. They repeat lines several times, as if echoing each other. Harp, violin and oboe can be faintly heard. When God gives the Satan permission to go ahead, only a tam-tam (percussion instrument, similar to a gong) can be heard, an ominous effect.[28]

Job 1.13-22

An atmosphere of accelerating doom is created by the entrance of each messenger announcing a new disaster directly on the heels of the messenger that is already present. Each messenger is the sole survivor of the disaster he describes. This sense of frenzy is re-created differently by each composer.

Before the scene with the messengers, Parry inserts a scene in which the Satan calls up the Sabeans, and then the wind, to do their damage. The Satan's entrance is a highly dramatic contrast with the preceding shepherd song (15, bottom). A dramatic chorus follows each of the Satan's pronouncements, exclaiming on what they are witnessing. Rapid orchestral passages, with dotted rhythms and a low tremolo (see Glossary), combine to create loud and frenzied music (17-20). This music pulls the listener into the drama as it brings the text to vivid life.

The music suddenly calms as the chorus sings 'The song of the shepherd has ceased in the land', referring back to the sweet and innocent shepherd's

---

28. There is no recording of this work; I obtained a recording of a live broadcast on RAI, Italian radio, from a private collector.

song just heard. In this poignant choral lament, the oboe plays a mournful transformation of the orchestral leitmotif heard in the first scene. Cellos and low violins interject expressive phrases. After a rising phrase in the orchestra, the chorus ends with 'O'er all the plains is silence, silence', sung almost sotto voce (very softly) and unaccompanied on the final repeat (22-23).

The messenger in Parry's libretto is the shepherd boy, deviating from the biblical text. Just before his entrance, the orchestra reprises the theme of his song, transposed (23, bottom). Verses 15-19 are omitted, since the actions described there are dramatized by the Satan and then the chorus, as in the previous section. The Satan's commands to the wind feature repeated triplets in the orchestra, a rhythm that gives his music tremendous momentum and power (26, 27). His music builds continually, up to a high *ff* A (*a'*) sustained for nine beats on the word 'Hasten' (29, 3rd staff, m. 2-4).

The full chorus responds to the disasters wrought by the Satan in excited and changeable music, sung as if they experience each disaster. This dramatic 'witness' account concludes with softer, poignant music. The phrase 'Lift up thy voice, O son of man, and cry' is sung a cappella and softly, exploding on the last word into an unexpected C-major (36, reh. X). This is usually considered the brightest key, but here it emerges as a cry of agony. The intense musical representation of this narrative creates both excitement and empathy in the listener. The sad mood continues to the end, in a lyrical and heartfelt melody accentuated by slurs (see Glossary) in the orchestra, a weeping sound (37). The orchestral postlude to this scene reprises the opening Job leitmotif, but in a very understated way (39). The biblicized text is by Parry.

Following this chorus, the narrator sings vv. 11-13 and 2.1, introducing Job's friends. Haunting oboe and cello solos, playing descending phrases, are woven into the orchestral background. The suspended harmonies underlining the phrase 'his grief was very great' add great emotion and new dimensions to the text.

In the biblical book, the entrance of the different messengers in rapid succession as they relate the incredible series of disasters is very effective. But Parry's oratorio intensifies the drama by relating it through witnesses as it happens and is experienced, rather than after the fact. Through the music, the listener is transported to the scene and can emotionally relate to the story.

In Dallapiccola, Job's entrance is introduced by sinuous flute passages, heard earlier on the oboe (17). The messengers rush in, and one after another they announce the disasters. Each announcement is preceded by a screamed 'Job!' starting on various pitches, but all sung on a descending augmented octave. The rapid and cacophonous atonal (see Glossary) music projects greater terror than the other works discussed here.

As the messengers enter, they begin to sing their own lines and echo each others', mimicking the effect of the messengers' arrival in the biblical version. Occasionally the tempo slows as a messenger relates another sad event. The voices all come together increasingly throughout the section, as the orchestra joins in. The feeling is relentless, and the repeated extreme high notes transmit a sense that everyone onstage is screaming. This is a far more violent scene than heard in any other musical work. The music recreates the terror that would have been experienced in the biblical narrative but that is not described.

The music dies down completely and slows for Job's entrance. His first words are 'Naked I came out of my mother's womb' (1.21), sung over soft and low single tones in the orchestra. As he continues, solo oboe and flute echo his voice with slurs descending on augmented octaves—a faint echo of the earlier choral cries of 'Job!' (28). After these few soft and poignant phrases, Job sings 'May God's name be blessed'. The chorus abruptly re-enters screaming, followed by very loud drum beats and a long silent pause (29). Then the narration resumes, spoken by the chorus as before with accompanying drum rolls and very low timpani beats. On the final verse 'Save his life' (2.6), a large tam-tam is heard (35, Reh. #35), adding drama to the words.

Davies does not include any of the scenes with the messengers, only vv. 20-22, in which Job bemoans his fate but continues blessing God. His words 'Naked I came from my mother's womb' are preceded by a lyrical orchestral interlude, prominently featuring strings. Job's baritone voice seems to emerge out of the low rumbling cellos.

Job 2.2-13

Only Davies includes the second scene between God and the Satan. God is again portrayed by mixed, dissonant (see Glossary) voices. In this scene, the Accuser is sung by solo tenor and baritone, not soprano and mezzo as previously. An orchestral interval follows the two scenes, dominated by very expressive strings. God speaks for the last time in 2.10,[29] until after 34 chapters of human speech. Verses 11-13 form a transition between the prologue and the dialogue. Job's three friends are introduced here; chaps. 3–31 consist of conversations between them and Job.

Job 3.1-26

Job's lament has been called the masterpiece of the book of Job by many commentators. Its importance lies in its complete focus on feeling and emo-

---

29. A great deal could be said, and has been written, about the role of Job's wife (2.9). But since she is not included in these three musical works, I am not discussing her portrayal or significance.

tion, without intellectual intrusions. The remainder of the book consists mostly of ideological questions about theodicy. But questions about the doctrine of retribution and the meaning of suffering are absent from this passionate and moving lament.

Parry's setting of Job's lament is considered the most innovative feature of his oratorio. The lengthy solo, 'the Lamentation of Job', is the emotional centre of the work and also a break with traditional oratorio form. No solo of this length (over five minutes, 17 pages) or emotional tension can be found in other oratorios of any era, particularly Parry's. Parry used verses not only from chap. 3, but also from chaps. 8, 9, 10, 14, 29 and 30. Though the vocal part is more recitative (see Glossary) than aria, the music has tremendous pathos and intensity. A descending theme—typical for depicting sadness—is repeated in the orchestra throughout, like a background to Job's grief.

The mood of the music changes continually, reflecting Job's confused and agonized thoughts. After the melancholy opening, with verses from chap. 3, Parry set vv. 1-11 of chap. 9 (singing God's praises) to triumphant and upbeat music. This might have been intended as an antidote to the preceding melancholy section. The tonality gravitates toward C-major, the key of earlier scenes. But the buoyancy is short lived, and the key returns to A-minor as Job realizes the hopelessness of his situation.

Parry followed this with verses from chap. 10 set as another melancholy recitative. He omitted 10.7, which is particularly significant because there Job claims not only that he is innocent, but also that God knows of his innocence. This is not an absent-minded or careless God, then, but an uncaring one. Job here compares himself to humanity at large and wonders why he was singled out.

Some sections of this lengthy solo feature many rests, to depict breathlessness (46, 3rd staff), and changed keys to reflect a new thought, as before Job states 'I will say unto God' (47, top; 10.3). In just two pages (48-49), the keys of A-flat, D-flat and E-major all appear, suggesting instability and uncertainty. When Job begins to recollect happier times (chap. 29), the mood and key change again, and both the voice and the orchestra are in a higher range (50, 3rd staff). Then when Job again complains of his lot (chap. 30), a tremolo rumbles under him, and uneasy chords accompany his phrase 'I cry unto Thee', in which the voice leaps from *e* to an unexpected *d-flat'*, reflecting not only anguish but a lack of any firm ground (53, 4th staff). As Job describes his agony, the music becomes increasingly dramatic.

The final phrase, 'For I know that thou shalt bring me unto death' (30.23), is a long descending phrase sung mostly unaccompanied (54, Reh. M). The closing orchestral measures strongly recall Wagner. The lament ends softly on an A-minor chord (54, bottom). The libretto jumps from the lament to chap. 38.

Fig. 1. Parry, 'Job's Lament'.

Davies's setting of Job's lament portrays anguish through the use of very low registers in cellos, basses, muted trombones, even an unusual and lugubrious marimbaphone (a rarely used tuned percussion instrument similar in sound to the marimba). These combine to create a vivid musical description of Job's suffering. Because Job is not depicted as an actual person in this work, his part is sung variously by baritone, soprano, mezzo and tenor. Some parts are sung solo, some as ensemble. In some sections, the chorus sings other text in the background while Job sings his lament. The orchestral music changes into almost nagging fragments, including a violin solo marked 'smarmy', as the three comforters approach. Their music could almost be labeled comical or buffoonish, a not-so-subtle message of Davies's personal impression of the friends.

In Dallapiccola, the measures leading up to Job's lament include several kinds of drum and organ (35, bottom), combining to sound like a thunderbolt. The tone of his lament fluctuates every few measures, from assertive to grieving and back to angry. The voice sings over a wide range of pitch and dynamics (36-38).

Fig. 2. Dallapiccola, 'Job's Lament'.

Job 4–6

Eliphaz tactlessly assures Job that he will have numerous offspring—this just after Job has lost his ten children! Eliphaz seems to care more about rhetoric than Job's personal circumstances. The poet is highlighting a bitter contrast between conventional piety and real suffering. Eliphaz's observations are all 'filtered through the distorting spectacles of a retributionist theology'.[30] So the chapter can be understood on two levels: on the surface, as a speech of encouragement to Job; on a deeper level, as an 'indictment of the cruelty of narrow dogma'.[31]

30. Clines, *Job 1–20*, pp. 134, 153.
31. Clines, *Job 1–20*, pp. 134.

Davies and Dallapiccola include parts of Eliphaz's and the other friends' speeches. In Davies, their voices are interchangeable, making the point that 'they share the same imagery for their doctrinaire claptrap'.[32] Even without this comment, it is obvious that the music is mocking the words of the friends. Near the end of these overlapping speeches, a tenor sings distant and expressive phrases echoed by alto flute, followed by a full choral plaint. This seems to universalize Job's situation before retreating to leave the single spotlight on Job. As the music shifts back to Job, it becomes more sombre and dark. When Job sings certain verses from chap. 6, the final words of each phrase are echoed hauntingly by a solo tenor: for example, the words 'sorrow, sorrow', and 'desperate, desperate sorrow'. Music is used effectively to highlight these words and create empathy in the listener.

Job 7–15

Job 7.1-18

Only Davies includes this speech, in which Job addresses God directly and begs to be left alone. Verses 17-18 are considered a bitter parody of Psalm 8.5-6.[33] Throughout this section, other voices moan echoes of Job's words. When Job sings assertively that he wants to speak to God to his face and defend himself, the tone of the music changes, and Job's words are suddenly taken up by a full chorus. This device, utilized by Davies throughout the oratorio, forces the listener to identify more with the text than with any individual character. He wants to create the sense that the text is all internal dialogue.

Before Job re-enters as a baritone soloist, slow cello passages mark the shift to Job's direct question to God: what has he done to warrant punishment? (Verses from chaps. 13 and 10 are interspersed.) As his complaint intensifies, it is once more sung by full chorus. The wide dynamic range reflects the constant change in Job's mood, from despairing to confrontational to questioning. Through the music, this Job is more human and vulnerable than his biblical counterpart. In the final part of this lengthy section, Job is sung by a solo tenor, alternating on every line with other solo voices and with the chorus in the background repeating, 'Like a cat, toying with a mouse' in staccato (see Glossary), sotto voce phrases. The section ends on the words 'black as night', sung by several solo voices in a dissonant tone cluster. It is a highly effective example of music's power to create a sense of grief, dread and hopelessness.

---

32. Quoting Davies in David Nice, CD liner notes, p. 7.
33. Clines, *Job 1–20*, p. 192.

Job 8.20-22

These verses re-state the retributionist theology. Of course, the very fact that Job is being unjustly punished completely invalidates that theology. But Bildad stands for traditional wisdom, and the author presents him in this ironic light to make his point. The description of the psalmist's 'enemies' sounds very much like Job's friends, who continue to insist on his guilt. This is yet another use of irony, showing that would-be comforters who accept the wisdom theology uncritically are transformed into enemies.

Part Two of *Davies's* work opens with this chapter. Job's friends are still sung by a variety of voices, including a coloratura soprano singing at a fever pitch in one brief section.

Dallapiccola includes a more extensive scene between Job and the three friends. The music introducing the three friends is marked 'Canon duplex', or double canon (see Glossary). There are three 3-part canons in the scene, effectively creating a conversational effect. The music is punctuated by snare drums, tambourine and kettle drum. The predominance of drums throughout this work heightens the drama and sense of foreboding.

Eliphaz is sung by a soprano, to represent a very young man. The lyrical music is simple and very soft. This tone changes abruptly on the text 'there is no death without sin', which is sung on strongly accented and rhythmical music (40, 2nd staff). Job responds that he is covered with worms, in music marked 'tumultuous', while his own part is marked 'darkly'.

Bildad is sung by a contralto in a very low range; her entrance is marked 'very calm'. Her unaccompanied music is simple and very soft (41, Reh. #65). When she tells Job to repent, Eliphaz re-enters and sings together with Bildad. They continue to echo each other for several measures. As they start to sing together, the eerie sound of the vibraphone is heard under their voices (42, 2nd staff). When the text 'there is no death without sin' is repeated, the music again becomes stronger and more rhythmic and harsh. Job responds to the friends 'tumultuously' (43, top).

After Job complains for a few measures, the third friend, Zophar, is heard, sung by a tenor. The three friends sing a trio, a kind of *fugato* (see Glossary), but each singing his own text (45, bottom). The word 'Repent!' is sung to increasingly stronger and more rhythmic music. Job argues while the three friends continue to sing high above his voice. As in a heated argument, all are 'shouting' at once (47). This effect is not realized in any other work, and it greatly amplifies the biblical text, in which only one character speaks at a time (as in any book). The friends then leave, one at a time, looking at Job with pity. He sings 'Pity!' several times as the music dies down. Dallapiccola maximizes music's ability to allow several characters to 'speak' at the same time.

Job 9.1-24

Job's speeches reach a new level of intensity and poignancy here. The interesting expression Job uses in v. 1, 'born of woman', is found nowhere else in the Hebrew Bible. The opening verses are full of despair and depression, as Job speaks of being trapped and powerless, wishing he had never been born and that God would leave him alone.

In vv. 5-10 Job praises God in a hymnic doxology to God's power (included in Parry, but in the earlier lament). In vv. 22-24 Job notes two facts: he is blameless and in despair (included in Davies). A god who allows those two conditions simultaneously must be cruel and indiscriminate. God rules the world with callous indifference, in this view. A basic premise of ancient wisdom was that there was an order to the universe, sustained by its Creator. Job abandons that premise here.

When Job wonders how he can refute God, Davies's music is frenzied, augmented by the unusual timbre of the marimbaphone. When he sings 'He does not care', Job's words are repeated like an echo in the chorus, almost a taunting effect.

Davies continues seamlessly from chap. 9 into chap. 29. Parry incorporates several verses from both chaps. 29 and 30 in Job's Lament (see above, chap. 3).

Job 29–31

Chapter 29 is the beginning of Job's final speech, which continues through chap. 31. In the opening verses, he reminisces about what his life had been, contrasting it with what it has become. Job continues to insist on his innocence in the subsequent chapters, which are scrambled and paraphrased in the librettos.

Dallapiccola set these chapters in music marked 'very slow, desolate' (49). The singer is to sing 'barely articulated, but very expressively' and extremely softly. The sound is like an internal soliloquy. The aria spans two octaves, from *A flat* to *a flat'*, difficult for a bass-baritone but highly effective in depicting mood. When he is reminiscing, the music remains soft and almost conversational. Short plangent phrases are played by horn, oboe and clarinet, effective musical suggestions of Job's emotional state.

A strident chord cluster in the brass interrupts this soliloquy, and Job bursts out with his questions about the injustice he sees in the world. The music becomes angry and harsh, reflecting his feelings. Job repeats the verses about 'those who sing and dance' several times in a high range, almost in a mocking tone and a dance rhythm (52, Reh. #35). After that, he virtually shouts his question to God, 'Why are they not punished?'(53, 2nd staff). Several very quick chords are followed by a long measure of silence. Then Job sings 'I, Job, ask Jahveh: answer me'. The word 'Job' is sung on a *fff a flat'* (very loud and high), followed by a descending octave leap on 'Jahveh' (54, bottom). This is a musical way of underlining the phrase.

When Job begins reminiscing in Davies, the music is calm, with only skittering violins playing in a high register in the background to suggest underlying anxiety. In Davies's setting, after an orchestral outburst, the vocal line climbs very high, sounding desperate and straining the baritone voice. When Job remembers his earlier situation, the dark colours of eerie low trombone notes yield to an almost garish and jazz-like orchestral evocation of strutting authority, with brass dominating. The Job who remembers his earlier status is sung by a high tenor, a subtle touch of parody which also suggests a younger man.

After these verses, a long orchestral interlude in Davies suggests Job is still remembering his past life. In the soft and understated climax of this section, the chorus repeats the four key words of Job's ecstatic reminiscences—silence, wisdom, majesty, courage—between his phrases. They suddenly burst out singing all four words, before the music dies out with soft percussion and solo cellos.

Davies's Part Three opens after chap. 29, but he inserts verses from chaps. 26 and 27 out of sequence here—Bildad's speeches and Job's responses. The music is martial, and uniquely here includes two bizarre percussion instruments: the *cuaca* (known as 'lion's roar') and the 'wobbling, wailing flexatone'.[34] Job still holds fast to his claim of innocence and insistence on confronting God. His proclamations are sung to insistent music. This leads straight to chap. 38.

Verses from chap. 30 are set only by Parry, as part of the lament (see chap. 3).

Job 38–40

In these speeches by Yhwh, humans are not included. Nor is an explanation of injustice in the world. By his silence, Yhwh is tacitly admitting that the world he created does not include any principle of retribution. God may be just, but his justice is not necessarily absolute. Divine justice is not part of reality; it is only a philosophy. Yhwh here depicts himself as a master architect of the world order. The wonders of the world are described and extolled, but all of Job's questions are ignored. In Yhwh's world, the wicked may prosper. Yhwh ironically suggests that Job can re-order the world himself by crushing the wicked.

---

34. David Nice, CD liner notes, p. 7.

Job 38.1-30

This is possibly the best-known chapter in the book, where God speaks to Job 'out of the whirlwind/tempest'. In one of his longest speeches in the Hebrew Bible, God speaks like the other interlocutors in the book, addressing Job yet ignoring his concerns. The speech has been interpreted in various ways. Some commentators believe God's answer lies simply in his revelation; others, that Yhwh's speech seems to insist only on his power, not on justice. The most intriguing question, which can never be answered definitively, is what tone we should hear in Yhwh's words. This must be interpreted by the reader, and is resolved in different ways by these composers.

Parry employs a full chorus to sing this chapter, in majestic pageant-like music, with prominent brass in the accompaniment. But the opening verse, 'Who is this that darkeneth counsel . . .' is sung by an a cappella four-part chorus (61, top). There is a striking transition to the verse 'Who shut up the sea with doors' (38.8), which is first sung by a female chorus, later joined by the men as it slowly builds (61). Flowing flute passages imitate rolling water, to introduce the verses about watercourses. These highly lyrical passages are like a love song, suggesting God's feelings for the sea.

Fig. 3. Parry, 'Voice from the Whirlwind'.

The mood changes entirely at the verses starting 'Hast thou commanded the morning . . .' (38.12), where the tempo quickens, the key changes and the accompaniment changes from a rolling one to bright groups of triplets in a high range (64-66). The mood changes again on 'Have the gates of death . . .', where several measures of slurs convey a sense of doom and grief (68). The chorus concludes on the phrase 'the face of the deep is frozen' (38.30). Very low notes are heard in the trombones, tubas, cellos and basses, creating unearthly timbres in a highly effective instance of word painting. The final chord is C-minor but in the third inversion (see Glossary), sounding unresolved (73, bottom).

The music of Dallapiccola for this chapter is marked 'broad and violently' (55, top). God's voice is represented by a full chorus, as in the other works. Initially they sing in unison, before breaking into parts. Before each of God's questions to Job, an organ solo is heard. This instrument's association with liturgical music is obviously meant to evoke God. The chorus sings the questions initially a cappella, then is joined by a strident, cacophonous accompaniment. Trombones and other brass play loudly onstage (indicated in score, 59, Reh. #25). The chorus repeats the text many times in a strident *fugato*. This section reaches a tremendous climax as the full chorus sings 'Job, answer me!' (Rispondimi!) on a *fff* unison A-flat (62, bottom). Then the next round of questions continues.

Fig. 4. Dallapiccola, 'The Voice from the Whirlwind'.

When God asks Job if his voice can thunder, the chorus representing God's voice is accompanied by onstage organ, horns, trumpets and trombone. This kind of obbligato instrumental group is found mostly in Baroque works. The onstage chorus sings a Gregorian *Te deum laudamus*.[35] It is a vivid and also oddly anomalous traditional musical depiction of God. The second section ends like the first, with a loud choral cry to Job.

Davies portrays the whirlwind with powerful orchestral passages, shrieking brass and percussion followed by eerie snatches of string passages. These passages build steadily to an explosive climax, when the chorus (as God) enters, assertively singing vv. 2-15. Strange percussion creates an otherworldly effect. The phrase 'All things are touched with colour, the whole world is changed' is repeated many times, initially with a high violin obbligato above it. This is an effective musical evocation of another world.

Job 39.1-30
The descriptions of the animals were irresistible to composers, who chose various instruments and timbres to paint their attributes in music. Parry chose only the horse (39.19), for which rapid staccato triplet groups convey prancing and continuous movement (74). The verses are sung in a fast, dramatic and scherzo-like chorus.

Davies playfully uses music pictorially to great effect. The lioness and her cubs are heard in shrill oboes; the antelope, in brass trills and quick ascending phrases; and the hawk, in luminous string passages. The previous 'All things are touched with colour' phrase is heard repeatedly in the background, as if to remind the listener of the reason for describing the animals.

Dallapiccola unfortunately did not set these verses.

Job 40–42

The parade of wonders offered by God in the final chapters is intended to excite awe and amazement at divine creativity. The author disregards the anthropocentrism of the rest of the Bible, claiming that ultimately God cannot be judged merely by God's manifestation in human society. We should be able to affirm God's work despite deficiencies in the moral realm through our sheer wonder at God's creativity in nature. Moral deficiencies are outside human judgment, in the writer's view. Wisdom, for humankind, consists of fearing God and rejecting evil; we can never know more than that.[36]

Clines brilliantly unravels why the entire final part of the book concentrates on 'one amazing creature, Leviathan the crocodile'. The poem

---

35. Raymond Fearn, *Italian Opera since 1945* (Amsterdam: Overseas Publishers Association / Harwood Academic Publishers, 1997), pp. 44, 45.
36. Greenberg, 'Job', p. 299.

settles for 'the lyrical over the didactic', completely altering the discourse from rationality and argument to delight and praise. In Clines's words, 'should we not be wary of poets who sweep questions of justice under carpets of delight? . . . Has this deity perhaps a little too much attachment to crocodiles?'[37] In these whimsical remarks, Clines has zeroed in on the disturbing undercurrent present in these final chapters. Yhwh is depicted as a god in love with the animals he created and uninterested in justice. As radical an idea as this sounds today, it must have been far more so when it was written.

Job 40.7-14

In these verses, Yhwh obviously baits Job, sarcastically challenging him to dress and act like the kind of god he thinks God should be. Then Yhwh returns to the theme of creation by praising Behemoth. The underlying message is that Job has not grasped God's purposes. He has not been evil or done wrong; he is only intellectually at fault for not really appreciating Yhwh's creations.

In Parry's extended symphonic chorus, God is referred to in the third person, rather than the first person as in the biblical text. The music for these crucial verses is similar to what preceded it: dramatic, powerful, surging. Some themes are repeated in ever higher keys, building great excitement. A brief *fugato* is heard, followed by a single unison passage (80-81). Absent, though, is any sense of sarcasm on Yhwh's part. Only 40.14 is differentiated musically from the preceding verses, sung as a soft a cappella chorale in six parts, reflecting the 'confession' contained within it.

Job 42.1-6

Job realizes he is dealing with a God disinterested in justice, and therefore he decides to withdraw his claim against him. If Yhwh will never answer questions about justice, there is no chance of Job's case being heard. An alternative possibility might be that Yhwh is embarrassed to admit his bet with the Satan, thinking it would place him in a bad light (which it would). Perhaps this is the reason he always changes the subject. But the end result is the same: Job must withdraw his suit without admitting guilt, because he will never get an answer from Yhwh. And the harsh message for humanity is that there is no underlying principle of justice in the world.

If Job does not admit wrongdoing, why does he seem to repent? Clines interprets the phrase usually translated 'I recant and relent' (JPS; אמאס ונחמתי, 42.6) to mean that Job brings his period of mourning to an end by accepting consolation for all his losses.[38] It can also possibly be read as a simple

---

37. Clines, *Job 38–42*, p. 1203.
38. Clines, *Job 38–42*, p. 1218.

expression of contrition. Job is not triumphant or defeated; he has come to realize that he will not get justice from God. The final verse of Job's last speech either means Job accepts he is only dust and ashes (that is, mortal), or he is still sitting on an ash-heap (על עפר ואפר).

Job's final words in *Parry* are introduced by his opening theme, but with a tremolo under it and with altered harmony (82, bottom), indicating musically that things are not exactly the same as they were at the beginning of the story. When Job says he has now seen God (42.5), Parry's music becomes romantic and soaring. Both Job's cello leitmotif and the theme from his lamentation are heard, but the opening theme is played in reverse—a very subtle musical message. The music is not only projecting an emotional experience but also suggesting textual meaning. Job's final phrase includes an astounding vocal leap: 'in dust and ashes' jumps from *a-flat* to *c'*—a full tenth. Yet the word 'ashes' is sung very quickly, on 16th-notes. This surprisingly abrupt conclusion seems to minimize Job's role in the whole drama.

Dallapiccola's extremely loud and dissonant rendition of God's confrontation with Job ends with a powerful organ chord, dying down immediately for Job's response. The music opens with soft violin passages, a great contrast with the previous scene dominated by brass. Job's words of contrition are sung to similar music as his lament, very soft and almost spoken. The conclusion is similarly understated, dying out on soft chords and a short ascending phrase on celesta (80).

Only Davies chose to end his work with Job's final words (rather than with the epilogue and happy ending). Job is clearly so dazzled by God's words that he is now content to simply exist. There is a huge dynamic range in the music for these opening verses. Job first sings very low and softly, but some of his words are then repeated by a very loud choral outburst. Perhaps this suggests a dissonance between his outer words and inner feelings. There is a rich orchestral postlude between Job's last words and a reprise of the opening plainsong-like chorus. Like Job's solo, the orchestra starts very softly and builds to a huge crescendo underlined by drums and unusual percussion. Then the music calms again for the chorus. The beginning and end of the work are one, and the music dies away to nothing. It is an intriguing and enigmatic conclusion.

Job 42.7-17 (Epilogue)

Unlike the prologue, there is no dialogue in the epilogue (after v. 8). The genre of both prologue and epilogue is legend, and the style is naïf, almost like a folktale.

In these final verses, Job never speaks again. His fortunes and family are all restored to him; he is granted a return to his previous idyllic existence, and he dies at a ripe old age. Several commentators have pointed out that God's repaying Job double what he took from him—in terms of possessions and even his life-span—constitutes an admission of guilt on God's part (based on Exod. 22.4). With this wry touch, the author suggests a tacit acknowledgment by God of wrongdoing.

Why does the author choose to end the book this way? Clines proposes that his focus shifted from questions about the meaning of the universe and justice to a search for 'what is important for an authentic human existence'. Is cosmic justice finally superseded by the importance of familial harmony?[39] The human spirit may crave answers and be oppressed by injustice, and the questions will never go away. But human life will go on even without answers.

Parry's concluding music reprises the bright C-major theme heard at the opening of the work. This is the musical way of suggesting he has come full circle, back to where he was at the start. The music is triumphant and expansive, leaving the listener with no doubts about the happy ending.

Dallapiccola also chose to end with the narrator's final words. The music is the same as that heard at the beginning of the work. Soft notes echo effectively in harp and celesta. For the final words, Dallapiccola chose 'Job's daughters were the most beautiful in the land' (42.15), an odd and stereotypically Italian choice.

Though Davies's ending is not as optimistic as Parry's and Dallapiccola's, the notion of coming full circle is present in his work as well. Is this a commentary by these composers on the nature of the story? After all he has gone through, is Job essentially back where he started? The book of Job has been read as a theological statement opposing the doctrine of retribution and also as the story of a spiritual journey. The friends seem to represent rigid doctrine, which overrides compassion and true justice. Job as 'Everyman' is both in confrontation with this rigid doctrine and a victim of it.

Conclusion

Music is an emotional medium, not an intellectual one. Job's suffering becomes intensely real in all three works, even though they span a century and represent vastly different styles. The story becomes a personal one, rather than one of a generic Everyman, by dint of being set to music. The drama of Job's suffering—both through a vivid depiction of the disasters that befall him and heartbreaking lament music—becomes the focus. As the listener is swept into the orbit of Job's suffering, attempts to explain or justify God's punishment of Job become insignificant. The emotional content of the music remains in the listener's ears, and no rational argument can erase the impression of a man who suffered deeply and undeservedly. In the end, Job accepts that he can never understand what happened to him.

---

39. Clines, *Job 38–42*, p. 1242.

But his path to this resignation is brilliantly and imaginatively brought to life through music.

Glossary of Musical Terms

A cappella: vocal music without instrumental accompaniment.

Atonal: music with no tonal centre or key signature. Certain composers, starting in the twentieth century, completely gave up the musical idea of 'expectation'. Their scales lack a root, or home, key, so the music is adrift and conveys a lack of grounding.

Canon: a melody followed by one or more imitations of the melody.

Chromatic/chromaticism: progressing in semi-tones (half-steps) (from Greek *chroma*, colour).

Dissonant/dissonance: unstable harmony that sounds harsh or unpleasant to most people.

Fugato: a passage that imitates a fugue but is not worked out strictly as a real fugue.

Fugue: a highly developed form of contrapuntal imitation, in which a theme is heard first in one part and then taken up successively by all participating parts (from Latin *fuga*, flight, describing the chasing of the theme throughout the parts).

Inversion: the notes of a chord do not follow their standard order, creating a sense of lack of resolution. The lowest note of an inverted chord is not the root of the chord.

Key: the series of tones that form a scale. The key is named after its key-note; that is, the C-major scale begins on a C. The *key signature* is the notation that indicates the key of a musical selection. *Major* keys commonly denote a happier mood than *minor* keys, though this is only a broad generalization.

Leitmotif: a theme associated with an event or character, especially in opera, that is repeated throughout the work.

Ostinato: a short, incessantly repeated musical pattern.

Plainchant (also called plainsong): unaccompanied music sung by a number of voices, associated with mediaeval church music.

Recitative: a style of declamatory singing in which lines are half spoken and half sung.

Rhythm: the relationship between the length of one note and another; a crucial part of what makes music.

Slur: two or more notes are played on one bow-stroke, in strings, or sung on one syllable, in vocal music. The slur mark indicates the phrase should be *legato*, or smooth. A *seufzer* (from German, sigh) is a descending slur.

Staccato: tones are abruptly disconnected, sounding jerky and detached.

Tremolo: the regular, rapid repetition of a single note, or a rapid alteration between two notes. It often represents a moment of suspense.

Twelve-tone: a method of composing in which all twelve tones of the chromatic scale are given equal importance, resulting in the absence of a key signature.

Any Dream Will Do?
Joseph from Text to Technicolor

J. Cheryl Exum

Abstract

Who but Joseph would have dreamed that the story of his life would become a hit musical? Yet *Joseph and the Amazing Technicolor Dreamcoat*, Tim Rice and Andrew Lloyd Webber's unpretentious, joyous romp through the biblical story of Joseph, has delighted audiences in countless theatres around the world, grossing well over two hundred million pounds at the Box Office (not to mention video, CD and DVD sales). It is obviously a successful version of the Genesis story. But what kind of version is it, and what accounts for its remarkable success? Will any dream do? In seeking some answers to these questions, the essay considers how Rice and Webber have adapted and changed the biblical story, how they interpret certain key moments in the story, and what overall 'message' their version gives to its audiences.

Who but Joseph would have dreamed that the story of his life would become a hit musical? Yet *Joseph and the Amazing Technicolor Dreamcoat*, Tim Rice and Andrew Lloyd Webber's unpretentious romp through the biblical story of Joseph (Genesis 37–50), has delighted audiences in London's West End, on Broadway and in countless theatres around the world, grossing over two hundred million pounds at the box office. It continues to tour extensively (in Sheffield, where I live, it plays every year or so), and it returned to the West End in July of 2007, following a nine-week BBC television talent search to find a 'new Joseph'—the programme appropriately entitled 'Any Dream Will Do'.[1] Alongside its many professional productions, it enjoys immense popularity among amateur companies, with some 500 school or amateur productions each year in the United Kingdom and over 750 in the United States and Canada alone. According to one estimate, the show has

---

1. Hosted by Graham Norton, with Andrew Lloyd Webber and a panel of judges. The winner was Lee Mead, who won over ten thousand hopefuls, with more than three million votes cast during the series finale. Mead then played Joseph in the revival of *Dreamcoat* at the Adelphi Theatre for eighteen months, with his last of six hundred performances on January 9, 2009.

been performed in around 20,000 schools or local theatres, involving over 700,000 performers of all ages, with an audience of more than 9 million.[2] *Dreamcoat* fans can listen to it any time, choosing from at least twelve different cast albums, or view it on video or DVD in a production starring Donny Osmond as Joseph, Richard Attenborough as Jacob and Joan Collins (in a small, walk-on role) as Potiphar's wife. For some of the many people who have seen it, *Joseph and the Amazing Technicolor Dreamcoat* is the only version of the biblical story they know. So what kind of version is it? An obviously *successful* retelling of the Genesis story, how does it rate as a *retelling*?

In raising this question I am not interested in whether, in taking the biblical story to the stage, Rice and Webber 'got it right' or 'got it wrong', as if there is a right and wrong interpretation. The Joseph story is not straightforward, though it may seem so.[3] My interest lies, rather, in how Rice and Webber present the story to their audiences, what they add and leave out, what changes they make and the effect these changes have on the story, how they interpret certain key moments in the story and what overall 'message' their version gives to its audiences.[4]

Every production of *Dreamcoat* is unique; a gesture can make a difference (as, for example, when Joseph, having suggested to Pharaoh that someone should be placed in charge of arrangements for the famine, sings, 'But who this man could be, I just don't know', and points flamboyantly to himself). So can facial expression, an exaggerated reaction, or, as *Dreamcoat* audiences have come to expect, hamming it up. The simplicity of the setting and the props is part of the fun, and makes it easy for amateur com-

2. These statistics are from the official website of Andrew Lloyd Webber's Really Useful Group (www.reallyuseful.com), accessed November 2007. Other interesting statistics include: the show has played in 13 different countries, and in over 80 cities in the United States. The 1991 London Palladium production ran for two and a half years, attracting an audience of two million, and earning approximately fifty million pounds. The song 'Any Dream Will Do' was voted the Broadway Song of the Year in 1981. This information is no longer available on the website, which also offers merchandizing: one can purchase stuffed toys, T-shirts, mugs, backpacks, key rings, etc., and even a £250-musical MP3 bear designed by Steiff.

3. See, e.g., Donald B. Redford, *A Study of the Biblical Story of Joseph (Genesis 37–50)* (VTSup, 20; Leiden: Brill, 1970), pp. 66-87; Hugh C. White, *Narration and Discourse in the Book of Genesis* (Cambridge: Cambridge University Press, 1991), pp. 237-75; Meir Sternberg, *The Poetics of Biblical Narrative: Ideological Literature and the Drama of Reading* (Bloomington, IN: Indiana University Press, 1985), pp. 285-308; Laurence A. Turner, *Genesis* (Sheffield: Sheffield Academic Press, 2000), pp. 159-209.

4. *Dreamcoat* offers a contemporary counterpart to oratorio. Handel's biblical oratorios were immensely popular in their time, and they continue to be performed on stage, some more than others, though, unlike *Dreamcoat*, they do not lend themselves to amateur performances and school productions.

panies to produce. Even the film relies on cardboard backgrounds, stuffed sheep, and stuffed Ishmaelites on a stuffed camel.

Joseph's transition from biblical story to musical began when Andrew Lloyd Webber was invited to compose a 'pop cantata' for the school choir at Colet Court, St Paul's Junior School, Hammersmith. He asked Tim Rice to compose the lyrics, and their decision to make the story of Joseph their topic could be called an inspired choice. The first performance of *Joseph and the Amazing Technicolor Dreamcoat* took place on March 1, 1968, and was only twenty minutes long.[5] It enjoyed some success, more material was added; but real fame came in the wake of another of Rice and Webber's immensely popular contributions to the biblical cultural industry, *Jesus Christ Superstar*, which debuted on Broadway in 1971.[6] It is easy to see why *Dreamcoat* has enjoyed such popularity with amateur companies and, especially, school groups. The plot is the stuff of great children's literature: a spoiled youth (with dreams of greatness) is sold into slavery by his jealous half-brothers, but after much tribulation he rises to a position of power that enables him to teach his brothers a lesson before revealing his identity to them. That a ruler would appoint a slave as the lord of the land because he happens to be able to interpret his dream is the stuff of fairy tales. And regardless of what we think of Joseph's test of his brothers, there is something satisfying in seeing them receive payment in kind from their wronged brother, since their test ends in reconciliation.[7] But to what should we ascribe *Joseph and the Amazing Technicolor Dreamcoat*'s wider success, a success that is, well, amazing?

5. *Dreamcoat*'s early stages are by now well known (with numerous Wikipedia articles). Tim Rice offers a personal perspective in his autobiography, *Oh, What a Circus* (London: Coronet Books, 1999), pp. 131-58; see also the discussion of *Dreamcoat* in Ian Bradley, *You've Got to Have a Dream: The Message of the Musical* (London: SCM Press, 2004), pp. 108-21.

6. *Superstar* originally appeared as a record because producers were unwilling to take a chance on such a controversial version of the story.

7. It seems unnecessarily cruel to punish his brothers so severely (*Dreamcoat*'s version would be quite sufficient), and Joseph appears unconcerned about the father who doted on him, never considering that he might die before his brothers' long trial is over. Redford, e.g., calls Joseph 'stubborn, bullying' and a 'brow-beating tyrant who plays with his victims like a cat with a mouse' (*The Biblical Story of Joseph*, p. 103); Turner speaks of 'his bizarre toying with his brothers' and 'the sadistic nature of Joseph's charges' (see his discussion in *Genesis*, pp. 179-91 [187]); Sternberg (*Poetics*, p. 286) asks 'why does Joseph torment his brothers?' and maintains, 'Since this gap forces a choice between inference and incoherence, no reader can afford to ignore it'. Beginning with the premise that 'Joseph's rough handling of his brothers causes the reader no undue worry about their ultimate fate' (p. 285), he examines various motivations that scholars have posited for Joseph (punishing, testing, teaching and dream fulfilment) and finds all at work (pp. 285-308).

Publicity poster for the 2012 production, The Lyceum Theatre, Sheffield

Surely the answer lies largely in *Dreamcoat*'s lively and memorable tunes, witty lyrics and great plot. Performance also plays a role. Watching the video is nothing like seeing the show performed on the stage, where, with an enthusiastic and energetic cast and a receptive audience, the enthusiasm is infectious. It has become customary for the Finale to reprise most of the songs, and the audience sings along (sometimes this happens during the performance). This can go on for an irritatingly long time, yet you find yourself leaving the theatre humming the songs, even when you try to get them out of your mind. *Dreamcoat*'s popularity can also be attributed to the facts that it is not overtly religious and it does not take itself seriously. The Bible is mentioned only a few times, and not in a pious way,[8] and God is never mentioned by name, though there may be an allusion to God in one song.[9] Since *Dreamcoat* retells a biblical story, some members of the audi-

8. In the songs 'Jacob and Sons' ('Way way back many centuries ago, not long after the Bible began / Jacob lived in the land of Canaan'); 'Potiphar' ('It's all there in chapter thirty-nine of Genesis'); 'Go, go, go, Joseph' ('Don't give up, Joseph, fight till you drop / We've read the book and you come out on top'); 'Those Canaan Days' ('Do you remember those wonderful parties? . . . The gayest the Bible has seen').

9. 'Close Every Door'. *Dreamcoat* could be said to resemble the biblical story, with its 'stress on God's hidden all-causality', well sketched by Ronald M. Hals, *The Theology of the Book of Ruth* (Facet Books Biblical Series, 23; Philadelphia, PA: Fortress Press, 1969), pp. 34-44; but note that, whereas the narrator tells us that God was with Joseph (39.2, 3, 21), blessed others because of Joseph (39.5) and made whatever he did prosper

ence might be inclined to find in it a religious dimension, but *Dreamcoat* never preaches to the audience and, because it does not take itself seriously, the audience need not do so either. There are many opportunities for hamming it up, with, among others, great roles for a good Elvis impersonator as Pharaoh and for an actor who can bring out the vamp in Potiphar's wife (like Joan Collins in the video). It's all good, clean fun, a 'classical family musical', as the jacket copy of the video describes it. Rather than any overtly religious message, *Dreamcoat* offers its audiences a feel-good message to go away with after the feel-good experience of the performance: 'You've got to have a dream, if you don't have a dream, how you gonna make a dream come true?'[10]

Dreamcoat's message is a far cry from the affirmation of the biblical story that everything that has happened is according to the plan of God for Israel's survival, or, as Joseph puts it, 'God sent me ahead of you to preserve for you a remnant on earth, and to save your lives by a great deliverance. So it was not you who sent me here, but God, and he has made me a father to Pharaoh and lord of all his house and ruler over all the land of Egypt' (Gen. 45.7-8).

Joseph and the Amazing Technicolor Dreamcoat brings the Bible into the modern world without its complexity or ambiguity (though it hints at these). Although it shows us low points in Joseph's life, the musical always has the positive outcome in mind. It maintains an upbeat mood, even in what are times of crisis for the protagonists, by diverting our attention from the seriousness of the situation with lively music and clever lyrics. At what in the biblical story are truly low points, Rice and Webber play with musical genres for their entertainment value, and in stage productions these become occasions for reprises of the lyrics accompanied by elaborately choreographed dancing.[11] When, for example, Jacob learns of Joseph's death in the biblical account, he is inconsolable: 'I shall go down to Sheol to my

(39.23), the crucial interpretation of the meaning of the events is placed in Joseph's mouth (45.5-8; 50.19-20). For Hals, 'it is absolutely out of the question to doubt that here the storyteller, and not just Joseph, is expressing his own view' (p. 35), both because of the strategic place of Joseph's declarations in the structure of the narrative and the fact that other major characters express the same view. Still, one could ask what this tells us about the character of Joseph and to what extent he and the narrator share the same point of view; see Yiu-Wing Fung, *Victim and Victimizer: Joseph's Interpretation of his Destiny* (JSOTSup, 308; Sheffield: Sheffield Academic Press, 2000).

10. These words, of course, are not from *Dreamcoat* but from another musical, Rogers and Hammerstein's *South Pacific*, but they capture the message of *Dreamcoat* perfectly.

11. Webber and Rice also play with musical genre to describe the crisis of the famine: Pharaoh's dream about the famine becomes an Elvis-Presley-style rock song ('Pharaoh's Story') and the situation of famine in Canaan is the subject of a French chanson ('Those Canaan Days').

son, mourning' (37.35). Rice and Webber turn the incident into a raucous Country and Western hoedown, in which the brothers, with tongue-in-cheek, seem to mourn, while actually celebrating, Joseph's death. 'There's one more angel in heaven', they tell their father, but 'let no tear be shed', for the things that Joseph stood for 'like truth and light never die'. At the lowest point in his fortune, when Joseph has been thrown into prison and sings the only heartrending song in the show ('Close Every Door'), he is consoled by the narrator and ensemble with the disco beat of 'Go, Go, Go, Joseph' ('Don't give up Joseph, fight till you drop. We've read the book and you come out on top'), and the prison is transformed into a discothèque. Another anxiety-arousing episode, when Joseph's cup is discovered in Benjamin's sack, after the sacks of all the other brothers have proved to contain only grain, is alleviated by the brothers' defence of Benjamin's innocence in a calypso: 'Oh no, not he/ How you can accuse him is a mystery / Save him, take me / Benjamin is straighter than the tall palm tree'.

Not only do we never have cause to worry very much about Joseph's future. Rice and Webber also soften the harshness of Joseph's test of his brothers by compressing the two visits they pay to Egypt in the biblical account into one, so that everything happens quickly, with the minimum of distress to all. As a result, Joseph does not appear so cruel as in the biblical story. The audience is spared the brothers' three-day ordeal in prison (42.17), their distress when Joseph demands that one of them remain in Egypt until Benjamin is brought before him (42.18-22), their dismay when they discover their money in their sacks ('What is this that God has done to us?', 42.28), Jacob's initial refusal to let Benjamin go back with them to Egypt and acquiescence only when there is no choice (42.36–43.14), the brothers' anxiety when they are brought to Joseph's house (43.18-19), Joseph's weeping (43.30), the brothers' dismay when Joseph's cup is found in Benjamin's sack (44.13), their guilt and fear that they will all be made slaves (44.16), Joseph's demand for Benjamin and Judah's touching plea to be allowed to take Benjamin's place (44.18-34), Joseph's inability to control himself any longer and the brothers' dismay when they learn his identity (45.1). Not least, Rice and Webber omit the ending, in which Joseph the former slave enslaves the Egyptians, which would definitely tarnish his 'nice guy' stage image.

The Tale of a Dreamer like You

Only by examining all the songs in *Joseph and the Amazing Technicolor Dreamcoat* can one appreciate the genius of this remarkable, and remarkably successful, musical version of the story of Joseph. *Joseph and the Amazing Technicolor Dreamcoat* owes its wonderful plot to the biblical story, with its many interesting episodes and its satisfying, balanced resolution.

Interestingly, Rice reports that his principal source text was not the Bible but *The Wonder Book of Bible Stories*.[12] Rice keeps things simple, and his lyrics are extremely effective in telling the story. There are few additions (apart from the Prologue and Finale, only two songs, 'Close Every Door' and 'Pharaoh's Story', do not represent incidents in the biblical text), some omissions (notably the brothers' second visit to Egypt in Genesis 43 and the events of chaps. 47–50), and few changes, though one of them (having only one visit by the brothers instead of two) is particularly significant for its effect on the story the musical tells. In order to show just how well *Dreamcoat* re-presents the biblical story, in what follows I discuss its treatment of the plot in some detail. As in the biblical story, characterization in *Dreamcoat* is less important than plot. Does Joseph change as a result of his experiences? What has he learned? And what about his brothers? Have they learned a lesson, and how have they changed by the end? To be sure, the biblical text leaves more room for speculation about character than the musical.[13] Although I will not consider such questions in depth, I will make some comments on characterization in the course of the discussion below.

It might help at the outset to give some idea of what parts of the biblical story are represented by the individual songs in *Dreamcoat*.

	Prologue Any Dream Will Do
Genesis 37	Jacob and Sons Joseph's Coat Joseph's Dreams Poor, Poor Joseph One More Angel in Heaven
Genesis 39	Potiphar Close Every Door
Genesis 40	Go, Go, Go, Joseph Pharaoh's Story
Genesis 41	Poor, Poor Pharaoh Song of the King Pharaoh's Dream Explained Stone the Crows

12. Rice, *Oh, What a Circus*, pp. 132-33.

13. Sternberg, *Poetics*, pp. 291-308, offers a detailed discussion of the changes undergone by Joseph as well as his brothers; see also White, *Narration and Discourse*, pp. 256-61.

Genesis 42	Those Canaan Days
42 combined with 44	The Brothers Come to Egypt
	Grovel, Grovel
Genesis 44	Who's the Thief?
	Benjamin Calypso

| Genesis 45 | Joseph All the Time |

| Genesis 46 | Jacob in Egypt |

| | Finale: Any Dream Will Do/ |
| | Give Me My Colored Coat |

Prologue; Any Dream Will Do

The biblical story is told by an omniscient narrator. Rice and Webber's use of a narrator to provide essential information enables them to tell the story in greater detail and to make the transitions from one episode to another smoothly. The narrator's lyrics carry the storyline, setting the scene and explaining what is happening. The narrator not only tells (that is, sings) the story to the audience, she also participates in what happens on stage, singing and dancing along with the characters and the ensemble.[14] Narrator and, in many productions, ensemble, which usually includes children, comment on events. Their presence is recognized by the characters, though not as part of the story. Typically members of the ensemble wear modern dress, which draws attention to the musical's status as a production taking place in the present for a modern audience (the film emphasizes this by using a school auditorium setting, with the teachers taking on roles as major characters).

The first song belongs to the narrator, who invites the audience to hear the story of 'a boy whose dream came true', and identify with him: 'And it could be you'. The narrator sings of people who have dreams and people who don't, and, although the narrator claims not to judge who is wrong and who is right, the assumption is that you should have a dream, and probably you do have one (though you may be too shy to admit it), since the story you are about to watch and hear is about 'a dreamer like you'.

Dreaming, as its title suggests, is a key theme in *Joseph and the Amazing Technicolor Dreamcoat*; twelve of the twenty-three songs mention dreams. But *Dreamcoat* gives the concept of dreaming two different meanings, only one of which is the sense it has in the biblical text. In the biblical text, dreams

---

14. Before 1978 the narrator's part was sung by a man; after 1978 by a woman.

are sent by God.[15] They foretell the future, future events that will come to pass regardless of what the dreamer might do. Not only Joseph's dreams but also the butler's, the baker's and the pharaoh's dreams come true.[16] Pharaoh's dreams of seven years of plenty followed by seven years of famine, for example, are realized; it is only through Joseph's interpretation of their meaning that he is able to avert disaster. Whereas *Dreamcoat* treats the dreams of the butler, baker and Pharaoh in the same way as the biblical text, it assigns a different significance to Joseph's dreams: 'if you think it, want it, dream it, then it's real / You are what you feel'. Dreaming becomes more than something that takes place when you sleep, dreams are goals. They are conscious, wishes you want to come true, ambitions you may have. *Dreamcoat*'s facile message that 'you are what you feel' has been called 'a terse statement of western relativist values'.[17] Wanting something, having a dream, will not make it real, though it may help you achieve your goals, depending on what those goals are. *Dreamcoat*'s Joseph may be 'a dreamer like you', but the biblical Joseph, who interprets what happens to him as part of a grand design, is not ('God sent me before you to preserve life', 45.5).

If we had any doubt about *Dreamcoat*'s message, the second song, 'Any Dream Will Do', sung by Joseph and the ensemble, makes it clear. Now no one thinks for a moment that Rice and Webber mean literally that any dream will do. What if you dream of making a lot of money through extortion? Or if you dream of revenge? What if you dream of being a suicide bomber to avenge wrongs inflicted upon your people? Who is to say which dreams will do and which will not? Rice and Webber have something different in mind, a feel-good message. You don't have to dream (as Joseph did) of being a ruler, or of being a world leader or a Nobel Prize winner or a pop star, the important thing is to have a goal for your life, something to strive for.[18]

---

15. On the nature of Joseph's dreams and Joseph as diviner, see Ron Pirson, *The Lord of the Dreams: A Semantic and Literary Analysis of Genesis 37–50* (JSOTSup, 355; London: Sheffield Academic Press, 2002), pp. 41-59, 86-90; and for developments in his reputation as a diviner, see Ljubica Jovanović, *The Joseph of Genesis as Hellenistic Scientist* (Hebrew Bible Monographs, 48; Sheffield: Sheffield Phoenix Press, 2013).

16. Joseph's dream that his father and mother and eleven brothers bow down to him (Gen. 37.9) does not precisely come true. On Rachel's 'presence' in the story, see Jürgen Ebach, *Genesis 37–50* (Herders Theologischer Kommentar zum Alten Testament; Freiburg: Herder, 2007), pp. 68-69. The text does not explicitly attribute Joseph's dreams to God.

17. Terence Copley, 'Children "Theologising" in Religious Education', *Education Today* 51 (2001), pp. 3-7; cited by Bradley, *You've Got to Have a Dream*, p. 120.

18. Whether *Dreamcoat*'s Joseph strives to fulfil his dreams of grandeur or succeeds simply because, as he puts it in 'Stone the Crows', 'Anyone from anywhere can make it / if they get a lucky break', is an interesting question.

In 'Any Dream Will Do', Joseph and the ensemble sing not only of having a dream but also of Joseph's wonderful multicoloured coat, which is snatched from him. If putting a narrator in the story was a inspired invention, the dreamcoat is another. Like dreaming, the coat takes on major significance in the musical. Whereas the coat in the biblical story is tangible evidence that Joseph is his father's favourite and provides the evidence by which Jacob recognizes that his favourite son has been killed, the coat in *Dreamcoat* serves as a concrete image of Joseph's dreams. He will call for it in the Finale, when he will repeat the song 'Any Dream Will Do'. Here at the beginning of *Dreamcoat*, the song seems to anticipate events to come, allusively and enigmatically in dreamlike fashion. Joseph sings of wearing his wonderful coat, when, suddenly, 'a crash of drums, a flash of light / My golden coat flew out of sight', leaving him alone. He concludes:

> May I return to the beginning,
> The light is dimming, and the dream is too.
> The world and I, we are still waiting,
> Still hesitating,
> Any dream will do.

As in a dream, the meaning of the details in 'Any Dream Will Do' is not transparent. Why is he, and the world with him, hesitating? For what are they waiting? According to Rice, the song's message is 'expressed in deliberately obscure terms', and his explanation of it should caution us against trying to read too much into his lyrics:

> The coat is the dream and the singer is only truly happy when he is asleep, when he can 'draw back the curtain' and see colours that are 'wonderful and new'. When he awakes he only wants to 'return to the beginning' of his dream.[19]

Jacob and Sons; Joseph's Coat; Joseph's Dreams; Poor, Poor Joseph; One More Angel in Heaven (Genesis 37)

The biblical story of Joseph begins with the words, 'These are the generations of Jacob'. The Bible devotes twelve chapters to the story of Jacob, who personifies Israel and whose sons are the eponymous ancestors of the twelve tribes (Genesis 25–36). Rice and Webber manage to set the stage with one song. 'Jacob and Sons' locates the story in time ('many centuries ago, not long after the Bible began')[20] and place ('in the land of Canaan') and identifies Jacob as the founder of the nation Israel. It tells us that they

---

19. Rice, *Oh, What a Circus*, p. 141.
20. Since the story takes place 'not long after the Bible began', if one did not know where to find it, one would look for it in the early chapters of the Bible.

lived by farming and raising sheep, and it introduces the twelve sons of Israel, who will play a major role in the tale, starting with Reuben, the eldest, and 'the next in line', Simeon and Levi.[21] There is the hint, then, that Reuben, as the firstborn, should be his father's successor and his father's favourite. In the biblical story, the first word after the introductory 'these are the generations of Jacob' is 'Joseph', indicating that Joseph is the favoured son, favoured by both Jacob and God. The next verse makes Jacob's preference for Joseph explicit: 'Israel loved Joseph more than all his other sons' (Gen. 37.3). Rice and Webber show Joseph's prominence by doing just the opposite, naming the other brothers first, 'which leaves only one'. The most important one, and last to be mentioned, is 'Joseph, Jacob's favourite son'.

With 'Joseph's Coat' we learn more about the situation: Jacob's excessive love for Joseph because he was the son of his favourite wife, the effect of this favouritism on Jacob's other sons ('it made the rest feel second best'), the danger of such favouritism and Jacob's blindness to the problem ('he could not imagine any danger'). Jacob, too, has dreams, dreams that seem to be realized in Joseph: 'He just saw in Joseph all his dreams come true'. All this is much more lighthearted than the biblical text, which draws a stark contrast between the father's love and the brothers' hatred:

> Israel loved Joseph more than all his other sons because he was the son of his old age, and he made him an ornamented robe.[22] But when his brothers saw that their father loved him more than all his brothers, they hated him and could not speak peaceably to him (37.3).

Dreamcoat makes the brothers' jealousy appear less severe, and the brothers more likeable. Although they are jealous ('Being told we're also-rans / Does not make us Joseph fans'), they are actually 'great guys but no one seems to notice'. The special robe, which in *Dreamcoat*, following a long tradition represented by the King James Version,[23] is a coat of many colours, a tangible sign of their father's favouritism that arouses the brothers' envy:

---

21. After that, the order in which they appear in the song corresponds to neither the story of their births in Genesis 29–30 nor the deathbed speech of Jacob in Genesis 49.

22. Following E.A. Speiser, who translates 'ornamented tunic', based on an Akkadian cognate (*Genesis* [Anchor Bible, 1; Garden City, NY: Doubleday, 1964], pp. 287, 289-90). The phrase *ketonet passim* appears elsewhere only in 2 Sam. 13.18-19, in reference to a garment worn by unmarried daughters of the king. Whatever the precise meaning, there is obviously something exceptional about the robe, since it arouses the brothers' jealousy.

23. As suggested by the Septuagint's *chitona poikilon* and Vulgate's *tunicam polymitam*. Some exegetes opt for 'a long robe' or 'a robe with sleeves' or 'a long robe with sleeves' (NRSV). Manfred Görg posits a connection to Egyptian *psj* (*kochen, färben*) and argues for a meaning 'coloured stuff' ('Der gefärbte Rock Josefs', *Biblische Notizen* 102 [2000], pp. 9-13); so the traditional 'coat of many colours' may be right. Ebach (*Genesis 37–50*, p. 60) acknowledges the various possibilities when he describes the

We had never liked him
All that much before.
And now this coat
Has got our goat.
We feel life is unfair.

If the biblical Joseph seems like a spoiled brat, in *Dreamcoat* he is something of a dandy:

I look handsome, I look smart;
I am a walking work of art.
Such a dazzling coat of many colors.
How I love my coat of many colors.

And how can the audience not take pleasure in it too, given the magnificence of the coat, the music and the lyrics?

It was red and yellow and green and brown
And scarlet and black and ochre and peach
And ruby and olive and violet and fawn
And lilac and gold and chocolate and mauve
And cream and crimson and silver and rose
And azure and lemon and russet and grey
And purple and white and pink and orange
And red and yellow and green and brown
Scarlet and black and ochre and peach
And ruby and olive and violet and fawn
And lilac and gold and chocolate and mauve
And cream and crimson and silver and rose
And azure and lemon and russet and grey
And purple and white and pink and orange
And blue.[24]

Whereas Genesis 37 reports that Joseph's brothers 'hated him even more' because of his dreams (vv. 5, 8, 11), matters are less serious in *Dreamcoat*, where the brothers are 'annoyed' and 'mad' and worried about the possible accuracy of Joseph's dreams.[25] Is the biblical Joseph a bit naïve to taunt

garment as 'ein knöchellanges, mit Ärmeln versehenes, vermutlich buntes Festgewand' (a long festive garment with sleeves, possibly many coloured).

24. Rice reports that this marvellous list of colours was put together by the class at Colet Court, for whom *Dreamcoat* was originally composed (*Oh, What a Circus*, p. 133).

25. The brothers hate Joseph because of his dreams, but do they consider them to be prophetic? Apparently not in the biblical story, where they believe that disposing of the dreamer will solve the problem of his dreams: 'Come now, let us kill him and throw him into one of the pits. Then we shall say that a wild beast has devoured him. We shall see what will become of his dreams' (37.20). (Ironically, they are actually saying more than they know.) *Dreamcoat* reflects this attitude in 'Joseph's Dreams': 'The accuracy of the dreams / We brothers do not know / But one thing we are sure about / The dreamer

them with his accounts of his dreams? Rice and Webber raise this possibility, both by Joseph's words ('My sheaf was quite a sight to see, / A golden sheaf and tall / Yours were green and second-rate / And really rather small'; 'Could it be that I was born / For higher things than you?') and his brothers' response, 'Not only is he tactless but he's also rather dim / For there's eleven of us and there's only one of him'. They conclude that 'the dreamer has to go', and, so the narrator informs us ('Poor, Poor Joseph'), on the 'next day, far from home / The brothers planned the repulsive crime'. This unsavoury act is treated much more concisely in *Dreamcoat* than in the biblical account; there is no objection by Reuben or Judah to shedding their brother's blood.

> *Brothers*: Let us grab him now
> Do him in, while we've got the time.
> *Narrator*: This they did and made the most of it
> Tore his coat and flung him in a pit.
> *Brothers*: Let us leave him here
> All alone and he's bound to die.
> *Narrator*: Then some Ishmaelites
> A hairy crew came riding by
> In a flash the brothers changed their plan.
> *Brothers*: We need cash.
> Let's sell him if we can.

As the narrator and ensemble point out, things look bad for Joseph. They pass judgment on the brothers, who tear Joseph's coat, attack a passing stuffed goat and smear the coat with its blood: 'You make a sordid group, hey, how low can you stoop?' But Joseph's plight is never allowed to become too serious. The entire episode is recounted with a light touch, as, for example, when the narrator observes that being sold as a slave and taken to Egypt 'wouldn't be a picnic he could tell', and Joseph adds, 'And I don't speak Egyptian very well'.

'One More Angel in Heaven', as noted above, takes one of the narrative's most distressing moments and recasts it with great fanfare as a celebratory song and dance with a hokey Western theme ('So long, little Joe, adios, buckeroo'). In the biblical story, the brothers bring the blood-stained coat to their father, and he draws his own conclusion: 'It is my son's robe; a wild beast has devoured him. Joseph has been torn to pieces' (v. 33). Here they tell him, but in a way that is so far-fetched, so exaggerated, that it becomes

---

has to go!' At the same time, however, they are apprehensive, voicing what the audience knows—they will come true: 'The dreams of course will not come true / That is, we think they won't come true / That is, we hope they won't come true / What if he's right all along?'

funny, rather than, as Reuben asserts, 'a tragic but inspiring tale of manhood in its prime'. What happened? Reuben or Levi sings the lead:

> When I think of his last great battle
> A lump comes to my throat
> It takes a man who knows no fear
> To wrestle with a goat.

The other brothers chime in, assuring Jacob that Joseph would not want him to grieve. He is now an angel in heaven, and 'his soul's in paradise', concepts quite alien to the biblical story but reassuring to the unhappy father. There may be (they sing) one more tear in his eye, and theirs, but theirs are crocodile tears, and the lively music and enthusiastic singing and dancing guarantee that the audience will not be shedding any tears.

Potiphar (Genesis 39)

Dreamcoat skips over the story of Judah and Tamar in Genesis 38, which, however important to the Joseph story it may be, seems to interrupt the flow of the plot.[26] *Dreamcoat* is only slightly terser than the biblical account in making the transition from Canaan to Egypt.

> Joseph was taken down to Egypt, and Potiphar, an officer of Pharaoh, the captain of the guard, an Egyptian, bought him from the Ishmaelites who had brought him there (39.1).[27]

> *Narrator*: Joseph was taken to Egypt in chains and sold/ Where he was bought by a captain named Potiphar.

Dreamcoat's Potiphar is one of Egypt's millionaires, having made a fortune buying shares. In pyramids. Joseph is a slave who 'liked his master' and advances because he 'was a cut above the average'. In the biblical story, in contrast, Potiphar prospers because God causes all that Joseph does to prosper. Consequently Potiphar elevates Joseph to the position of overseer of his

---

26. The relationship of Genesis 38 to the rest of the Joseph story has long been debated. Is it an insertion? An interlude? An essential part of the story? See, *inter alia*, Gerhard von Rad, *Genesis: A Commentary* (trans. John H. Marks; Philadelphia, PA: Westminster Press, 1961), p. 351; Claus Westermann, *Genesis 37–50* (trans. John J. Scullion; Minneapolis, MN: Augsburg, 1986), p. 49; Victor P. Hamilton, *The Book of Genesis: Chapters 18–50* (Grand Rapids, MI: Eerdmans, 1995), p. 431; Gordon J. Wenham, *Genesis 16–50* (Word Biblical Commentary, 2; Dallas, TX: Word Books, 1994), pp. 363-65; Ebach, *Genesis 37–50*, pp. 119-21; and, on Genesis 38 as an integral part of the larger narrative, the classic study of U. Cassuto, 'The Story of Tamar and Judah', in his *Biblical and Oriental Studies, Volume 1: Bible* (Jerusalem: Magnes Press, 1973), pp. 29-40.

27. The same information appears in Gen. 37.36, thus providing a frame for the interlude in chap. 38.

house (39.2-6). Joseph is in charge of everything; the only thing Potiphar keeps back from him is his wife, says Joseph (v. 9).

Joseph is a handsome man, and, after some time, Potiphar's wife desires him: 'Lie with me' (v. 7). She attempts to get Joseph to have sex with her, he refuses and she falsely accuses him of assault, which lands him in prison (vv. 7-20). But *Dreamcoat* tells a different story. For one thing, its version is highly condensed; for another, it prejudges Potiphar's wife, based on stereotypes of the biblical figure: 'she was beautiful but evil, saw a lot of men against [Potiphar's] will'—a picture that in no respect corresponds to anything in the biblical story.[28] Potiphar's wife is given only one line, 'Come and lie with me, love'. Joseph's response is nothing like his objection in the text, when he refuses to 'do this great evil and sin against God' (v. 9); rather, Rice and Webber aim for humour: 'Please stop, I don't believe in free love'.

The entire scene offers an opportunity on stage for the performers to enjoy hamming it up. Potiphar's wife is played as a vamp, whose exaggerated overtures can include pinching Joseph's bottom and blowing in his ear. While performances differ, often her attendants start undressing Joseph and stroking him (discreetly, of course). Potiphar is counting shekels in his den below the bedroom (not away from the house, as in Gen. 39.16), hears the 'mighty rumpus', bursts through the door and cries, 'Joseph, I'll see you rot in jail / The things you have done are beyond the pale'. There is no accusation of Joseph by Potiphar's wife, no garment left behind as evidence. In *Dreamcoat*, in spite of his demurral, Joseph can be played as enjoying the proceedings, though they are hardly serious enough to land him in prison.

Close Every Door

In prison Joseph sings one of the two songs in the musical that does not correspond to an episode in the text. As a rule, *Dreamcoat*, like the biblical story, is less interested in characterization than plot. Here, however, by focusing on Joseph's reaction to being thrown into prison, it fills a gap in the biblical story, which is not interested in Joseph's feelings but only in the

---

28. For important critical readings of the biblical account, see Mieke Bal, 'Myth *à la lettre*: Freud, Mann, Genesis and Rembrandt, and the Story of the Son', in *Discourse in Psychoanalysis and Literature* (ed. Shlomith Rimmon-Kenan; London: Methuen, 1987), pp. 57-89; Alice Bach, *Women, Seduction, and Betrayal in Biblical Narrative* (Cambridge: Cambridge University Press, 1997), pp. 38-65 *et passim*. On retellings of the story, see Bach, *Women, Seduction and Betrayal*, pp. 82-127; Athalya Brenner and Jan Willem van Henten, 'Madame Potiphar through a Culture Trip, or, Which Side Are You On?', in *Biblical Studies/Cultural Studies: The Third Sheffield Colloquium* (ed. J. Cheryl Exum and Stephen D. Moore; Sheffield: Sheffield Academic Press, 1998), pp. 203-19; Bernhard Lang, *Joseph in Egypt: A Cultural Icon from Grotius to Goethe* (New Haven, CT: Yale University Press, 2009), pp. 115-76.

fact that God was with him. But that is not all. For the first and only time *Dreamcoat* becomes serious, as it looks beyond itself with what could be seen as an allusion to the Holocaust.[29] 'Close Every Door' also contains a rare allusion to God:[30]

> If my life were important I
> Would ask will I live or die
> But I know the answers lie
> Far from this world.

The melody is haunting, the lyrics sombre, as Joseph, no longer the rather flat character he has been up to this point, sings of his feelings of abandonment. Earlier he could be self-centred and brash ('I look handsome, I look smart, I am a walking work of art'). Now he seems almost out of character as he becomes introspective and philosophical:

> Just give me a number
> Instead of my name
> Forget all about me
> And let me decay
> I do not matter
> I'm only one person
> Destroy me completely
> Then throw me away.

But lest Joseph seem too downcast, the mood of *Dreamcoat* become too serious and the audience begin to worry, the song has a countertheme:

> Children of Israel
> Are never alone
> For I know I shall find
> My own peace of mind
> For I have been promised
> A land of my own.[31]

---

29. There is a curious allusion to the Holocaust, the rhyming of shoah with Noah, in 'Stone the Crows', where Joseph is called the 'greatest man since Noah / Only goes to shoah'.

30. Rice says that 'even in our light-hearted re-telling of [the story] the presence of God is inescapable' (*Oh, What a Circus*, p. 134); Bradley rightly disagrees, though he thinks that 'far from being inescapable, the presence of God is completely missing' (*You've Got to Have a Dream*, p. 114).

31. Interestingly, in the biblical text, the so-called promises to the fathers of land and descendants are repeated to Abraham, Isaac and Jacob, but not to Joseph or any of Jacob's sons, though they are, of course, clearly the recipients of the promises. The musical replaces God's loyalty to Joseph with Joseph's faith in God.

'Close Every Door' combines despondency with assurance. The promised land is a source of hope, and 'children of Israel are never alone', a
declaration of faith (and a further allusion to God that calls to mind the
biblical text's 'the Lord was with Joseph and showed him loyalty', 39.21).
The final chorus, in which Joseph is joined by the ensemble, becomes 'For
we know we shall find / Our own peace of mind / For we have been promised / A land of our own'. In the film version, the children in the ensemble
are schoolchildren in an auditorium, both watching and participating in the
performance. In this scene the auditorium is darkened, and they all hold
candles. Joining in the song, they walk slowly onto the stage, and, in an act
of solidarity, surround Joseph in his prison cell, offering him comfort.

Go, Go, Go, Joseph (Genesis 40)

The next song brings the mood back full circle to one of gaiety. Joseph is
encouraged by fellow prisoners with 'Hey dreamer, don't be so upset' and
'Hey Joseph, you're not beaten yet', and by the narrator and ensemble with
'Don't give up Joseph, fight till you drop / We've read the book and you
come out on top'. All this, of course, changes the way we look at the imprisonment: it is only a temporary setback, not a cause for despair.

Succinctly but effectively the lyrics tell the story of the butler's and the
baker's dreams and their interpretation. The only reason the biblical text
gives for their imprisonment is that 'the butler of the king of Egypt and
his baker offended their lord the king of Egypt' (40.1), which Rice captures nicely with 'Both men were servants of Pharaoh the king / Both in
the doghouse for doing their thing'. In the biblical story they are in prison
for some time before their sleep is disturbed by dreams that leave them
troubled because 'there is no one to interpret them'. Joseph replies, 'Do not
interpretations belong to God? Tell them to me, please' (v. 8). Later, when
he is brought before Pharaoh, he will again attribute his ability to interpret
dreams to God ('Not I; God will give Pharaoh a favourable answer', 41.16).
In *Dreamcoat* the explicit attribution of the interpretation of dreams to God
is not made, and Joseph seems initially slightly tentative about his abilities:
'Though I cannot guarantee / To get it right, I'll have a go'. As in the biblical
text, the butler tells his dream first and hears its favourable interpretation;
then the baker, 'hoping it would have a similar theme', tells his (an admi-
rable rendering of 'When the chief baker saw that the interpretation was
favourable, he said to Joseph, "I also had a dream"', v. 16). The bad news
that 'your execution date is set' is somewhat offset by 'Don't rely on all I
said I saw'. But the next line, 'It's just that I have not been wrong before',
shows that Joseph is not so tentative about his abilities. On stage, the baker
typically faints upon hearing this.

In *Dreamcoat* Joseph never protests his innocence (what would he be
protesting?) nor complains about being sold into slavery, as he does in the

biblical text when he asks the butler to remember him and bring his plight to Pharaoh's attention: 'For I was indeed stolen out of the land of the Hebrews, and here also I have done nothing that they should have put me into the dungeon' (40.15).[32] Why at this point in the biblical narrative Joseph thinks being mentioned to Pharaoh will get him out of prison is not clear. The butler does remember Joseph and mentions him to Pharaoh, just not right away; it happens at the logical place in the plot. That it is two years before Pharaoh has a dream that will require Joseph's interpretation seems unnecessarily long; no wonder *Dreamcoat* gives the impression that little time has passed.

'Go, Go, Go, Joseph' is a victory celebration even before Joseph is released from prison to appear before Pharaoh. As the disco theme becomes ever stronger and the prison becomes a discothèque with strobe lights, populated by singers and dancers in wild costumes, the dreamcoat reappears in the lyrics to symbolize the realization of Joseph's dreams. Dancing and singing, the energetic ensemble repeats enthusiastically:

> Go, go, go, go, Joseph, you know what they say
> Hang on now Joseph, you'll make it some day
> Sha la la Joseph, you're doing fine
> You and your dreamcoat ahead of your time.

Pharaoh's Story

Although it does little to advance the plot, 'Pharaoh's Story' provides background information for the audience and sets the stage for what follows. It also, since it comes between Joseph's interpretation of the butler's and baker's dreams and the report of Pharaoh's dream, provides some suggestion of the passage of time. Pharaoh is introduced as 'a powerful man / With the ancient world / In the palm of his hand', and the audience learns that 'strange as it seems / There's been a run of crazy dreams', which keeps the dream theme in the foreground. There is a clever allusion to Gen. 39.21-23 in the narrator's description of Joseph's time in prison: 'For even though he is / In with the guards / A lifetime in prison / Seems quite on the cards'. Nevertheless, the narrator and ensemble see a glimmer of light at the end of the tunnel:

> A man who can interpret
> Could go far
> Could become a star . . .
> Could be a big success
> Could be famous
> Could be a star.

---

32. He is noticeably vague about the circumstances when he speaks of being 'stolen out of the land of the Hebrews' and not sold into slavery by his brothers.

Poor, Poor Pharaoh; Song of the King; Pharaoh's Dream Explained;
Stone the Crows (Genesis 41)
The biblical text launches immediately into Pharaoh's dream: 'After two
whole years, Pharaoh dreamed that he was standing by the Nile . . .' (v. 1).
'Poor, Poor Pharaoh' tells only about the dream, not about its contents:

> *Narrator*: Guess what?
> In his bed Pharaoh
> Had an uneasy night
> He had had a dream that pinned him
> To his sheets with fright.
> No one knew the meaning of this dream
> What to do, whatever could it mean.

The butler says that Joseph could explain its meaning. Because there is no
mention of the butler having forgotten Joseph or of the time that has passed
since Joseph interpreted the butler's and the baker's dreams, Joseph's time
in prison seems much shorter—in fact, extremely short—in *Dreamcoat* than
in the biblical story, where God lets him remain in prison for some time.
This not only makes Joseph's ordeal less onerous, it makes God look better.
The narrative and ensemble show some sympathy for Pharaoh that recalls
their earlier sympathy for Joseph when he was sold into slavery ('Poor, poor
Joseph, what'cha gonna do? / Things look bad for you, hey, what'cha gonna
do?') and when he was imprisoned ('Poor, poor Joseph, locked up in a cell /
Things ain't going well, hey, locked up in a cell'):

> Poor, poor Pharaoh
> What'cha gonna do?
> Dreams are haunting you, hey
> What'cha gonna do?

The solution is at hand. Joseph is brought before Pharaoh, 'chained, bound,
afraid and alone', and not, as in the biblical story, having had his hair cut
and changed his clothes (41.14; Pharaoh's attendants will change his clothes
on stage when Joseph is made overseer of Egypt).

Pharaoh's dream ('Song of the King') is often a show stopper. Pharaoh, dressed like Elvis Presley, sings an Elvis-style song, with a reaction
of swooning and adoration from his court. The details of the dream are all
there in an entertaining song that includes such allusions to Elvis songs as
'don't be cruel', 'all shook up' and 'treat me nice'. Rice and Webber are
also on form with 'Pharaoh's Dream Explained'. Following seven surplus
years, 'Egypt's luck will change completely overnight /And famine's hand
will stalk the land'. Whereas the biblical story has Joseph repeatedly affirm
that God has revealed to Pharaoh what he is about to do (vv. 16, 25, 28, 32),
Rice has Joseph sum it up nicely in a way that, at least on the surface, seems
to credit Joseph for the interpretation:

> Noble king, there is no doubt
> What your dreams are all about
> All these things you saw in your pajamas
> Are a long range forecast for your farmers.

Joseph, accompanied by the ensemble, suggests the solution, an overseer to lead Egypt through the years of famine. Although Joseph sings, 'who this man could be I just don't know', there is an opportunity in performance for him to point to himself, giving Pharaoh the idea of appointing Joseph as his 'number two' in the song 'Stone the Crows'.[33]

Narrator and ensemble report the seven years of plenty and of famine, but what happens to the Egyptians is a far cry from the biblical story, according to which Joseph makes slaves of the Egyptians, first selling them grain and then, when their money is gone, trading them food for their cattle, horses, donkeys, flocks and herds, and then for themselves.[34] Joseph the former slave who makes slaves of others is not the Joseph of *Dreamcoat*. In *Dreamcoat* 'the first recorded rationing in history was a hit', and the Egyptians fawn over their saviour:

> Joseph how can we ever say
> All that we want to about you
> We're so glad that you came our way
> We would have perished without you.

To which Joseph replies modestly, 'Anyone from anywhere can make it / If they get a lucky break'—a far more cavalier attitude than that of the biblical Joseph, who steadfastly attributes his success to God. With Joseph's fortunes at their height, the narrator reminds us of Joseph's family in Canaan and what the famine means for them.

Those Canaan Days; The Brothers Come to Egypt; Grovel, Grovel; Who's the Thief?; Benjamin Calypso (Genesis 42 and 44)
The change of scene is less abrupt than Gen. 42.1 because the narrator prepared us for it at the end of 'Stone the Crows'. Rice and Webber use 'Those Canaan Days' as another occasion to play with musical genre. The song provides an entertaining interlude, in which the brothers and their father reminisce about the good old days in the style of a French chanson, and the dancing at the end usually features an Apache dancer:

> Those Canaan days we used to know
> Where have they gone, where did they go?

33. Rice and Webber skip over Joseph's marriage and the birth of his sons, Manasseh and Ephraim; perhaps it would make Joseph appear too old. It is in any event irrelevant to their story of a boy whose dreams come true, though for the biblical narrator the continuation of the line of Abraham is crucial for the ongoing story.
34. Except the priests; Joseph's wife, Asenath, is the daughter of a priest.

> Eh bien, raise your berets
> To those Canaan days.

As good fun and family entertainment, *Dreamcoat* never lets Joseph suffer too much or the brothers seem too bad. The brothers, who told us early on that they were 'great guys but no one seems to notice', seem to have had a change of heart about Joseph, who was a part of their family in better times:

> It's funny but since we lost Joseph[35]
> We've gone to the other extreme[36]
> Perhaps we all misjudged the lad
> Perhaps he wasn't quite that bad
> And how we miss his entertaining dreams.

From here on, things happen much more quickly and simply than in the biblical story. Down to their very last sheep, the brothers, including Benjamin, resolve to go to Egypt for food. In the midst of the seriousness of the famine, *Dreamcoat* inserts a bit of humour:

> They've got corn, they've got meat,
> they've got food and drinks.
> And if we have time
> we could see the Sphinx.

They are there in literally no time, grovelling at Joseph's feet. This is *Dreamcoat*'s major departure from the biblical text. In Gen. 42.1-4 Joseph's ten brothers are sent to Egypt by their father, who keeps Benjamin at home with him for fear that harm might befall him, and only later, after they have eaten all the food that they brought back, does he send them back to Egypt. But first they must convince him that they cannot return without Benjamin (43.1-15). I discussed above how the compression of the brothers' two visits to Egypt into one —the first without Benjamin, the second with him—enables *Dreamcoat* to spare the characters and the audience the trauma that the brothers and their father Jacob experience and the pain that Joseph feels. Indeed, in contrast to Joseph's weeping when he sees Benjamin (43.30) and when he makes himself known to his brothers (45.1-15), in *Dreamcoat* 'Joseph found it a strain not to laugh because / Not a brother among them knew who he was'. His test of them is not the drawn-out difficult ordeal of the biblical account: 'I shall now take them all for a ride / After all they have tried fratricide'.

---

35. Their statement that they 'lost' Joseph is reminiscent of the way the biblical Joseph speaks of being 'stolen out of the land of the Hebrews' without placing responsibility on his brothers.

36. They are referring here not to their feelings but to the contrast between the good old days and the present famine, as the earlier stanzas of the song make clear.

When he sees his brothers, as in the biblical story Joseph remembers his dreams, and in 'Grovel, Grovel' he reminds the audience of their content. He accuses his brothers of being spies (cf. 42.9), but since Benjamin is present, there is no test of their honesty by requiring the ten of them to produce their other brother. Nor do they admit their guilt (though there may be an allusion to this in the next song), in contrast to their admission of guilt in the biblical story, which they do not realize Joseph understands, since there is an interpreter between them ('Indeed we are guilty concerning our brother, in that we saw his distress, when he pleaded with us and we did not listen; therefore this distress has come upon us', 42.21). In *Dreamcoat* Joseph's words only subtly suggest his brothers' earlier mistreatment of him: 'Why do you think I should help you? Would you help me?'

In Gen. 42.11 Joseph's ten brothers deny the charge of spying, 'We are all sons of one man, we are honest men, your servants are not spies', and in Gen. 42.13 they repeat their denial, 'We, your servants, were twelve brothers, the sons of one man in the land of Canaan. The youngest however is now with our father, and one is no more'. In *Dreamcoat* their response to the charge that they are spies, amid their grovelling, is simply 'We are just eleven brothers, good men and true. . . . Honesty's our middle name.' Joseph gives them food and the rest of the story unfolds quickly:

> Then, unseen, Joseph nipped out around the back
> And planted a cup in young Benjamin's sack
> When the brothers were ready to go
> Joseph turned to them all
> With a terrible stare and said
> 'No! No! No! No! No!

He continues ('Who's the Thief?'):

> Stop! You robbers—
> Your little number's up!
> One of you has stolen
> My precious golden cup!

The sacks are searched and the suspense of the biblical story's 'he [Joseph's steward] searched, beginning with the eldest and ending with the youngest', is captured by the emptying of each brother's sack in turn, ending with Benjamin. When Joseph decrees that Benjamin be locked in a cell and the key thrown into the Nile (in the biblical version slavery is to be his penalty), the other brothers are dismayed: 'Jail us and beat us, we should be blamed'. Do they mean they should be blamed for the fact that the cup was found in Benjamin's sack (although they insist 'he must have been framed')? Or should we hear this as a recognition of their guilt for what they did to Joseph, 'a reckoning for his blood' (42.22)? If the latter, Benjamin is just as guilty as they are, for in Rice and Webber's version Benjamin is included among the guilty brothers from the beginning and participates in the selling of Joseph to the Ishmaelites. In Genesis, in contrast, the situation is more complicated. The biblical narrator, in relating how Joseph came to be cast into the pit and then sold to Ishmaelite traders, does not mention all of the brothers by name. The repeated references to 'his brothers' and their conversations suggest that all Joseph's brothers are involved except Benjamin, an assumption confirmed by the fact that later Benjamin is the means by which the ten guilty brothers are tested.[37]

It is a tense moment in *Dreamcoat*, and so time for some comic relief, which the next song, 'Benjamin Calypso', provides. Judah appropriately leads, but all the brothers, as well as the ensemble, join in to sing choruses of:

> Oh no, not he
> How you can accuse him is a mystery
> Save him, take me
> Benjamin is straighter than the tall palm tree.

All the brothers, and not just Judah, as in the biblical account, volunteer to take Benjamin's place. They assure Joseph that 'Benjamin is honest as coconuts', whose reputation for honesty is well attested. Judah again declares the brothers' guilt and Benjamin's innocence:

> Sure as the tide wash the golden sand
> Benjamin is an innocent man
> sure as bananas need the sun
> We are the criminal guilty ones.

With everyone on stage dancing the calypso, it is difficult to get too worked up about what the outcome for Benjamin will be.

Joseph All the Time (Genesis 45) and Jacob in Egypt (Genesis 46)
The biblical story has five more chapters to go. *Dreamcoat*, on the other hand, is rapidly drawing to a happy conclusion. Hearing all his brothers offering to take Benjamin's place convinces Joseph 'that his brothers now were honest men'. The brothers have learned their lesson, and no one has

---

37. He thus cannot be guilty himself. We might assume that Benjamin is too young to be away shepherding the flock with his brothers. The young Joseph is not tending the flock with them either, but is sent by his father to bring back a report of them (37.12-14). Ebach draws attention to the 'problem' of Benjamin and asks if, at this point in the story, Benjamin has been born (though 37.9 assumes eleven brothers). Benjamin, he points out, is more of a figure than a person in the story (*Genesis 37–50*, pp. 59, 69-71). When he begins the test, Joseph does not know of Reuben's innocence; he discovers it only when the brothers speak in his presence, thinking he does not understand (42.18-23).

suffered unduly. Joseph reveals his identity, there is kissing and hugging and cheering, and the entire ensemble celebrates. All that is needed now is to reunite Joseph with his father. Jacob comes to Egypt, where he is met by Joseph in his chariot of gold. *Dreamcoat's* Jacob is not the embittered Jacob of the Bible, whose first words to his son are 'Now I can die, having seen for myself that you are still alive', and who tells Pharaoh, 'Few and evil have been the days of the years of my life'. Often in performance, the joyous Jacob brings the dreamcoat with him, for Joseph's dream has come true.

Finale: Any Dream Will Do; Give Me my Coloured Coat
Inclusio is a well-known biblical structuring device. In good biblical fashion, *Dreamcoat* ends by returning to the beginning, with the song 'Any Dream Will Do' and the coda, 'Give Me my Coloured Coat':

> May I return to the beginning
> The light is dimming, and the dream is too
> The world and I, we are still waiting
> Still hesitating
> Any dream will do
> Give me my coloured coat
> My amazing coloured coat
> Give me my coloured coat
> My amazing coloured coat.

The amazing technicolor dreamcoat is returned to the dreamer, whose dream has been realized. Since he has achieved everything he could want, power, fame, reunion with his family, for what is he, and the world, waiting? Now, the song seems to suggest, it is up to you, who have heard the tale of a boy whose dream came true, to follow your dream, any dream, wherever it leads you. Any dream will do? The baker would not agree.

Epilogue

Let me return to the beginning, and to my question, How does *Joseph and the Amazing Technicolor Dreamcoat* rate as a retelling of the biblical story of Joseph? In its treatment of the plot, it gets high marks for its attention to detail, its adherence to the storyline and its few departures from it (with its one significant change, only one trip by the brothers to Egypt, making it a less distressing story). As a less than two-hour performance (unless the reprises go on even longer), it can hardly be expected to match the dramatic complexity or the grand programme of its biblical source, which, as part of a larger, on-going story, forms a bridge between the world of the patriarchs and the exodus. *Dreamcoat's* characters are essentially one-dimensional (except for Joseph's sombre reflections in prison). They do not undergo the hardships and vicissitudes faced by the biblical figures, and they do not change as the result of their experiences. Nothing really threatening happens, and the story ends well in the end (which is also true of the biblical story). The musical can, of course, be faulted for its facile message. But, after all, it was written for entertainment, not serious study. *Joseph and the Amazing Technicolor Dreamcoat* was written for children, but adults love it. Whereas the biblical story was written for adults, because its plot lends itself to retelling for children, it has often been made the subject of children's literature.

As an accessible retelling, I have found *Dreamcoat* to be a very effective teaching resource. Many of my students have seen it dozens of times, a few have even performed in school productions of it, and they all know it, some by heart. For some—because if scheduling permits the entire class attends a performance—it is their first experience of going to the theatre. They never have any criticisms of *Dreamcoat*. But they also easily recognize its message that any dream will do as glib and unrealistic. Comparing *Joseph and the Amazing Technicolor Dreamcoat* to the biblical text—analysing what parts of the biblical story it represents and how, the effects its omissions, changes or particular slant on events have on the story—requires that they read the narrative carefully, with attention to detail, and, in the light of their close reading, consider not just what the biblical story's 'message' might be but, more important, evaluate it critically.[38]

---

38. Comparing and contrasting the Josephs of *Dreamcoat* and the biblical account can also be illuminating. Readers over the centuries may have found in Joseph a model of wisdom or piety or self-restraint, but is the biblical Joseph a role model? Compare, for example, Anita Diamant's unflattering characterization of Joseph in *The Red Tent*.

LITERATURE

History and its Contagions: Rethinking the Legacy of Genesis 22 in A.B. Yehoshua's 'Early in the Summer of 1970'

Nathan Paul Devir

Abstract

This article offers a first-ever close reading of the entirety of 'Early in the Summer of 1970', a long-neglected short story by celebrated Israeli author A.B. Yehoshua. In particular, this study examines how the allegorical tale's narrative superstructure, predicated entirely upon the legacy of the 'Binding of Isaac' story from Genesis 22, functions as an impetus for the meta-historical perspective on Zionism advocated by the author. The study demonstrates how this perspective ultimately offers an opportunity for the (Israeli) reader to undergo a process of introspection by elucidating Yehoshua's uses of the story's symbolically charged (archetypal) and realistic (local) elements within the context of the mythical structures and patterns of Jewish history. It also breaks new ground by examining recent extra-literary statements by Yehoshua regarding the legacy of Genesis 22 and the Abraham/Isaac motif as a significant part of the chain of signifiers through which 'Early in the Summer of 1970' might be read. Finally, it proposes a contextual lens through which to view the rhetoric of sacrifice as it appears in Yehoshua's work as a whole.

1. *Introduction*

This article demonstrates the ways in which Israeli writer A.B. Yehoshua's short story *Betkhilat kaiytz 1970* ('Early in the Summer of 1970') (1972) links itself symbolically with recurring tropes, motifs and characters from the intertextual reservoir of Judaic culture.[1] In particular, this study analyses Yehoshua's re-envisioning of the story of the *'akedah*, or Binding of Isaac (known in Christianity as the Sacrifice of Isaac), from Genesis 22. In Yehoshua's rewriting of this traditional tale, he revises commonly held perceptions of the story into an unabashedly irreverent recasting of sacrosanct

---

1. All references in this article to the story 'Early in the Summer of 1970' will follow the most standard versions available in both the English translation and the Hebrew original. These are found, respectively, in the volumes *The Continuing Silence of a Poet* and *Kol hasipurim*.

archetypes, which he executes along the lines of emphatically secular, left-leaning Israeli concerns. The transformations of these images and patterns as they inhabit the personae in 'Early in the Summer of 1970' help to elucidate what Joseph Cohen has called the two main 'albatrosses' in Yehoshua's work: biblical heritage and political Zionism (1990: 46). Each debunking undertaken by the author therefore heightens the (Israeli) reader's growing awareness of the dangers of such 'albatrosses' (as Yehoshua sees them) through those archetypes' interaction with the intertextual, realistic and allegorical components of the narrative. The intellectual confrontation that this narrative technique provokes also forms the building blocks by which a new kind of perspective, modeled on Yehoshua's desired brand of Israeli identity, will ultimately offer an opportunity for the reader to undergo a process of introspection.

Much of the understanding of the subcultural specificities in Yehoshua's early literary work is predicated on the awareness of his reexamination and frequent subversion of conventional Judaic archetypes, including the ways in which contemporary avatars of traditional Judaic textual practice intermingle with those very archetypes within the context of the narrative of political Zionism. However, in the cultural (in this case, literary) production of that narrative, we can also pinpoint particular subcultural patterns, embodied by characters or themes in the texts. In many cases, such patterns represent the dissonance (historical, ethical and political) that exists between fathers and sons in the Zionist paradigm. Yehoshua's work relies heavily upon ancestral imagery—in the present case, by using the figures of Abraham and Isaac—to elucidate such discord. As Gershon Shaked notes, the importance of the father–son conflict in Yehoshua's fiction rests primarily upon the .ways in which the father figures impose prescribed meanings upon actions committed by the state, while their incredulous sons often consider these meanings disjointed or illusory (1972: 154). Both of the symbolically charged (archetypal) and realistic (local) elements of these actions draw upon the mythical structures and patterns of Jewish history to foreground their supposed significance.

Needless to say, Yehoshua was not the first writer of his generation to invert biblical archetypes (including those of Abraham and Isaac) for the purposes of political or aesthetic expression. As Alan Mintz notes, authors such as Amos Oz, Haim Gouri and Yehuda Amichai all played with the myth of the Binding of Isaac before Yehoshua did, as part of their engagement in the battle over what Mintz calls the 'loss of meaning and the baffled search for a way to overcome that loss' (1978: 67). In other words, the 'loss of meaning' that Mintz describes hearkens back to the recognition that, for Israel's besieged youth, the metanarratives of old can no longer be thought of as sufficient grounds for the justification of the sacrifices that they are expected to carry out.

Avi Sagi, in his wide-ranging article on the use of the myth in Modern Hebrew letters, notes that the sacrificial motif in the story of Isaac 'epitomiz[es] the Zionist revolution and the sacrifices it exacted, [and simultaneously] rejects both the myth and its implications' (1998: 45). In Sagi's comprehensive outline of the various ways in which the myth functions as a pivotal kind of 'DNA' for the symbolic structure of the stories of many of the giants of Modern Hebrew literature, he mentions such celebrated writers as Shmuel Yosef Agnon, Yehuda Amichai, Yariv Ben Aharon, Amir Gilboa, Haim Gouri, Uri Zvi Greenberg, Yitzhak Laor, Hanoch Levin, Aharon Megged, Moshe Shamir, Avraham Shlonsky and S. Yizhar, to just name a few.[2] However, Yehoshua's well-known reappropriations of the story of Isaac, predominantly in the short story 'Shloshah yamim veyeled' ('Three Days and a Child') (1965) and in the novel *Mar mani* ('Mr Mani') (1990), seemed to have touched a nerve in a way that the other writers' work did not. As Gila Ramras-Rauch explains, this may be attributed to the fact that Yehoshua's cheekily grotesque portrayals of biblical figures and motifs surpassed the more subtle models provided by his literary peers. From that perspective, Yehoshua proved himself to be not only 'adept at the art of ironic inversion—inverting not only the basic myths and archetypes, and the expectations of the reader—but also the conventional values of Israeli society' (1989: 145).

This article contributes to existing scholarship on the aforementioned inversions in Yehoshua's literary corpus in three ways. To begin, it offers a first-ever close reading of the entirety of 'Early in the Summer of 1970', which is one of the author's long-neglected short stories; it is also one in which the narrative superstructure, predicated entirely on the legacy of Genesis 22, is seldom included in any discussion surrounding his many later subversions of the Abraham/Isaac motif.[3] Next, it breaks new ground

2. The literary works to which Sagi refers may be found in the following: Agnon 1966: 8-9; Amichai 1996: 21; Ben-Aharon 1966: 116; Gilboa 1981: 560; Greenberg 1972: 145-47; Gouri 1981: 565; Laor 1985: 70; Levin 1987: 33-56; Megged 1970: 80-145; Shamir 1960: 18-25; Shlonsky 1954: 136; and Yizhar 1958: 804. For an analysis of the trope of the Binding of Isaac in Modern Hebrew literature, see, for example (this list is by no means exhaustive): Yisrael Cohen 1981: 51-74; Coffin 1987: 293-308; Feldman 2010; Kartun-Blum 1995: 185-202; Melman 1991: 53-72; and Shamir 1960: 332. Also, see Zanger 2003 for a description of the *'akedah* trope in Israeli cinema.

3. Notable exceptions are as follows: There is a very brief discussion of this story in Feldman (2010: 240-42), which is the most wide-ranging study of the Binding of Isaac in Israeli cultural production. Joseph Cohen (1990: 54-56) and Ramras-Rauch (1989: 146) also discuss the text, albeit in passing. Morahg (1988) has, to date, the most detailed and insightful analysis on this particular story, although his reading of it (315-21) focuses on individual-versus-collective paradigms, as opposed to biblical recastings. Adia Mendelson Maoz (2010) offers an intriguing comparison of this story and one of

by examining recent extra-literary statements by Yehoshua regarding the legacy of Genesis 22 as a significant part of the chain of signifiers through which 'Early in the Summer of 1970' might be read. Finally, it proposes a contextual lens through which to view the rhetoric of sacrifice as it appears in Yehoshua's work as a whole.

2. *Notes on the Author and his (Inter-)text*

Avraham (A.B.) Yehoshua was born in Jerusalem in 1936, a fifth-generation Jerusalemite on his father's side. Since the late 1960s, Yehoshua has been one of Israel's leading public intellectuals, frequently participating in debates over contentious national issues such as the fate of the Occupied Territories, the psychosocial makeup of Jewish history, the obligations of the Arab-Israeli minority and relations with the Jewish Diaspora.[4] From very early on in his intellectual development, Yehoshua has related to his Jewish experience as a primarily national (Israeli) phenomenon, in which Jewish religion is not a necessary component in order to be a Zionist.

Literary criticism has had much to say about the ways in which Yehoshua uses traditional Jewish symbolism to portray the Israeli reality, while, at the same time, he subverts the supposed static nature of those traditional symbols. In doing so, he creates a world that is quintessentially Israeli, often disassociated from conventional Jewish rhetoric and focused on the interiorization of human relations within the Israeli reality. Joseph Cohen, for example, notes that Yehoshua 'interiorizes reality, undermining temporal and spatial linearity, and . . . has a gift for lyricism in his prose that lifts us out of the ordinary world and propels us into a subjective one where "real" life goes on inside peoples' heads rather than in their external environment' (1990: 45). Gilead Morahg, the foremost Yehoshua scholar to date, states that 'Yehoshua's protagonists are often the victims of the combined force of their inner need for confirmation and (Israeli) society's relentless demand for conformity' (1979: 142). Even the uber-conservative Israeli critic Baruch Kurzweil, who was infamously disparaging of most of the writers

---

Yehoshua's recent novels, *Esh yedidutit* (Friendly Fire) (2007). Articles by Mordechai Shalev (1993) and Yosef Haefrati ('Ktzat') explore the treatment of Genesis 22 in this story alongside several other early works by Yehoshua, although, given the dates of their publication, neither Shalev nor Haefrati had access to more recent, extra-literary statements by Yehoshua (not to mention later fictional works) that would elucidate the author's use of the myth. By the same token, most scholarship that references such extra-literary statements focuses exclusively on remarks made by Yehoshua in 1995 ('Sikum'), but only in relation to his novel *Mar Mani* (Mr Mani) (1990).

4. Readers interested in Yehoshua's essays on political issues should see, in particular, the following volumes: *Between Right and Right*; *Israël, un examen moral* (1981); and (with Frédéric Brenner) *Israel* (1988).

of Yehoshua's generation, maintains that the strength of Yehoshua's fiction is that it 'metilah 'aleinu mevukhah rabah' (1982: 307, 'casts upon us great embarrassment'), in that it propels to the forefront of Israeli letters some of the most sensitive and divisive issues facing the nation.

'Early in the Summer of 1970' is the tale of an elderly Bible teacher, who, after having refused for many years the call to retire from his position at a public high school, must explain the death of his only son. The son, who had lived for an extended period of time in the United States, returns to Israel with his American wife and child, and is reported as having been killed during a stint of reserve duty on the Jordanian front during the War of Attrition (1967–70). When the father arrives at the army base to identify his son's body, he realizes that a mistake has been made and that the son is in fact alive. At the end of the story, the reader realizes that the entire account of the son's death is simply a fantasy of the deranged old man. The Bible teacher imagines himself playing the role of the bereaved father during a high school graduating-class assembly, where he lectures to his students and their parents on the importance of sacrifice. Yehoshua suggests that the father feels compelled to undertake a public display of grief in order to save face vis-à-vis the students, whom he feels he has duped with his emphasis on the biblical pretexts of Israel's founding, as well as with his seeming justifications (based on biblical praxis) of the Israeli government's present-day undertakings. The old man relates how, in a conversation with the headmaster several years earlier, when the teacher was 'deeply agitated', and with his hands 'trembling' (Yehoshua 1991: 256), the latter had tried to explain to his supervisor why he could not retire yet, 'telling him in halting phrases that I did not see how I could leave them now, that is to say, now that we were sending them to their death' (256).

The old man tells this story in first person, but the actual sequence of events is never quite clear, since the opening changes each time he starts over. Moreover, his insistence upon reiterating the more redundant details of the story again and again, much in the same way that he had mercilessly drilled his students in the arcane minutiae of the Hebrew Scriptures, is seen as the clearest key to his impending madness. The absurd rationalization of sacrifice that the father attempts to convey to the graduating class, who will soon be inducted into the army, has all the morality and dogma inherent in the religious texts that had occupied him pedagogically; only this time, while lecturing on the corruption of Israeli youth, 'as one who was a father and is so no more' (272), the father now negotiates the meaning of those biblical concepts based on their application to the subcultural praxis of secular political Zionism. For, despite the fact that the overtly secular father figure in 'Early in the Summer of 1970' still has a link to the Bible, as part of the shared intertextual and discursive relation of the Israeli subgroup to the Judaic religious tradition, the way in which the teacher carries out his role betrays an almost 'religious' duty. Indeed, this character's entire existence seems based on obsessive devotion to (and unquestioning reliance upon) the commemoration of the Judaic textual tradition, or what the teacher refers to as 'the tyranny I enforce by means of the Bible' (277). More specifically, the father unconsciously equates his grief over the sacrifice of his son to the grief felt by the biblical Abraham over the near-sacrifice of his son Isaac. As a father who had been similarly conditioned to accept the sacrifice of his son for an ideal, the teacher preaches in a semi-deranged fashion to the crowd about how he, like his biblical counterpart, 'was prepared for his [that is, the son's] death in a manner, and that was my strength in that fearful moment' (272). Thus, the ostensibly 'personal' grief felt by the mourning father is not only made collective and used for pedagogical purposes, in the context (and for the benefit) of the modern Zionist enterprise. It is also justified by, and paralleled with, the archetypal grief expressed in one of the founding myths of the Judaic textual tradition, as attributed to the original father of the Jewish people, Abraham of Ur. The myth referred to is the *'akedah*, or the Binding of Isaac, an act that Abraham performs after being instructed by God in Gen. 22.1-19 to carry out the sacrifice of his son. Thus, in 'Early in the Summer of 1970', the father is the patriarchal figure who also serves as the incarnation, the recasting, or the modern-day avatar of Abraham.

The original story involves the directive issued by God to the progenitor of the Jewish people, Abraham, to sacrifice his own son as a burnt offering on Mount Moriah. In the biblical tale, Abraham is ready to carry out God's will and prepares the sacrifice as instructed. However, as he is bringing the knife down, the body of Isaac is replaced with that of a ram. God is pleased with Abraham for having been willing to kill his only son and indicates that he will reward him for his piety. Given below is the English translation of the biblical text:

> And it came to pass after these things, that God did prove Abraham, and said unto him: 'Abraham'; and he said: 'Here am I'. And Abraham rose early in the morning, and saddled his ass, and took two of his young men with him, and Isaac his son; and he cleaved the wood for the burnt-offering, and rose up, and went unto the place of which God had told him. On the third day Abraham lifted up his eyes, and saw the place afar off. And Abraham said unto his young men: 'Abide ye here with the ass, and I and the lad will go yonder; and we will worship, and come back to you'. And Abraham took the wood of the burnt-offering, and laid it upon Isaac his son; and he took in his hand the fire and the knife; and they went both of them together. And Isaac spoke unto Abraham his father, and said: 'My father'. And he said: 'Here am I, my son'. And he said: 'Behold the fire and the wood; but where is the lamb for a burnt-offering?' And Abraham said: 'God will provide Himself the lamb for a burnt-offering, my son'. So they went both of them together. And they came to the place which God had told him of; and Abraham built the altar there, and laid the wood in order, and bound Isaac his son, and laid him on the altar, upon the wood.

And Abraham stretched forth his hand, and took the knife to slay his son. And the angel of the LORD called unto him out of heaven, and said: 'Abraham, Abraham'. And he said: 'Here am I'. And he said: 'Lay not thy hand upon the lad, neither do thou any thing unto him; for now I know that thou art a God-fearing man, seeing thou hast not withheld thy son, thine only son, from Me'. And Abraham lifted up his eyes, and looked, and behold behind him a ram caught in the thicket by his horns. And Abraham went and took the ram, and offered him up for a burnt-offering in the stead of his son. And Abraham called the name of that place Adonai-jireh; as it is said to this day: 'In the mount where the LORD is seen'. And the angel of the LORD called unto Abraham a second time out of heaven, and said: 'By Myself have I sworn, saith the LORD, because thou hast done this thing, and hast not withheld thy son, thine only son, that in blessing I will bless thee, and in multiplying I will multiply thy seed as the stars of the heaven, and as the sand which is upon the seashore; and thy seed shall possess the gate of his enemies; and in thy seed shall all the nations of the earth be blessed; because thou hast hearkened to My voice'. So Abraham returned unto his young men, and they rose up and went together to Beer-sheba; and Abraham dwelt at Beer-sheba (Gen. 22.1-19).[5]

While a full-fledged summary of the postbiblical interpretations of this myth is impossible here, suffice it to say that the story of the Binding of Isaac has been largely considered by Jewish commentators to be the prime example of Jewish devotion to God via a martyrdom based on adherence to, or sanctification of, traditional notions of Judaic theodicy.[6] In that sense, Jews persecuted throughout the centuries have looked toward Abraham's compliance to God's decree as the example on which to base their own decisions regarding the necessity of sacrifice, in light of challenges to their maintaining a religious or ethnic doctrine. Especially relevant to Yehoshua's transformation of this tale, in which the secular state assumes the role of the deity, is the notion of God 'testing' (rendered as 'prove[ing]' in the first line of the above translation) Abraham's dutifulness in the wake of such a horrible request. Also significant for the modern recasting of the story is the idea that, in both cases, the result of the father's willingness to sacrifice his only son presupposes the legitimacy of sacrifice for the continuation of a particular creed, despite the fact that in both cases a substitute is offered in place of the actual son.

As stated, the biblical imagery surrounding the characters in 'Early in the Summer of 1970' is very indicative of the comical, often pathetic, figures

5. All English translations from the Hebrew Scriptures will follow the translation of the *Jewish Publication Society* (ed. Max Leopold Margolis; 1917 edn).

6. I encourage the interested reader to consult Spiegel's volume on the Binding of Isaac (by far the most comprehensive on this trope in Judaic history and lore) for more background information and variant readings. Also recommended are the studies of Boehm 2007, Chilton 2008 and Delaney 1998.

that inhabit much of Yehoshua's early stories. Instead of functioning like conventional archetypes who may, on one hand, act as imposing, authoritarian types, or givers of wisdom on the other, Yehoshua's Abraham is a dried-up curmudgeon, disconnected from the intricacies of current political and social realities, and more often than not at odds with the very generation for which he is supposed to function as an authority figure worthy of emulation. In this case, the patriarch is part of the generation of founding fathers who built the state and promulgated its values.

3. *Public Pedagogy or National Pathology?*

In this story, the psychological tension between the Abrahamic figure, embodied by the elderly teacher, and the current Zionist reality, personified both by the returning son and the high school students, is perceivable early on in the text when the old man enters the classroom. Archetypally speaking—and especially in the context of the collective unconscious of 'the people of the book'—the classroom may be considered the epicenter of the senex experience, especially when the subject matter to be taught is the Bible. However, Yehoshua subverts the common associations of the conventional Judaic practice of honoring the 'giver of wisdom' and promulgator of values in his natural environment by portraying the teacher as ridiculous, even somewhat demented. In the opening scene, we learn that the old man has become so isolated in his outdated world, both symbolically and literally, that the lack of contact with the other teachers in the school, not to mention with the headmaster, has prevented him from receiving the news that a younger replacement has been hired to force him out; he only discovers the fact upon entering the classroom on the first day of the school year. The younger teacher's reaction provides an indication of the extent of the old man's lunacy, as the elderly teacher relates how the younger one 'thought I had gone out of my mind' (257). This is an instance in which the father's unyielding code reveals a kind of pathological reliance upon structure and its perpetuation, evidenced by the old man's actions. The elderly teacher says, 'Before he [the younger teacher] has time to recover I have mounted the platform, taken out my ragged Bible' (257). It is telling that the term 'ragged' (257), used as a qualifier for the state of the copy of the old man's Bible used for instruction purposes, also applies to the physical and mental state of the teacher, whose psychosis is directly informed by his obstinate reliance on that text to substantiate the never-ending military conflict in modern-day Israel. In Yehoshua's worldview, this psychosis is directly linked to a credo of the unending necessity of sacrifice.

This fixation is contrasted by the arrival of the elderly teacher's son, who has returned to Israel after accepting a position as a professor at the Hebrew University of Jerusalem. The son has come back to Israel for mainly professional reasons and expresses little support for the mainstream Zionist ethos. Upon his arrival from the United States via the Far East, the old man notes, 'I hardly recognized my son in him. Bearded, heavy, soft, my son's hair was already sprinkled with grey, and, in his movements, some new, slow tranquility' (258-59). The reciprocity of the father's sentiment is manifested when the son wakes up from his post-arrival slumber: 'He [the son] gave a brief start, as though for an instant not recognizing me' (260).

In the first serious conversation between father and son, the son asks the old man if he is still teaching Bible. The response betrays a dangerous stringency: 'Yes, of course. Only Bible' (260). After having been asked to tell the father about his own field of study, the son 'sits there and smiles, begins to talk, flounders, has difficulty explaining, doesn't think I'd understand him' (263). The misunderstanding between the two men is compounded by the fact that the son's writings are in English, for 'Even if he [the son] should give me stuff to read he doubts I'd be able to follow, the more so as it is all in English' (264). When the conversation turns to the political situation in Israel and the elderly teacher recounts how his students are being killed in the War of Attrition, the son is uninterested concerning what his father despairs as 'history disintegrating' (264). This remark coincides with the son's baby-boy babbling in English, and the American daughter-in-law (who, it is suggested, is not Jewish), 'not understand[ing] a word I say' (264) with respect to the Hebrew conversation. In a prelude to the notion of the son's eventual sacrifice, the father remarks that his son reminds him of his students (a clearly delusional parallel on the old man's part, if understood from the perspective of solely physical characteristics, since the son has already been described as having aged considerably), because 'the absent look in his eyes [is] familiar, unhearing, already elsewhere, alien, adrift' (264).

The fact that the father somehow equates the physical appearance of his aging, professor son (who is now also a father) with that of his students is an obvious sign of the old man's increasing inability to distinguish fantasy from reality. However, we might well conjecture that Yehoshua inserts the account of the supposed similarity between them as a way of emphasizing the role of shared attributes in the collective Israeli paradigm. After all, both his son (who had been away from the country for years) and his students are about to be called up for military service, to perform reserve duty and compulsory duty, respectively. There are at least two other indications that this manner of introducing the concept of collective responsibility is in fact a deliberate narrative technique on the part of Yehoshua to implement the *mise en abyme*, or the self-reflective directive, of the story. But as we will see later, this idea of collective responsibility should not be confused with ineffectual sacrifice.

First, when the headmaster of the school informs the teacher about the supposed death of his son, the headmaster insists on accompanying the old man back to his home. It had been stated earlier on in the story that there was no love lost between the elderly teacher and the headmaster, who had numerous confrontations regarding the former's refusal to retire; and yet, the headmaster's outpouring of grief at the death of the old man's son goes far beyond that of a polite reaction of a sympathetic colleague. The teacher notes, 'There are tears in his eyes, as though not my son but his had fallen' (262), a remark that highlights the ritual of collective mourning, in tandem with the tendency, very characteristic of early Zionist practice, to rhetorically appropriate grief from the private sphere for nationalistic purposes.[7] Second, this collective aspect is further highlighted during the sequence in the story in which the old man takes the bus to Jerusalem in order to begin the process of identifying his son's body. During this time, the parallel between the narrative of 'Early in the Summer of 1970' and its biblical antecedent becomes more apparent, since Jerusalem is both the site at which the near-sacrifice of Isaac took place as well as the locale which Sidra DeKoven Ezrahi has appropriately referred to as the 'Ground Zero' of the Hebrew imagination (2007: 220).[8]

During the trip to the city of Jerusalem, the father begins to speak for the first time in the second person, as if to the Israeli reader: 'You find yourself on the way to Jerusalem . . . there is no knowing anymore whether one goes up to Jerusalem or down . . . and suddenly you cry out, or think you do' (Yehoshua 1991: 265). The reference in the above citation to being unsure as to whether 'one goes up [to Jerusalem] or down' is a nod to the traditional use of the Hebrew verb *la'alot*, which means 'to ascend'. In the Hebrew Scriptures, one always 'ascends' to Jerusalem (as opposed to simply 'traveling' to the Holy City). This usage has carried over to the modern

---

7. The interested reader will find a detailed account of the historical and political contexts of Israeli mourning rituals in 'History, Collective Memory, and Countermemory' (see Zerubavel 1995: 3-38).

8. The debate surrounding the exact location (i.e., whether it was actually in a 'settled' Jerusalem or in the wilderness) of the purported near-sacrifice of Isaac at the site 'ordained by God' (*moriah* in Hebrew) is too long and involved to discuss here. I therefore confine myself to the following (brief) explanation: Despite the fact that the Hebrew Scriptures offer contradictory accounts (Gen. 14.18-20; 1 Chron. 11.4; 1 Kings 5) as to the actual site of Moriah, which is not a single peak, but, rather, an extended ridge commencing from the Kidron and Hinnom valleys, traditional Judaic lore places the locus of Abraham's test at what is now the city of Jerusalem; as such, the importance of its association in Yehoshua's story remains highly relevant (and taken as a given for the reader familiar with Judaic symbolism). For a critical discussion surrounding the linguistic and historical ambiguities of the biblical text, see Walvoord and Zuck 1983–85: 61-66.

day, inasmuch as it is possible to discern the religious and/or nationalistic leanings of a traveler to Jerusalem by the way in which s/he delineates the symbolic act of the journey: whether it is *la'alot* ('ascending') to Jerusalem, or *linso'a* ('traveling') there. The fact that the father in 'Early in the Summer of 1970' takes this linguistic palimpsest one step further by suggesting that 'ascent' to the Holy City is no longer self-evident, even going so far as to imply the contrary—that a pilgrimage to the capital city of Israel might be equated with the notion of 'descending' (265)—conveys the feeling of a representational rollercoaster ride upon which the perceptions of tradition and propriety held by the father are constantly under threat of teetering off into the abyss. The elderly teacher's physical reaction to this upset is therefore no surprise: he becomes ill on the bus and requests that the bus driver pull over to the side of the road before continuing.

The old man's confusion regarding the question of 'ascent' to Jerusalem may be seen as a direct parallel with the language of Gen. 22.2, in which God instructs Abraham to sacrifice his son Isaac, 'to offer him there for a burnt-offering' at a mountain in the Moriah range, which is located in the Old City of present-day Jerusalem. The term *'olah* ('burnt offering', literally, something that 'goes up', referring to the smoke wafting toward the heavens) possesses the same root as the verb used to indicate the ascent to Jerusalem in Yehoshua's text, *la'alot*. Taking into account the old man's expressed uncertainty (which he articulates in the second person, as if encouraging the Israeli reader to also undertake a similar line of questioning) regarding the status of the site that Jews have held sacred for nearly three thousand years, we may consider the linguistic parallel with the biblical story as a kind of intertextual prelude to Yehoshua's call to reflect, ultimately, on the notion of sacrifice for Zionism's *'ilah* ('cause'), another term that shares the root of 'to ascend'—and not least of all because Yehoshua's ultimate subversion of the traditional Judaic myth of Abraham and Isaac rests upon the subcultural specificities of the national Israeli subgroup to which he belongs, and which therefore acts as a filter through which these two archetypes are presented in his fictitious, yet entirely possible, exposé of Israeli reality.

Compounding the shock of the journey to Jerusalem is the old man's arrival at what he calls 'the apartment I never knew' (266), probably an abandoned Arab home, where he meets the Palestinian woman who works as a cleaning lady for his son's family. He wants to tell her about the son's death, but communication between them is impossible because of his poor Arabic and the woman's inability to speak Hebrew. His attitude toward the woman, whom he describes as a 'withered monkey' (266) who attempts to communicate with him by 'gesturing and yelling' (267), is rife with the ethnocentrism and imperialism characteristic of the old guard in Israel, as he relates how she 'understands at once that I belong here, that I have rights, and perhaps perceives traces of others in my features' (266). Quite symbolically, the failure of the so-called authority figure to communicate with the 'Other' is only the first in a series of uncomfortable encounters with the people from whom he is psychically estranged, first and foremost from the younger generation. The next encounter takes place when his daughter-in-law (who, like the Arab woman, is an outsider in his eyes) returns home, and he 'mumble[s] the morning's tidings in an ancient, Biblical Hebrew, and [I] know she will not understand, the words dart back at me' (268); the father characterizes this as 'the confusion of generations' (268). Searching the house, he finds among the dead son's notes 'something genuinely his' (268), a book manuscript written half in Hebrew, half in English, entitled (the title is only given in the English version of the story) 'Prophecy and Politics' (269). This discovery of a concentrated version of his son's thoughts, which, as the title suggests, has to do with the place of religious history in the affairs of the modern Israeli state (and which is assumed to be a study in the field of sociology, a discipline the son had earlier declared his father to be incapable of understanding) provides further evidence concerning the usurpation of the old guard by the younger generation, not to mention foreshadowing the eventual downfall of the Abrahamic figure. Curiously, the father had remarked upon his son's return that the now-bearded man resembled a 'prophet' (259); once again, we see how the father utilizes biblical imagery and terminology to communicate the obstinate reliance upon textual tradition for which the son expresses his scholarly disdain in the title of the aforementioned manuscript.

The old man's following series of encounters takes place on Mount Scopus, the location of one of the campuses of the Hebrew University of Jerusalem, and also the symbolically charged vista that looks out on the panorama of the Old City. When he asks one of the clerks at the university the whereabouts of his son, he notes that they 'take me for mad . . . a crank wishing to draw attention to himself' (270). Another key incident involving the teacher is when he stumbles upon a group of Jewish-American foreign exchange students, with whom dialogue is also impossible, since they do not speak Hebrew, and his meager English does not suffice for even basic communication. Although these students are Jews, they are depicted as just as foreign to the old man as are the Arab cleaning woman and the Gentile daughter-in-law. Here, too, he demonstrates contempt for them: 'I butt in, start walking among them, over them, step on their flabby diaspora limbs' (271). The jeers of these students who, unlike the Israeli high school students, are able to freely ridicule him, reinforce the impotence of his authority, as they label him, in English, 'you old man' (271).

When the father finally gets into a taxi to go down to the Jordan valley, where the supposed death of his son took place, he sees along the way 'olive groves, stone walls, flocks of sheep, the beauty of it, [an] ancient kingdom changeless for thousands of years' (273). The fact that the 'giver of wisdom' at this point in the story still insists on equating the landscape of the Occupied Territories, captured from Jordan three years earlier in the Six-Day War, to any kingdom described in the Bible points to an unmistakably delusional worldview, based on a dogmatic vision of biblical prophecy and on historical entitlement. It also recalls a comment by Avner Falk, according to whom 'Modern Israel was a fantasy that became a reality [and] the price for living in that fantasy has been high' (1999: 728). In essence, Falk's assertion means that despite the cost, in human terms, of the fantastical origins of modern political Zionism, the Israeli state, although secular, possesses the 'religiously' dangerous tendency to cancel out the recognition of fantasy as such in the pursuit of territory or dominion. The old man, of course, does not acknowledge that his comparison of a twentieth-century Judean landscape with that of the biblical Israel smacks of pathos. And yet, since this is his first time in the territories, it seems as though the descent into 'death', as it were, much like the ambiguous 'ascent' into Jerusalem, does render some kind of heightened state of consciousness in the old man, as he looks out on the hills of Moab. The thought that biblical history is repeating itself is, for him, felt in a very visceral manner, as he explains, while looking out on the horizon: 'Heavily does this fearful land seize me by the neck' (Yehoshua 1991: 273).

4. Directives for the Jewish State: The Bible, History, or the Present?

Descending into the Judean desert is a symbolic action performed by many of Yehoshua's early characters against the backdrop of Zionist settlement activity, especially since such an action is archetypally equated, in the Jewish psyche, with God's promise to Abraham (Gen. 17.8), according to which he and his seed would have 'everlasting possession' of the land in which they were strangers. This idea would have seemed even more poignant to the Israeli reader in the aftermath of the 1967 war, during which the idea of *Eretz yisrael hashlemah* ('the Greater [Land of] Israel')—according to which the biblical classifications of the Land of Israel as set out in Gen. 15.18-21; Num. 34.1-15; and Ezek. 47.13-20 should determine the present borders of the current Israeli state—was at its zenith, in light of the recently acquired Israeli sovereignty over areas captured from Jordan.

The mention of Moab, which in Aramaic (*moav*) means 'from the father', and refers to the outcome of the incestuous relation between Lot and his eldest daughter (Gen. 19.37), is also an allusion to the supposed sacrifice of the old man's son. The linguistic symbolism of the plateau of Moab's name has to do both with its above-mentioned meaning, as well as with its current geographical position. Moab is located in present-day Jordan, a country which, before September 1970, was used by the Palestinian Liberation Organization (PLO) as the launching ground for attacks against the Jewish state. However, 'early in the summer' in the year of 1970 (before King Hussein of Jordan drove out the PLO from his territory in a bloody operation known as 'Black September'), the PLO, and not the Egyptian forces with whom the limited War of Attrition was fought, still used the Jordanian side of the border to launch attacks against Israel. While these attacks and the Israeli retaliations that they brought on were not part of the official conflict, the Jordanian front was still a place in which many Israeli soldiers met their deaths. Thus, in addition to the symbolism that the name Moab ('from the father') evokes—that is, inasmuch as the Abrahamic figure has bequeathed to his descendants a legacy of conflict and bloodshed, now epitomized by the supposedly dead son—it also sheds an intertextual light, from the perspective of the father, on the historical reasons for which the Israelis and Jordanians are in confrontation. More specifically, the reference is to two other warring peoples, the Israelites and the Moabites, who share a common ancestry through Terah, son of Nahor (Gen. 11.27). From the father's viewpoint, then, the Bible may still be used as an informative, instructive tool to explain, or more importantly, to justify, the ongoing killing which has, he believes, now taken his son from him.

Upon arriving at his son's base in the Jordan valley, the old man meets another figure who is portrayed as ridiculous and as out-of-touch as he is: the company's army chaplain. The chaplain is depicted as awkwardly attempting to preserve a specific hierarchy and propriety through his practical (as opposed to textual, as in the case of the elderly teacher) reverence toward biblical dogma. In one of the rare appearances by a rabbi in the oeuvre of Yehoshua—rare because Yehoshua's main local association with figures of authority, like that of most secular Israelis, is usually with those involved in either the top echelons of the political, military, or educational systems— this particular character, who notes that 'something very deep has gone awry' (278) with respect to the death of the son, also unconsciously articulates what is fundamentally wrong with a system that thrives on a strict adherence to behavioral norms and on the expunction of individualism.

What precisely had gone awry in order that the buffoonish chaplain should make such a statement? The chaplain has shown the old man the body of a fallen soldier who is not his son. However, since for all they know the son might actually be dead (and the insinuation is that, in any case, one dead body equals another in a culture where collective sacrifice and mourning are the norm), the chaplain is unsure about whether or not to instruct the man to tear his garment (279). In Judaism, the traditional ritual mourning act of *kriy'ah*, or 'tearing', may be traced back to Gen. 37.34, when Jacob performed the first tearing of his garment when he believed, erroneously, that his son Joseph was dead. Here, the symbolism of the father's *kriy'ah*

is twofold: first, it implies that all fathers of Israel are bereaved, since sacrificing the younger generation is portrayed as one of the patriarchal duties
of Zionism. Second, it hints that obdurate reliance on antiquated religious
custom is incompatible with present-day reality, since the rabbi, who is supposed to be (by way of his vocation) an expert on the finer points of Jewish
ritual, does not even know the correct way to advise the old man to mourn,
let alone how to ascertain the reason for the mix-up regarding the as-of-
yet-unidentified body. The chaplain's ineptitude is further evidenced when
he abandons the confused old man at the base, driving like a maniac (a
potentially suicidal act which in and of itself endangers life for the sake of
preserving religious praxis) in order to return to Jerusalem before the onset
of the Sabbath (279).

While at the base, the father casually notes that he never served in the
army—another indication that his Zionism, which is based on canonicity
(as opposed to real-lived experience), has no connection with current geopolitics. His observations about the areas around him, similar to his early
references to Moab, bear witness to this fact: for instance, instead of speaking about the enemy coming from Jordan, he comments on how he 'smell[s]
ancient hosts about me' (280). Later, while riding in a jeep to his son's
encampment, he tries to 'look at once for signs of a dead, distant, biblical
deity among the arid hills flanking the road' (283).

When he finally arrives at the encampment where his son has been sta-
tioned, someone shouts, 'The old father's arrived!' (283), as if the emphasis
upon his ancestral quality were a fact that already went without saying. The
soldiers there are awed by his strange Hebrew, and look at him 'as though
I were a sacred figure' (283). He attributes their silence to the fact that his
use of the language, which still has some 'rhetoric' (285) left in it, must
puzzle them. If we consider that rhetoric, properly defined, is persuasive
speech (or, from a more pejorative perspective, meaningless or exaggerated
language), it becomes apparent that even outside the classroom, this man's
obstinate and archaic way of looking at the world manifests itself even in
his verbal expression. This is also an embodiment of the Judaic textual tradition, since the high register of the Modern Hebrew language the old man
is referring to relies mainly upon biblical vocabulary and syntax to distinguish it from its modern variant.[9]

Fascinated with the elderly teacher's appearance, one soldier at the
encampment comments that he used to have a teacher who had the same
look in the eyes as the old man does, and inquires as to what kind of history
he teaches (this is first time in the story that the old man is referred to as a

---

9. For a summary of the differences between Biblical and Modern Hebrew, as
well as for an explanation of the linguistic registers in Israeli Hebrew, see Zuckermann
(2008).

teacher of history and not of the Bible). The exchange between the soldier and the father is as follows: The soldier asks, 'What history?', to which the old man responds, 'Jewish history'. The old man then inquires, 'And he [the other teacher] looked like me?' The soldier responds, 'Yes. Despite the difference'. 'What difference?' the old man wonders. The soldier explains that he means the difference 'between history and Bible'. The old man, exasperated, asks, 'Why difference?' (286). Here again, the father is not able to distinguish the physical, normative existence of Israel as a geopolitical reality; he insists upon seeing it through the eyes of a textual continuum.

In the final, fateful encounter between father and son (which we now know has only taken place, like the entire tale, in the mind of the senile father), the father asks the son how he is faring on his reserve duty. The old man recounts their conversation: '"You can see for yourself . . ." he [the son] whispers with something of despair, with bitterness, as though it were I who issued call-up orders, "such a loss of time . . . so pointless . . ."' (289). The son's insinuation, played out in the mind of the father, that the old man has actually had some part in issuing the call-up orders for an army in which he never served further concretizes the point that he is seen by the younger generation as the bearer of a stagnant, conservative consciousness. This accusation seems to spur the old man on, for, in the last version he tells of the story, he muses with bitter sarcasm:

> As though everything we taught them—the laws, the proverbs, the prophecies—as though it had all collapsed for them out there, in the dust, the scorching fire, the lonely nights, had all failed the test of some other reality. But what other reality? Lord of Hosts, Lord God—*what* other reality for heaven's sake? Does anything really change? I mean, these imaginary signs of revolution (292).

While the father sees revolution (that is, political transformation) as imaginary, the son strives to move Israel out of the imaginal realm to which the father insists on clinging. The fissure between the two plays itself out in the old man's final vision, in which he is lecturing to his students and their parents during yet another assembly. He states, with a quasi-religious, deterministic attitude: 'For to say it plainly and clearly—there is no history. . . . All further research is futile' (266). The old man's derogatory assertion that 'history', as the objective study of events and their consequences, does not exist, is in stark opposition to the beliefs of his son, who wishes to complete his work on 'Prophecy and Politics', the findings of which he will also (to quote another disgruntled revolutionary) 'shout from the rooftops' to the young people of Israel, but without the qualifying cover of traditional Judaism upon which his father relies. Thus, the chasm of psychological tension between the two generations is never really bridged, even by the possible loss of the son, because by effectively killing the drive for intellectual reform and the rethinking of statehood as advocated by the son, the father ends up metaphorically sacrificing him anyway. The story ends with the old man imagining himself picking up 'Bibles on the floor' (293) of the high school (an intimation of Yehoshua's ideas regarding the role of religion in the state's educational apparatus), and the teacher's same illusory vision of the headmaster informing him of the death of his son (293).

5. *Subversion as Ideology*

The father/son relationship in 'Early in the Summer of 1970' highlights one of the overarching themes of Yehoshua's early work as a whole: that which Joseph Cohen refers to as 'generational conflict' (1990: 46) played out in the realm of phylogeny. I concur with Cohen that the negative portrayals of the instigators of these conflicts, especially as personified by the elderly father in 'Early in the Summer of 1970', also point to the danger of the 'unconscious destructive urges', which he says are indicative of a 'trench mentality' in Israel (1990: 46). In the paragraphs below, I build on the psychosocial frame of mind mentioned by Cohen in order to demonstrate the ways in which the modern Israeli paradigm is reflected through the representations of the archetypal, or symbolically charged, configurations in the above-mentioned story, which provides a fertile starting point to analyse the subversion of the Judaic tradition through Yehoshua's secular lens of the Israeli subculture.

What Ramras-Rauch has called a reexamination of 'the conventional values of Israeli society' (1989: 145) in Yehoshua's work is the tacit premise lurking beneath the symbolic structure of 'Early in the Summer of 1970', evidenced in a large part by the special role played by the Abrahamic figure. Because the father in the story insists on perpetuating the belief that the sacrifice of his son has some ultimate meaning, he seeks not only to justify current geopolitics by way of the biblical praxis of the ancient Kingdom of Israel; he also establishes, whether consciously or unconsciously, an archetypal connection between himself and the biblical Abraham, the patriarch of the Jewish people. Although there is no divine commandment to sacrifice his son, there is a national one, and so the father sees himself as someone who would, and indeed should, turn out to be a mourner worth of praise. Inasmuch as Judaic religious propriety is patterned on patriarchal religiosity, modern individuals are sometimes not fully aware that any natural insistence upon order and authority mirrors almost precisely the religious elements of psychic life, now cached in secularism. And this secular commandment issued by the state, one that calls for the sacrifice of its sons, has been given without much attention to the opinions of the current generation. That generation, as symbolized by the son, does not want to be sacrificed. And, like his biblical counterpart Isaac, the son is not a 'believer' in the commandment-issuing entity (Isaac was not aware of the divine imperative for his near-sacrifice), because his knowledge of actual lived experience differs from the father's reliance on the textual tradition—and these texts justify, to a large extent, the nationalistic imperative handed down by the Israeli government. Moreover, through his research, the son has become the conscientious and methodical opposite of the father figure, standing for a different kind of behavioral norm based on observation and evaluation. Although this son is ultimately not sacrificed for the state's political agenda, the 'sacrificed' Isaac in the story still exists (the dead soldier for whom the teacher's son was mistaken); and so the killing continues.

By looking at this story archetypally, we may see that the novella's message has to do with debunking the notion that perpetuating sacrifice should go without saying in contemporary Jewish life. By playing with the places, characters and themes of one particular passage from the Hebrew Scriptures, Genesis 22, Yehoshua transforms the story of the Binding of Isaac into one in which the moral injustice is seen, and may therefore be acted upon. In Yehoshua's version of the tale, the slaughter is allowed to take place (since there is, in fact, a dead son to be mourned by someone), and so Yehoshua subverts the common association of that archetype with its original meaning.[10] In doing so, he uses that very archetypal symbolism to create a new meaning, a meaning that will resound even more profoundly with his Jewish readers, precisely because of the historical, linguistic and psychological weight of the symbolism of the biblical subtext and the archetypal structure on which it is based. The fact that neither the father's nor the son's names are given is also a way for the Israeli reader to strongly identify with the challenges that the characters must face, whether it is because of the intertextual association the reader is already unconsciously aware of between the characters in the story and the characters in Genesis 22, or because the reader has already had lived experience of similar consciousness making its impact felt on the nascent Israeli society.

So what is the exact meaning of this recasting of biblical archetypes for Yehoshua? Why did he choose to present his moral allegory in such a fashion? As an atheist, Yehoshua thinks that the story of the Binding of Isaac is inherently immoral. He points out (2001: 63) that in the Hebrew Bible, there are no other references to the story, which he sees as an indication of its obviously dubious moral quality. Yehoshua believes that Christianity's version of the myth, which incorporated the corrective of a man-god sacrificing

---

10. Although the biblical account has Isaac spared from slaughter, there are several *midrashim* (homiletic interpretations/expansions of biblical texts) that refer to Isaac as actually having been killed. These may be found in the following: *Shibboleh haleket* 9a-b; *Taanit* 16a; *Zevachim* 62a-b; *Gen. Rabbah* 56.4-8; and *Pesiktah Rabati* 39. For secondary material on alternate versions of the myth of the Binding of Isaac, see Davies and Chilton 1978; Ginzberg 1909–38: I, 281f., and V, 251; Goodenough 1953–69: IV, 183-84; Schoeps 1946: 389; and Spiegel 3-4, 28-37.

himself for the entirety of humanity, is much more morally coherent than the Jewish version. His secular reading of the story is that Abraham simply staged the event along with his invention of monotheism: 'Such a linkage, in which religion is connected to a specific familial religion, to 'seed' in the biological sense, [was] created by Abraham to repair his own break in the biological chain through his abandonment of his father's house and family' (2004: 210).

More importantly, Yehoshua thinks that the Binding of Isaac is one of the detrimental myths of the Jewish people that must be re-evaluated in order for the state of Israel to blossom into a healthy society. By using the term 'myth', Yehoshua's intent is to recall the Greek *muthos*, a traditional story or legend, often accepted as history, that may therefore explain the world-view of any given people. Yehoshua proposes that these 'founding myths', or 'metastories' (2004: 205), among which are the Exodus from Egypt and the Destruction of the Temple, form the basis of Jewish identity, in lieu of a proximate *material* culture to which Jews could refer throughout the ages. Just like the French have the Louvre, he says, the Jews have always had their narratives (quoted in Horn 1997: 102). These narratives, for better or worse, have structured the ways in which Jews from assorted civilizations regarded their common roots. This is the reason that during Passover, every Jew is supposed to view himself as if he had actually left Egypt.

6. Conclusion

In the best-case scenario, Yehoshua considers Zionism as a rejection of the reliance on the rhetoric of ritual: he regards it as 'a return to history' that advocates 'a consciousness that subjects itself to criticism and examination in the interest of extrication from a sense of fatefulness, and of a return to real historical activity that leads to change and progress' (2004: 205). In his view, making sure that Zionism promotes a consciousness tied to true chronological time, in the sense that historical activity, including its progress and its problems, might be looked at objectively (instead of by divinely or textually inspired decrees) will help to correct the Jews' 'out-side-of-history' sort of identity. The lunacy of the father in 'Early in the Summer of 1970' functions as a symbolic warning of what may happen to Israeli society if irrationally motivated nationalist concerns outweigh all others. And, although the state of Israel is the first self-governing Jewish entity in over two thousand years, Yehoshua maintains that the danger of the Jews taking historical cues from their metastories is ever present, since Jewish history is rife with instances of the myth of the Binding of Isaac exerting destructive influence. In his view, 'Abraham's descendants bring themselves to situations of conflict with their surroundings, in which they are threatened with extermination and destruction, with the knife waving overhead, and at the last minute they are rescued, or supposed to be rescued, by God's voice' (2004: 210). With respect to the influence of the Abraham/ Isaac metanarrative on current Israeli life, Yehoshua cautions: 'The knife game is prefigured in our history. It must be borne in mind that whoever brandishes the slaughtering knife—whether as intimidation or as a game—cannot always restrain it' (2001: 65). With these words, Yehoshua offers the reader an articulation of the ideological message of 'Early in the Summer of 1970' that could not, I would venture, be any clearer.

Bibliography

Agnon, Shmuel Yosef
    1966   'Lefi hatza'ar hasakhar' ['As the Sorrow, the Retribution'], *Haesh vehaetzim* [*The Fire and the Wood*] (Tel Aviv: Schocken), pp. 8-9.
Amichai, Yehuda
    1996   *The Selected Poetry of Yehuda Amichai* (trans. Chana Bloch and Stephen Mitchell; Berkeley, CA: University of California Press).
Ben-Aharon, Yariv
    1966   *Hakrav* [*The Battle*] (Tel Aviv: Sifryat po'alim).
Boehm, Omri
    2007   *The Binding of Isaac: A Religious Model of Disobedience* (New York: T. & T. Clark International).
Chilton, Bruce
    2008   *Abraham's Curse: Child Sacrifice in the Legacies of the West* (New York: Doubleday).
Coffin, Edna Amir
    1987   'The Binding of Isaac in Modern Israeli Literature', in *Backgrounds for the Bible* (ed. Michael Patrick O'Connor and David Noel Freedman; Winona Lake, IN: Eisenbrauns), pp. 293-308.
Cohen, Joseph
    1990   *Voices of Israel: Essays on and Interviews with Yehuda Amichai, A.B. Yehoshua, T. Carmi, Aharon Appelfeld, and Amos Oz* (Albany, NY: State University of New York Press).
Cohen, Yisrael
    1981   *Bekheviyon hasifrut ha'ivrit: hasifrut ha'ivrit leor mishnato shel K.G. Yung* [*In the Secret Places of Hebrew Literature: Hebrew Literature in the Light of Jungian Theory*] (Tel Aviv: 'Eked), pp. 51-74.
Davies, Philip R., and Bruce D. Chilton
    1978   'The *Aqedah*: A Revised Tradition History', *Catholic Biblical Quarterly* 40, pp. 534-35.
Delaney, Carol Lowery
    1998   *Abraham on Trial: The Social Legacy of Biblical Myth* (Princeton, NJ: Princeton University Press).
Efrati, Yosef
    2010   'Ktzat tekstim vekheresim: "betkhilat kaiytz 1970" umekomo beiyn sipurei A.B. Yehoshua' ['A Few Texts and Shards: "Early in the Summer of 1970" and its Place among the Stories of A.B. Yehoshua'], in *Mabatim mitztalvim: 'iyunim beyitzirat A.B. Yehoshua* [*Intersecting Perspectives: Essays on A.B.*

Yehoshua's Oeuvre] (ed. Amir Banbaji *et al.*; Bnei Brak: Hakibbutz hameu-khad), pp. 94-71.

Ezrahi, Sidra DeKoven
2007   "'To What Shall I Compare You?" Jerusalem as Ground Zero of the Hebrew Imagination', *Proceedings of the Modern Language Association* 122.1, pp. 220-34.

Falk, Avner
1999   *A Psychoanalytic History of the Jews* (London: Associated University Press).

Feldman, Yael
2010   *Glory and Agony: Isaac's Sacrifice and National Narrative* (Stanford, CA: Stanford University Press).

Gilboa, Amir
1981   'Yitzkhak', in *The Penguin Book of Hebrew Verse* (trans. T. Carmi; New York: Viking), p. 560.

Ginzberg, Louis
1909–38   *The Legends of the Jews* (7 vols.; Philadelphia, PA: Jewish Publication Society).

Goodenough, Erwin R.
1953–69   *Jewish Symbols in the Greco-Roman Period* (13 vols.; Princeton, NJ: Princeton University Press).

Gouri, Haim
1981   'Yerushah' ['Heritage'], *The Penguin Book of Hebrew Verse* (trans. T. Carmi; New York: Viking), p. 565.

Greenberg, Uri Zvi
1972   'Korban shakharit' ['Morning Offering'], *Sulam* 13, pp. 145-47.

Horn, Bernard
1997   *Facing the Fires: Conversations with A.B. Yehoshua* (Syracuse, NY: Syracuse University Press).

Kartun-Blum, Ruth
1995   'The Aqedah as a Paradigm in Modern Hebrew Poetry', *The Shaping of Israeli Identity: Myth, Memory, and Trauma* (ed. Robert S. Wistrich and David Ohana; Portland, OR: F. Cass), pp. 185-202.

Kurzweil, Baruch
1982   *Khipus hasifrut hayisraelit* [*In Search of Israeli Literature*] (ed. Zvi Luz and Yedidya Yitzkhaki; Ramat Gan: Bar-Ilan University Press).

Laor, Yitzkhak
1985   'Hametumtam hazeh Yitzkhak' ['This Fool, Isaac'], *Rak haguf zokher* [*Only the Body Remembers*] (Tel Aviv: Adam), p. 70.

Levin, Hanoch
1987   'Malkat haambatiyah' ['Queen of the Bathtub'], *Mah ikhpat latzipor?* [*What Does It Matter to the Bird?*] (Tel Aviv: Hakibbutz hameukhad), pp. 4-31.

Megged, Aharon
1970   *The Living on the Dead* (trans. Misha Louvish; London: Cape).

Melman, Yosef
1991   '"Zekhor et asher 'asah avikha"—'akedat Yitzkhak: yesodot mashma'utah basipur hamikrai vegilgulah beshirat hamekha'ah bat yameinu' ['"Remember What your Father Did"—The *Akedah:* Its Foundations in the Biblical Narrative and its Transformation in the Contemporary Poetry of Protest'], in *Ha'akedah:*

mitos, temah, vetopos basifrut [*The Binding of Isaac: Myth, Theme, and Literary Topos*] (ed. Zvi Levi; Jerusalem: Magnes Press), pp. 53-72.

Mendelson Maoz, Adia
  2010 'The Bereaved Father and his Dead Son in the Works of A.B. Yehoshua', *Jewish Social Studies* 17, pp. 116-40.

Mintz, Alan
  1978 'New Israeli Writing', *Commentary* 65, pp. 64-67.

Morahg, Gilead
  1988 'Facing the Wilderness: God and Country in the Fiction of A.B. Yehoshua', *Prooftexts: A Journal of Jewish Literary History* 8, pp. 311-31.
  1979 'Outraged Humanism: The Fiction of A.B. Yehoshua', *Hebrew Annual Review* 3, pp. 141-55.

Ramras-Rauch, Gila
  1989 *The Arab in Israeli Literature* (Bloomington, IN: Indiana University Press).

Sagi, Avi
  1998 'The Meaning of the *Akedah* in Israeli Culture and Jewish Tradition', *Israel Studies* 3, pp. 45-60.

Schoeps, Hans Joachim
  1946 'The Sacrifice of Isaac in Paul's Theology', *Journal of Biblical Literature* 65, pp. 385-92.

Shaked, Gershon
  1972 'Lo rak mukdam bekaiytz 1970' ['Not Only Early in the Summer of 1970'], *Siman kriyah* 1, pp. 154.

Shalev, Mordechai
  1995 'Chotam ha'akedah bisheloshah yamim ve-yeled, bitekhilat kayitz 1970, uve *Mar mani*' ['The Seal of the Binding of Isaac in "Three Days and a Child", "Early in the Summer of 1970", and *Mr Mani*'], in *Bakivun hanegdi: Kovetz mekhkarim al Mar Mani shel A.B. Yehoshua* [*In the Opposite Direction: Essays on Mr Mani by A.B. Yehoshua*] (ed. Nitza Ben Dov; Tel Aviv: Sifriyat po'alim), pp. 399-448.

Shamir, Moshe
  1960 *Bekulmos mahir* [*Quick Notes*] (Tel Aviv: Sifriyat po'alim).

Shlonsky, Avraham
  1954 'Khulin' ['A Secular Object'], *Ktavim* [*Writings*], II (Tel Aviv: Sifriyat po'alim), p. 136.

Spiegel, Shalom.
  1967 *The Last Trial: On the Legends and Lore of the Command to Abraham to Offer Isaac as a Sacrifice* (trans. Judah Goldin; Woodstock, VT: Jewish Lights Publishing).

Walvoord, John F., and Roy B. Zuck
  1983–85 *The Bible Knowledge Commentary: An Exposition of the Scriptures,* I (Wheaton, IL: Victor Books).

Yehoshua, A.B.
  1981 *Between Right and Right* (trans. Arnold Schwartz; New York: Doubleday).
  1990 *Mar Mani* [*Mr Mani*] (Tel-Aviv: Hakibbutz hameukhad).
  1991 *The Continuing Silence of a Poet: The Collected Stories of A.B. Yehoshua* (New York: Penguin).
  1992 *Mr Mani* (trans. Hillel Halkin; New York: Harcourt Brace).
  1993 *Kol hasipurim* [*The Collected Stories*] (Tel Aviv: Hakibbutz hameukhad).

1995 'Sikum: levatel et ha 'akedah 'al yedei mimushah' ['Conclusion: Annuling the Binding of Isaac through its Fulfillment'], *Bakivun hanegdi: Kovetz mekhkarim al Mar Mani shel A.B. Yehoshua* [*In the Opposite Direction: Essays on Mr Mani by A.B. Yehoshua*] (ed. Nitza Ben Dov; Tel Aviv: Sifriyat po'alim), pp. 388-94.

2001 '*Mr Mani* and the Akedah' (trans. Rivka and Amnon Hadary), *Judaism* 50, pp. 61-66.

2004 'From Myth to History' (trans. Harvey N. Bock), *Association for Jewish Studies Review* 28, pp. 205-12.

2005 *Israël, un examen moral* [*Israel : A Moral Test*] (trans. Denis Charbit; Paris: Calmann–Lévy).

Yehoshua, A.B., and Frédéric Brenner
1988 *Israel* (New York: Harper & Row).

Yizhar, S.
1958 *Yemei Tziklag* [*The Days of Ziklag*] (Tel Aviv: 'Am 'Oved).

Zanger, Anat
2003 '*Hole in the Moon* or Zionism and the Binding (Ha-Ak'eda) Myth in Israeli Cinema', *Shofar: An Interdisciplinary Journal of Jewish Studies* 22, pp. 95-109.

Zerubavel, Yael
1995 *Recovered Roots: Collective Memory and the Making of Israeli National Tradition* (Chicago: University of Chicago Press).

Zuckermann, Ghil'ad
2008 *Yisraelit safah yafah* [*Israeli, a Beautiful Language: Hebrew as Myth*] (Tel Aviv: 'Am 'Oved).

The Flood Story in Middle English:
The Fourteenth-Century Alliterative Poem, *Cleanness*

David J.A. Clines

ABSTRACT

The fourteenth-century didactic work known as *Cleanness,* or *Purity,* one of the finest examples of Middle English poetry, is a 1,812-line allitera-tive poem extolling the virtue of cleanness, moral and physical purity. It contains elaborations of three biblical stories as exempla that portray the divine attitude to cleanness: the Flood, Sodom and Gomorrah, and Bel-shazzar. The author is thought to have been the poet of *Sir Gawain and the Green Knight* (a much better-known work than *Cleanness*), and a con-temporary of Chaucer. The present paper focusses on the c. 300 lines nar-rating the Flood, with special reference *inter alia* to (1) their portrayal of the divine wrath that brings about the Flood (as distinct from the biblical picture of divine grief), (2) the sympathetic characterization of the humans and animals that are to be drowned in the Flood (the victims of the Flood are given no subjectivity in the biblical text), (3) the vision of the Flood as an act of divine cleansing rather than of punishment ('I schal waken vp a water to wasch alle þe worlde'). The moral of the present paper is that alternative realizations (such as *Cleanness* offers) of a fabula attested in the Bible can alert us to silences and repressions in the biblical text as well as heighten our awareness of the contours of the biblical text.

The fourteenth-century didactic work known as *Cleanness*, or *Purity*, is one of the finest examples of Middle English poetry.[1] It is a 1,812-line allitera-

---

1. The poem itself bears no title, and both *Cleanness* and *Purity* have been applied to it by editors. Since 'cleanness' (*clannesse*) is the very first word of the poem, it seems a little perverse not to use that as a title. For the present study, I have used the editions by Charles Moorman, *The Works of the* Gawain-*Poet* (Jackson, MS: University Press of Mississippi, 1977), pp. 101-95 (with glossary); Malcolm Andrew and Ronald Waldron, *The Poems of the* Pearl *Manuscript: Pearl, Cleanness, Patience, Sir Gawain and the Green Knight* (Exeter: University of Exeter Press, 5th edn, 2007), pp. 111-84 (with glossary). Quotations of *Cleanness* are taken from the online edition by Ian Lancashire at rpo.library.utoronto.ca/poems/cleanness.

The verse translations quoted are from Marie Borroff, *The Gawain Poet: Complete Works* (New York: W.W. Norton, 1967), pp. 33-107; her free vivacious verse translation reproduces effectively the flavour of the original's alliteration.

The prose translations cited in the footnotes are taken from the CD-ROM accompanying Andrew and Waldron's *The Poems of the* Pearl *Manuscript.*

tive poem extolling the virtue of cleanness, by which it means both moral and physical purity. It contains elaborations of three biblical stories as exempla (tales that inculcate a moral), portraying divine attitude to cleanness: the Flood, Sodom and Gomorrah, and Belshazzar's Feast. The author is generally believed to have been the poet of the Arthurian romance *Sir Gawain and the Green Knight* (a much better-known work than *Cleanness*), and a contemporary of Chaucer. The poem was written in the late fourteenth century, in a northwest Midland dialect of Middle English. It survives in a single manuscript, Cotton Nero A. x,[2] in the British Library, together with the other works of the Gawain poet.

The Flood narrative, together with the account of the corruption of the earth as told at the beginning of Genesis 6, and a concluding homily reflecting on the lessons of the Flood, occupies lines 249 to 600 of *Cleanness*.[3] The purpose of the present paper is to explore some points at which *Cleanness* differs from its biblical prototype.

1. *The Anger of God*

It is a feature of the poem *Cleanness* that God is depicted as having a special hatred of its opposite (*contrare*), namely, uncleanness (*unclannesse*) or filth (*fylthe*). This hatred is foregrounded in the opening lines:

For wonder wroth is þe Wyȝ þat wroȝt alle þinges
Wyth þe freke þat in fylþe folȝes Hym after.

For the Maker of all things is irked beyond measure
When the folk of his following affront him with filth (lines 5-6).

The Flood called forth the divine anger to a hitherto unknown degree. In the scenes that precede the Flood narrative, there had been grave sins, which

2. The 1,400 manuscripts collected by Sir Robert Bruce Cotton (1571–1631) included the Lindisfarne Gospels, *Magna carta*, and the unique manuscript of *Beowulf*. Cotton is recognized as the first benefactor of the British Museum (and thus the British Library). The British Library retains his system of shelf marks, according to which each manuscript was housed in a case surmounted by the bust of a Roman emperor. The notation Cotton Nero A. x means that it belongs to the case surmounted by Nero, and is on the top shelf, the tenth manuscript from the left.

3. I have benefited from the following works, especially W.A. Davenport, *The Art of the Gawain-Poet* (London: Athlone Press, 1978); Lynn Stanley Johnson, *The Voice of the Gawain-Poet* (Madison, WI: University of Wisconsin Press, 1984); Ad Putter, *An Introduction to the* Gawain-*Poet* (London: Longman, 1996); A.C. Spearing, *The* Gawain-*Poet: A Critical Study* (Cambridge: Cambridge University Press, 1970). For the place of *Cleanness* in the literature of its period, see James H. Morey, *Book and Verse: A Guide to Middle English Biblical Literature* (Urbana, IL: University of Illinois Press, 2000).

sorely displeased the deity, but which did not rouse him to anger such as that engendered by the *fylthe* of the generation of the Flood.[4] For example, when the angels had rebelled and were cast out of heaven, his punishment of them was 'in the measure [i.e. moderation] of his anger, his mercy nevertheless' (*In þe mesure of His mode, His metz[5] neuer þe lasse*, 215). And when Adam was punished it was all by measure and mercy that the vengeance was carried out (*Al in mesure & meþe watz mad þe vengiaunce*, 247). But never has the deity been so roused to anger as by the filth of the generation of the Flood:

> Bot neuer ȝet in no boke breued I herde
> Þat euer He wrek so wyþerly on werk þat He made,
> Ne venged for no vilte of vice ne synne,
> Ne so hastyfly watz hot for hatel of His wylle,
> Ne neuer so sodenly soȝt vnsoundely to weng,
> As for fylþe of þe flesch þat foles han vsed;
> For, as I fynde, þer He forȝet alle His fre þewez,
> & wex wod to þe wrache for wrath at His hert.

> Never have I seen it set down in a book [elsewhere]
> That He punished so impatiently the people He had made,
> Nor avenged Him so violently on vice or on sin,
> Nor so hastily did harm in the heat of His anger,
> Nor so severely and swiftly sought to destroy
> As for filth of the flesh that fools have practiced,
> For then, I find, He forgot all His courteous forbearance
> And maddened past relenting (*wex wod to þe wrache*, waxed angry to vengeance), moved to take revenge (197-204).

And a little later,

> Þer watz malys mercyles & mawgre much scheued,
> Þat watz for fylþe vpon folde þat þe folk vsed,

> Then was [God's] ill will (*malys mercyles*) unstinted, ire unrestrained,
> Because the folk had fallen into filthy ways (250-51).

---

4. Their *fylthe* seems to be essentially homosexuality, though there is also a hint of a breaking of boundaries by the sons of God who intermarry with human women in Genesis 6. Elizabeth B. Keiser notes how it is not until lines 695-96, after the story of the Flood and in the introduction to the exemplum of Sodom, that male homosexuality is explicitly identified as the *fylþe of þe flesch* (*Courtly Desire and Medieval Homophobia: The Legitimation of Sexual Pleasure in Cleanness and its Contexts* [New Haven, CT: Yale University Press, 1997], pp. 44-45).

5. Taking the word as an error for *meth* or *meþe*, 'moderation, mercy' (as Moorman, *The Works of the* Gawain-*Poet*, p. 114 n. 215).

And his heart is touched by 'cruel afflicting anger (*felle temptande tene*)':[6]

> … Þat þe Wyȝe þat al wroȝt ful wroþly bygynnez.
> When He knew vche contre coruppte in hitseluen …
> & vch freke forloyned fro þe ryȝt wayez,
> Felle temptande tene towched His hert.
> As wyȝe wo hym withinne, werp to Hymseluen:
> 'Me forþynkez ful much þat euer I mon made,
> Bot I schal delyuer & do away þat doten on þis molde,
> & fleme out of þe folde al þat flesch werez,
> Fro þe burne to þe best, fro bryddez to fyschez;
> Al schal doun & be ded & dryuen out of erþe
> Þat euer I sette saule inne; & sore hit Me rwez
> Þat euer I made hem Myself; bot if I may herafter,
> I schal wayte to be war her wrenchez to kepe.'

> … that the Author of all things grew angry (*wroþly*) at last.
> When each country's corruption was clear in His sight,
> And they that lived in each land no longer loved virtue
> Then anger (*tene*) grew hot in the heart of our Lord;
> Like a man mourning within, He mused to Himself,
> 'Much do I repent me that ever I made man,
> But I shall wreak my revenge on all wrong-headed folk;
> Of all creatures clad in flesh will I cleanse the world [lit. banish from
>   the world] —
> Both men and every beast, both birds and fish
> All shall be doomed [lit. down] and dead and driven from the earth
> That ever I set soul in, and sorry I am
> That I myself made them; but if I may hereafter
> I shall watch them well, and be wary of their tricks [or, deceitful
>   deeds]' (280-92).

As the Flood comes and the animals and humans alike cry out for clemency, the divine anger is still on show:

> Þat amounted þe masse, þe mase His mercy watz passed,
> & alle His pyte departed fro peple þat He hated.

> But the maelstrom grew madder; His mercy was no more,
> And his pity passed away from people that He hated (395-96).

6. Spearing, *The Gawain-Poet*, p. 46, and Davenport, *The Art of the Gawain-Poet*, p. 65, note the contrast between the deity's reaction to the fallen angels and to Adam and his response to the uncleanness of the generation of the Flood.

This divine anger is not solely a feature of the divine character; it is experienced on earth in the savagery of the Flood, the terror implicit in the biblical narrative being heightened by the poet of *Cleanness*:

> Thus *Cleanness* emphasizes more strongly than the Vulgate the terrifying violence of the forces unleashed against the human race. The flood gates are not simply opened (*apertae sunt*), but they burst ('torent'). Rain is no longer 'made' on earth (*facta est pluvia super terram*), but 'rusched to þe erþe'. The breaking of all the riverbanks (365), the shredding of the clouds (367), and the presentation of the Flood as a collision between earth and a world of water (371) are all nonbiblical, and contribute to the awesomeness of the poet's description.[7]

Nevertheless, the biblical story requires a further change of heart on the part of the deity beyond his decision to flood the earth: his scheme for the ark effectively amounts to a plan for the undoing of his will for the destruction of life on the planet, and the finale of the story will be a blessing, not a cursing, of humanity, even though it will remain just as wicked as it was before the Flood (Gen. 8.21).[8] The transition from the original justified divine anger to the subsequent subversion of the divine decision to destroy the world and then to the unconditional postdiluvian blessing is one that is difficult to negotiate. On this matter, *Cleanness* follows the biblical sequence pretty closely, and has little of its own to contribute. God announces to Noah that he is about the destroy the whole world, and commands Noah to make himself an ark. He makes his covenant with Noah because righteousness and reason have always ruled Noah (*For þou in reysoun hatz rengned & ryȝtwys ben euer,* 328). God's undoing of his own original plan never rises to the surface either in the biblical text or in *Cleanness*, and the deity brings the Flood to an end simply when he thinks it good to do so:

Bot quen þe Lorde of þe lyfte lyked Hymseluen
For to mynne on His mon His meth þat abydez,
Þen He wakened a wynde on watterez to blowe.

But when God thought it good, who governs the sky,
To make known to His man His mercy unfailing,
He wakened a wind over the wide waters (435-37).

7. Ad Putter, 'Sources and Backgrounds for Descriptions of the Flood in Medieval and Renaissance Literature', *Studies in Philology* 94 (1997), pp. 137-59 (140).

8. I have discussed this point at length in my paper 'The Failure of the Flood', in *Making a Difference: Essays on the Hebrew Bible and Judaism in Honor of Tamara Cohn Eskenazi* (ed. David J.A. Clines, Kent Harold Richards and Jacob L. Wright; Hebrew Bible Monographs, 49; Sheffield: Sheffield Phoenix Press, 2012), pp. 74-84.

When the dove returns to the ark with the olive branch, the poet remarks:

Þat watz þe syngne of sauyte þat sende hem oure Lorde,
& þe saȝtlyng of Hymself with þo sely bestez.

That was the sign of salvation sent by our Lord,
How He had reconciled Himself with those simple beasts (489-90).

Why just with the beasts? I do not know. Perhaps it is in prospect of the ensuing animal sacrifice that will be related in the coming lines. For it is 'when the beasts burned briskly and smoke billowed forth' (509) that he 'addresses His man in companionable kindness, with courteous words':

'Now, Noe, no more nel I neuer wary
Alle þe mukel mayny [on] molde for no mannez synnez.'

'Now, Noah', He said, 'nevermore shall I curse
All the mighty mass of earth for any men's sins' (513-14).

The deity's motivation for the turn to mercy is quite mysterious, as it is in the biblical narrative. But in the homily addressed to the reader (lines 541-600) that follows the Flood story proper the poet picks up the theme again, as if dissatisfied by his own narrative, and rehearses the rationale for the divine actions. Let us be clear, the poet seems to be saying, that

1. It was because human 'vileness and villainy had vanquished his patience' (544) that God 'sore repented that He had made human beings to inhabit the earth' (557-58); he became 'sorry that He had set and sustained them on earth' (561).

2. The result of this divine sorrow (more often in *Cleanness* it is divine anger) was that God inflicted on his human creation a dread disaster and chastised them harshly (542-43). 'Their fall into filth He fearsomely avenged' (559).

3. Thereafter he retreated from his own decision, sorrowfully recognizing that he had acted too severely: 'that He harshly had harmed them seemed hard to Him after'. So 'when sorrow assailed Him and softened His heart, He crafted a covenant to keep with mankind' (562-64). And he kept that covenant even in evil days after (569).

That is the logic of events in the mind of God as the poet sees it, but the effect of the poet's homily that concludes the Flood story is quite other than this more or less rational sequence. For the overwhelming emphasis of the homily is upon how quickly God can be angered. There are indeed a couple of lines on the 'mild magnanimity and merciful will' (565) of the deity, but there are at least 25 about the fierceness of his fury, his hatred of evil and his abhorrence of the wicked whom he harries from his kingdom. The depiction of his anger comes to a head with the lines,

> Bot of þe dome of þe douþe for dedez of schame,
> He is so skoymos of þat skaþe, He scarrez bylyue;
> He may not dryȝe to draw allyt, bot drepez in hast:
> & þat watz schewed schortly by a scaþe onez.

> … when the folk fall into foul deeds of defiling lust,
> He loathes so that lewdness, He lashes out at once,
> Cannot bear to hold back, but abruptly strikes,
> And that was openly proven by a punishment once (597-600).

With that, the homily concludes, and therewith the whole Flood episode in *Cleanness*.

The divine anger seems to be a new feature in this telling of the Flood story, since the scholastics denied that God could be moved by a human emotion such as anger.[9] It is true that God also 'deeply regrets' (*sore hit Me rwez*[10]), a much milder term, but the anger is unmistakable.

In this respect *Cleanness* departs significantly from the biblical text, where it is remarkable how restrained the divine response is, emotionally at least; the violence of the universal cataclysm makes the detachment of the deity even more chilling than anger.

2. *The Experience of Humans and Animals at the Flood*

A striking feature of *Cleanness* is its sympathetic characterization of the humans and animals that are to be drowned in the Flood, in contrast to the biblical narrative, in which the victims of the Flood are given no subjectivity.

> Þer watz moon for to make when meschef was cnowen,
> Þat noȝt dowed bot þe deth in þe depe stremez;

9. 'The *Gawain*-poet is exceptional among mediaeval writers in portraying God as someone who is occasionally overcome with nausea and bouts of ill temper' (Putter, *Introduction*, p. 212). Nevertheless, the anger of the deity appears already in the Flood narrative as told in the twelfth-century versified *Bible* of Henri de Valenciennes: 'God was enraged , and showed his anger' (*Molt fu Diex correciez, si mostra sa fierté*, line 210, quoted by Putter, 'Sources and Backgrounds', pp. 144-45). On Henri de Valenciennes, see Jean Bonnard, *Les traductions de la Bible en vers français au moyen âge* (Paris: Imprimerie Nationale, 1884). Against Spearing, I do not see that the phrase 'as a man (*As wyye*)' in line 284 is an express assertion that God felt in his anger like a man, since the phrase is evidently to be taken with what follows, his self-reflection.

10. That is, 'it sorely rues me', that is, I sorely rue.

Water wylger ay wax, wonez þat stryede,
Hurled into vch hous, hent þat þer dowelled.
Fryst feng to þe fly3t alle þat fle my3t;
Vuche burde with her barne þe byggyng þay leuez
& bowed to þe hy3bonk þer brentest hit wern,
& heterly to þe hy3e hyllez þay [h]aled on faste.
Bot al watz nedlez her note ...[11]

They who marked the mischief lamented their fate,
That they were doomed to drown in the deep streams.
Torrents towered higher, toppled down houses,
Rushed raging into rooms where wretches harbored,
All fled at the first shock whose feet would serve them.
Women with children wended their way
To banks and bluffs that abode above water,
And all made for the uplands, where hills were highest,
But their efforts were futile ... (373-81).

Whereas the biblical narrative does not linger for a moment on the anni-hilation of all living beings, the poet imagines the Flood 'no longer as the apparently instant cause of death of the Old Testament, but as a remorseless and painful process'.[12] In *Cleanness*, Putter remarks, 'human beings and animals can see the Flood coming. It chases people out of their houses and pursues them as they climb up the mountains. Even there the water soon rises to their feet, and men and women prepare for death in a final grand and selfless gesture.'

Bi þat þe flod to her fete flo3ed & waxed,
Þen vche a segge se3wel þat synk hym byhoued.
Frendez fellen in fere & faþmed togeder,
To dry3her delful deystyne & dy3en alle samen;
Luf lokez to luf & his leue takez,
For to ende alle at onez & for euer twynne.
When the swift-swelling flood swirled around their feet,
Not a soul but saw he must sink and be lost;

---

11. In the prose translation of Andrew and Waldron: 'There was cause for lamentation when the calamity was known—that there was no help for it but to die in the deep streams; the water grew ever more powerful, destroying homes, rushed into every house, seized those who lived there. First, all who could flee took to flight; each woman with her child leaves the house and went to the high ridges where it was steepest, and quickly they hastened to the high hills. But their efforts were all in vain. . . .'

12. Putter, 'Sources and Background', p. 141.

> Comrades crowded round and clung to each other
> To endure the dire doom that destiny decreed;
> Lover looked to lover in last fond farewell,
> To end once for all, and ever be parted (397-402).

Equally remarkable are the sympathies of the poet of *Cleanness* for the animal creation, whose fate and dismay are portrayed with no less tenderness than that of the humans:

> Syþen þe wylde of þe wode on þe water flette;
> Summe swymmed þeron þat saue hemself trawed,
> Summe styȝe to a stud & stared to þe heuen,
> Rwly wyth a loud rurd rored for drede.
> Harez, herttez also, to þe hyȝe runnen;
> Bukkez, bausenez, & bulez to þe bonkkez hyȝed;
> & alle cryed for care to þe Kyng of heuen,
> Recouerer of þe Creator þay cryed vchone.

> The wild things went to water, when woods were drowned;
> Some set out to swim, in search of safe harbor;
> Some, stranded on the steeps, stared up to heaven
> With heart-rending roars that reechoed afar;
> Hares and harts hastened to the high ground;
> Bucks, badgers, and bulls beset the steep banks;
> All called, confounded, on the King of heaven
> Cried out for clemency to the Creator of all (387-94).

In a comparable vein, the raven sent out by Noah is given its own subjectivity. Though it is a creature that is by nature 'unruly, rebellious at heart', as its coal black colour no doubt signifies, and though its selfish failure to return to the ark is judged harshly, it too has feelings and desire (for unclean carrion, as is only hinted at in the Bible at Gen. 8.7):

> ... he fongez to þe flyȝt & fannez on þe wyndez,
> Halez hyȝe vpon hyȝt to herken tyþyngez.
> He croukez for comfort when carayne he fyndez
> Kast vp on a clyffe þer costese lay drye;
> He hade þe smelle of þe smach & smoltes þeder sone,
> Fallez on þe foule flesch & fyllez his wombe,
> & sone ȝederly forȝete ȝisterday steuen,
> How þe cheuetayn hym charged þat þe kyst ȝemed.
> Þe rauen raykez hym forth, þat reches ful lyttel
> How alle fodez þer fare, ellez he fynde mete.

… he speeds into space on outspread wings,
Hovers high in heaven, intent to learn tidings.
When he came upon carrion, he croaked for joy,
That had drowned and drifted up on a dry ledge.
The stench smells sweet to him; he swoops down at once,
Falls on the foul flesh, and fills his belly.
He has dismissed from his mind the command that came
From the mouth of the man who was master of the ship.
He keeps his own course, concerned no whit
Whether all creatures starve, so his craw be stuffed (457-66).

The obedient dove, by contrast, though much praised by Noah, and though beautifully pictured taking 'her turn in the weather on taut-webbed wings' (*Ho wyrle out on þe weder on wyngez ful scharpe*, 475), and resting at last, one evening, on the bow of the boat with a branch of olive in her beak, 'graced all with green leaves that grow from the stem' (488), is, perhaps surprisingly, accorded no such subjectivity.[13]

The last scene in the Flood story is given wholly to the animals. Noah has offered sacrifice, God has promised in 'courteous words' never again to 'curse all the mighty mass of earth for any men's sins' (512-14), and in a mere two lines has sent Noah forth from the ark to 'grow great, beget many heirs' (521-12). The climax to the narrative is however the 12-line depiction of the animals leaving the ark and spreading out over the landscape:

Þerwyth He blessez vch a best, & bytaȝt hem þis erþe.
Þen watz a skylly skyualde, quen scaped alle þe wylde,
Vche fowle to þe flyȝt þat fyþerez myȝt serue,
Vche fysch to þe flod þat fynne couþe nayte.
Vche beste to þe bent þat þat bytes on erbez;
Wylde wormez to her won wryþez in þe erþe,
Þe fox & þe folmarde to þe fryth wyndez,
Herttes to hyȝe heþe, harez to gorstez,
& lyounez & lebardez to þe lake-ryftes:
Hernez & hauekez to þe hyȝe rochez,
Þe hole-foted fowle to þe flod hyȝez,
& vche best at a brayde þer hym best lykez;
Then he blessed each beast, bade them overspread the earth.
Wittily [i.e. knowledgeably] through the wide world the wild things
    scattered:

<hr>

13. The dove is, however, focalized in line 483, where it 'skims over the seascape and scouts all about'.

Each fowl took to flight on well-feathered wings;
Each fish sought out seas, where fins served best,
The livestock found level lands where lush grass grew;
The long snakes glided into lairs under ground;
The fox went to the forest, the fitchew [polecat] as well;
Harts to the highlands, hares to the thickets,
And lions and leopards to the rain-lashed canyons.
Eagles and hawks to the highest rocks,
The web-footed fowl to the fresh-flowing streams,
And each beast abides where best he may prosper (528-39).

As a pendant to this discussion of the poet's sympathy with the humans
and animals caught up in the Flood, I mention his depiction of the ark itself,
which is treated almost as a living creature, another victim of the deluge:

Þe arc houen watz on hyȝe with hurlande gotez,
Kest to kythez vncouþe þe clowdez ful nere.
Hit waltered on þe wylde flod, went as hit lyste,
Drof vpon þe depe dam, in daunger hit semed,
Withouten mast, oþer myke, oþer myry bawelyne,
Kable, oþer capstan to clyppe to her ankrez,
Hurrok, oþer hande-helme hasped on roþer,
Oþer any sweande sayl to seche after hauen,
Bot flote forthe with þe flyt of þe felle wyndez.
Whederwarde so þe water wafte, hit rebounde;
Ofte hit roled on rounde & rered on ende;
Nyf oure Lorde hade ben her lodezmon hem had lumpen harde.

The ark was hurled about by heaving waves ,
Carried close to the clouds in countries unknown.
It wallowed on the wide sea, went where it would,
Drove over the deep, in danger, it seemed,
Without boom crutch, or mast, or bowline made taut,
Cable or capstan to secure their anchors,
Helm to keep a course, or hand-held tiller,
Or any swelling sail to speed them to harbor,
But floated forth, flogged on by furious winds,
From each buffet of the brine it rebounded in turn;
Often it rolled round and reared up on end.
Had the Lord not been their helmsman, their lot had been dire
    (413-24).

It is a surreal picture, the 'buoyant box' (*þat lyftande lome*, the heaving vessel, 443), lacking every feature of a proper ship—without boom crutch, mast, bowline, cable, capstan, anchors, helm, tiller, or sail—carried by the waves over strange lands (*kythez vncouþe*) and upwards, 'close to the clouds' (*þe clowdez ful nere*, 414), and rearing up at the last on its end, a primeval Titanic. The ark, no less than the drowned humans and animals, suffers at the hands of the divine *malys mercyles* (line 250) that brings on the Flood.

By comparison with the ark itself, the survivors of the Flood, Noah and his family, are not subjects of much interest to the poet. Noah is introduced as a dutiful servant of the Lord:

> Þenne in worlde watz a wyȝe wonyande on lyue,
> Ful redy & ful ryȝtwys, & rewled hym fayre,
> In þe drede of Dryȝtyn his dayez he vsez,
> & ay glydande wyth his God, his grace watz þe more.

> Now one man there was in the world at that time
> Ever ready to do right, and ruled himself well.
> In dread of the dear Lord he disposed his days,
> And as he walks with his God, he wins the more grace (293-96).

God gives him elaborate instructions for building the ark, in a 37-line speech, and Noah 'briskly … set about to obey God's behests' (line 341). The Lord checks with him whether 'each seam [is] made seaworthy, sealed well with clay' (line 346), and Noah replies, 'Yes, Lord, by your leave … I have worked by your word and wit you lent me' (lines 347-48). Only one scene featuring Noah and his family comes alive: when the dove returns,

> Þen watz þer joy on þat gyn where jumpred er dryȝed,
> & much comfort in þat cofer þat watz clay-daubed.
> Myryly on a fayr morn, monyth þe fyrst,
> Þat fallez formast in þe ȝer, & þe fyrst day,
> Ledez loȝen in þat lome & loked þeroute,

> Then bliss was in the box where before all was gloom,
> Much comfort in that cabin that was clay-daubed.
> Merrily one fair morning—the first month it was,
> That falls foremost in the year, and the first day,
> They laughed in that little boat, and looked all about (491-95).

But the writing in the scenes about Noah and his family is mostly stilted. There is no hint of the Noah who usually figures in painting and carving and mystery plays of the late Middle Ages: the boat-builder, the hen-pecked husband, the simple and honest man.[14]

3. *Cleansing*

It is a surprising aspect of the biblical Flood narrative that the deluge is never represented as a washing or cleansing of the earth. The water of the Flood is viewed solely as a means of annihilation, not of cleansing. The word *rāḥaṣ* 'wash' does not occur, and even the word *māḥâ* 'wipe out', which occurs four times in the Flood narrative (Gen. 6.7; 7.4, 23 [*bis*]), does not suggest a washing or a wiping clean. It is indeed used in 2 Kgs 21.13 for wiping a dish clean, but that seems to mean removing the last crumbs of food from it rather than washing it.[15] The term *māḥâ* in Genesis refers to destroying or annihilating the world.

The rather obvious gap in the biblical narrative (that is, the question why it should be a flood of water that is used to punish the earth) is filled by *Cleanness*. The obverse of cleanness being filth (*fylthe*), it would seem evident that the Flood should be seen as a washing away of the filth of the antediluvian world. *Cleanness* does not develop the theme extensively, and it makes only three explicit connections between the Flood and washing. Nonetheless, the connection must have been fundamental to the poet, for why else would he have chosen to illustrate the theme of cleanness with the story of the Flood?

The first connection between washing and the Flood occurs in God's address to Noah announcing the sending of the Flood:

... I schal waken vp a water to wasch alle þe worlde

... I shall waken up a water to wash all the world (323).

---

14. The point is made by Davenport, *The Art of the Gawain-Poet*, p. 65.

15. That will fit well with the next clause about turning the plate over, which indicates satiation (so too Mordecai Cogan and Hayim Tadmor, *II Kings: A New Translation with Introduction and Commentary* [AB, 11; New York: Doubleday, 1988], p. 269). I think Luis Alonso Schökel is incorrect in thinking the dish is being wiped 'with the help of water' ('מָחָה *māḥâ*', in *Theological Dictionary of the Old Testament*, VIII [ed. G. Johannes Botterweck, Helmer Ringgren and Heinz-Josef Fabry; trans. Douglas W. Stott; Grand Rapids, MI: Eerdmans, 1997], pp. 227-31 [228]). In Prov. 30.20 the verb *māḥâ* means to wipe the mouth clean of food. In Num. 5.23 *māḥâ* is explicitly associated with water: the curses against an unfaithful wife are written by a priest on a scroll and then 'wiped off' into water. The words are not washed off *by* the water, however, but apparently scraped or rubbed off *into* the water that the woman will have to drink (NJPS 'rub it off into the water of bitterness'; RSV, NRSV, NAB, NIV, NJB and REB have 'wash off', wrongly in my opinion).

Nevertheless, there is no explicit connection at this point between washing and the filth that is to be washed away. It was twenty lines earlier in his address to Noah that he gave 'filth' (*gore*) as his reason for sending the Flood, and there was no verbal connection there with washing:

> With her vnworþelych werk Me wlatez withinne;
> Þe gore þerof Me hatz greued & þe glette nwyed.

> The sight of their unseemliness (*vnworþelych werk*, shameful conduct)
>   sickens me within;
> The great glut of their grossness (*Þe gore þerof*, the filth thereof) grieves
>   me sore (305-306).

The second reference to washing is, however, more explicit. As the Lord instructs Noah to enter the ark, he warns him that after seven days he will begin the Flood:

> I sende out bylyue
> Such a rowtande ryge þat rayne schal swyþe
> Þat schal wasch alle þe worlde of werkez of fylþe

> I shall swiftly dispatch
> A tempest so terrible, such teeming rains
> As shall flood away the filth that infects the world (lit. that shall wash
>   all the world of works of filth) (353-55).

The third reference comes near the beginning of the homily that concludes the Flood element in *Cleanness*:

> Forþy war þe now, wyȝe þat worschyp desyres
> In His comlych courte þat Kyng is of blysse,
> In þe fylþe of þe flesch þat þou be founden neuer,
> Tyl any water in þe worlde to wasche þe fayly.
> For is no segge vnder sunne so seme of his craftez,
> If he be sulped in synne, þat syttez vnclene;
> On spec of spote may spede to mysse
> Of þe syȝte of þe Souerayn þat syttez so hyȝe.

> Wherefore beware, you who wish for a worthy place
> In the company of the court of the King of bliss,
> Lest filth of the flesh infect you so deep
> That no water in the world can wash it away.
> For though a man's demeanor be much to admire,
> If he be steeped in sin that has stained his soul—
> One speck or one spot of aspect foul
> Can hinder us from beholding the King high enthroned (545-52).

Here the poet deviates from the more obvious sense of the Flood as wash-ing to envisage a filth so deep that no water in the world can wash it away. He does not appear to be thinking of the divine promise that the world will never again be invaded by a universal Flood, but has narrowed his vision from humanity in general to the individual human, who can be at risk of incurring filth that is incapable of removal, worse, then, than the filth of the antediluvians. No, it is far worse than that: one does not need to be deep-dyed in filth, or steeped in sin to bring upon oneself the divine wrath; even having 'one speck or one spot of aspect foul' (*on spec of spote*, 551) can be enough to deprive a person of the sight of the 'King of bliss' in his 'fair court' (*comlych courte*, 546).

By this point, it is not too easy to see just what the moral of the Flood story is, according to the poet of *Cleanness*. If the dreadful wickedness and filth of the generation of the Flood brought upon them the destruction of their world, and necessitated the washing clean of the whole world, where stands one speck or spot in comparison? Presumably to be shut out from the court of the King of bliss is an even worse fate than being drowned in a Flood, so perhaps our poet thinks that the generation of the Flood got off lightly: they had the freedom to sin on a massive scale before they had to be annihilated, whereas the reader may expect to suffer a worse fate for a trivial speck or spot.

What is at issue in the present article is, however, no more than the con-ceptualization of the Flood as the washing away of sin. Our poet, though no doubt much indebted to some predecessors, does not appear to have derived this element from any of them and may be credited with this important inno-vation in the history of reception the Flood narrative.

Conclusion

From the point of view of biblical scholarship this study has reinforced the conviction that engagement with alternative realizations of biblical narra-tives can bring fresh light to the study of these almost over-researched texts. In three respects *Cleanness* has offered us a new insight into how the story of the Flood can or could be told and thus into the specificity of the biblical narration.

In the biblical text, God is grieved by human sin; in *Cleanness* he is angered. In the biblical text, the Flood is divine punishment and the impact on the animals and humans who drown in it is not of consequence; in *Cleanness* their subjectivity comes to the fore and their reaction is depicted on a scale that raises an implicit challenge to the justice of the divine deci-sion. In the biblical text, the water of the Flood is, strangely, never con-ceived of as a cleansing agent; in *Cleanness*, though its washing function is referred to only three times, the fact that the Flood story serves as one of the three biblical exempla of cleanness shows that this is the principal significance of the narrative for the poet.

The differences between the hypotext (in this case, the biblical narrative) and the hypertext (in this case, *Cleanness*) are no less important for the understanding and interpretation of one text than for the other. The story of the Flood in *Cleanness* can, of course, be read for itself, without regard to its background; but a new level of appreciation for the poet's work and its distinctivess is gained by comparison with its biblical antecedent. And the character of the Flood story in the biblical narrative is indelibly altered by reading it again after *Cleanness*: what biblical interpreter can then fail to notice (as interpreters generally have done in the past) the cold determination of the deity, the disregard of the experience of the victims of the Flood, human and animal, and the surprising absence from the narrative of the idea of 'cleanness'?